THE GREEN SUPERMARKET SHOPPING GUIDE

——————— ✓✓✓ ———————

"*The Green Supermarket Shopping Guide* gives you common sense, straightforward advice, and information on what's what when you shop. Wasik has reduced a mountain of research into a practical, easy–to–understand, consumer guide that cuts through the confusion. I found it most useful, indeed."

—INGRID NEWKIRK, National Director of People for the Ethical Treatment of Animals, and author of *Save the Animals!* and *The Compassionate Cook*

"Extremely thorough and well-researched. In fact, I think it is the most comprehensive guide of its kind."

—JACQUELYN A. OTTMAN, President, J. Ottman Consulting; author of *Green Marketing: Challenges and Opportunities for the New Marketing Age*

"The great strength of *The Green Supermarket Shopping Guide* lies in its straightforward assessment of some of the most complex questions facing responsible consumers. Not only consumers, but socially responsible investors will find this an invaluable resource."

—AMY DOMINI, Domini Social Index Trust; co-author of *Investing for Good*

The text of this book was
printed on recycled paper.

THE GREEN SUPERMARKET SHOPPING GUIDE

JOHN F. WASIK

WARNER BOOKS

A Time Warner Company

Thanks to
Kathleen, Stan and Linda from SCS,
Woody, and, most of all,
Mom and Dad.

WARNER BOOKS EDITION

Copyright © 1993 by John F. Wasik

Cover design by Julia Kushnirsky
Cover illustration by David Frampton

Warner Books, Inc.
1271 Avenue of the Americas
New York, NY 10020

 A Time Warner Company

Printed in the United States of America

First Printing: October, 1993

10 9 8 7 6 5 4 3 2 1

Contents

Foreword

The Power of Information

History teaches us many lessons. One of the most important of these is the power of information. From the discovery of the wheel to the invention of the computer chip, new information has transformed civilizations, challenging existing worldviews and propelling society toward deeper levels of understanding. Tyrants, fearing information, have imposed censorship to keep their populations under control. Democracies, on the other hand, have recognized the free exchange of information as the key to vital, healthy societies.

It comes as no surprise, therefore, that in seeking to solve the world's environmental problems, we must be as informed as possible about their causes and the potential solutions. No matter who we are or what we do, each of us has a role to play. However, only when we know all the facts can we make informed decisions.

As consumers, information can help us turn the "power of the purse" into a powerful force for environmental change. But this information must be accurate and reliable if it is to be of use. Every day, the number of products making environmental claims grows. It is up to each of us to determine what these claims mean and how significant they are for the environment. For example, the claims "recyclable" and "recycled" are often mistakenly assumed to mean the same thing. In the first case, the product has the *potential* to be recycled—that is, its components may be reused to manufacture new products. This potential will only be realized, however, if the product is put in a curbside recycling bin or taken to a recycling center, and if there is a market for the material. All too often, though, recyclable products end up as landfill. In the case of "recycled" products, this potential has already been realized. A recycled product is one that is made, at least in part, with materials that were recovered from used products.

We must also be willing to reexamine and, if necessary, shed our preconceptions about what is good and bad, so that we can look realistically at the facts. It does little good to give up one manufactured product for another if we are simply trading one environmental problem for another. We are far better off knowing the full environmental costs of our options before we choose. This is the consumer's fundamental right to know. It is also the consumer's responsibility.

As long as we fail to understand the basic causes of our environmental problems—global warming, the ozone hole, acid rain, smog, deforestation, and so on—we will not be able to distinguish real solutions from cosmetic ones. CFCs (chlorofluorocarbons), for example, are associated with the destruction of our atmosphere's protective ozone layer, while sulfur dioxide emissions lead to generation of ground-level smog and contributes to acid rain. Without this basic environmental literacy, we are vulnerable to manipulation by companies who try to sell us products that may be hazardous to the environment. We may also fail to distinguish those companies that are taking significant, legitimate actions to reduce their negative impact on the environment.

We must also recognize that we cannot rely solely on the government to prevent deceptive claims from reaching the store shelf. Although the government plays an important role, it can monitor only a fraction of the claims made by manufacturers. It is up to us to critically evaluate the claims we see in the marketplace and to ask for the information that will help us make the best decisions.

Some product marketers view the American consumer as ignorant of and uninterested in the facts. This attitude has led to the kind of hype and distortion that have made so many consumers skeptical of environmental claims.

With this book, John Wasik brings important information about environmental claims to the American consumer. In a commonsense, straightforward way, he demystifies the claims that have caused such commotion and confusion and explains the path we must take together to become more informed shoppers. More important, he not only provides us with the information that is available today but lets us know what information we still lack and must strive to attain. In other words, the path to knowledge is before us; it is up to each of us to take the first step.

—Stanley Rhodes, Ph.D.,
president, Scientific Certification Systems,
Oakland, California

Preface

This book rates 219 consumer goods manufacturers, more than 2,000 products, and 102 large supermarket chains in the United States for various environmental qualities. We've identified products by their parent companies to make you aware of who makes what. While we would have liked to survey every company and every product available, we focused on national brands and large regional supermarket chains. The best choices in product categories are highlighted in bold face. Since there was limited available independent information on company environmental policies, we studied packaging, labeling, and consumer information most closely. We encourage you to read labels, compare products, and ask questions. We did—and in the process discovered much about our disposable society.

If the companies or products you patronize are not rated highly, let them know that you won't give them any more of your business unless they shape up. Even if they are rated highly, there is likely much they can do to improve their products and policies. Remember, there's lots of competition for your dollars.

If you want to get more involved, call or write the companies (see resources section) and ask them about their environmental policies. If you don't like something, let them know. They will listen. Let us know, too. Ideas and action acquire power when grown from the seeds of compassion.

Introduction

Fate thrust me into writing this book, but not for the usual reasons or in the usual way. It had more to do with horses, my wife, and the American dream (though not in that order). When I wed my Belfast beauty, Kathleen, she had a dream of owning a horse. Having grown up in strife-torn Belfast, she yearned for something that transcended the typical suburban life. Now she had a new car, was well paid for her talents as a sales executive, and was living fairly comfortably with her journalist spouse. But something was missing. She mused about memories of horseback riding in the mountains cradling Belfast.

She wanted a horse—one that she could ride and show. So, we began our search for a horse that (1) wouldn't kill the rider, and (2) came with a warranty. We were told by all of the sages in the equine business that we should avoid mares (temperamental), ex-racehorses (crazy and lame), and thoroughbreds (all of the above to the extreme). Of course, we ended up with a thoroughbred mare off the track. We named her Tara, which is Irish for "friend."

When I finally got up the nerve to ride her, I brilliantly jumped on her back behind her ribs, thinking I would ride her bareback. This, I learned, is the quickest way to find a horse's maximum discomfort zone, from which my two-hundred-pound frame was hurled some twenty feet.

Then one day when I was at a writer's conference, Kathleen called to tell me that Tara had had a baby. "They called me about seven o'clock this morning to tell me there were two horses in Tara's stall," she said.

After all our careful planning, we had managed to purchase a pregnant horse. Doubled our investment, doubled our expenses.

Kathleen named the filly Alcyone, after the daughter of the Greek god of the winds. Our adorable little Alcy had a white blaze on her forehead that Kathleen called a "little Gorby" (as in Mikhail Gorbachev). Neither of us could part with her. Several months later, it was clear that the bond was also financial—in a big way. Keeping the two horses boarded, fed, vetted, and trained cost more than our monthly mortgage payments. So, we moved to a ramshackle house on two and a half acres with a barn. It was zoned for horses, fifty miles from Chicago, and beautiful in its own way. Oaks towered along the edge of the property, a 150-year-old cottonwood lorded over the front lawn; a thousand-acre farm was our backyard and deer grazed on the front lawn. We were now twice as much in debt, feeding twice as many horses, in need of at least seventy thousand dollars' worth of remodeling on the house, and commuting twice as long. But this downward mobility would teach us about the earth—and ourselves.

It very quickly became apparent that I had a mounting solid-waste problem. Horses kept in stalls generate some two hundred pounds of solid waste (including soiled wood shavings) *per week*—and it must be disposed of somewhere. Throwing it in the trash can doesn't work, because the can fills up quickly and then there's no room for your *other* household garbage. So there I was, a reluctant horse breeder and country gentleman—with a landfill problem. The previous owner had thrown manure behind the barn—tons of it—which we eventually had to move. At last we found a way to compost the manure to make it decompose, and built a huge paddock to keep the horses outside more.

Shoveling manure every weekend got me to thinking about other kinds of waste: energy waste, landfill waste, water waste, and product packaging waste. Suddenly, I realized I could now evaluate these things firsthand. Since my house had its own well, I could easily imagine the horrible consequence of my only source of water being poisoned by a landfill. I became curious about which poisons I couldn't put into my septic system because if the bacteria in it died, we'd have an even bigger waste problem, since I wasn't hooked up to a city sewer line. I wanted to learn everything I could about these things, and other compelling issues such as natural pesticides (horses attract tremendous numbers of flies in the summer). At about that time, the twentieth anniversary of Earth Day inundated all who would listen with earth issues. But the torrent of information also included a wave of false and misleading claims about the environmental quality of consumer products. As a would-be farmer who was becoming "one with the earth," I took these affronts personally. So, I started the New Consumer Institute and the *Conscious Consumer* newsletter to inform consumers, businesses, and the media about these "gray" green areas.

While others were driving their gas-guzzling luxury cars to environmental soirees, I started to "audit" my garbage to see what I was throwing away. I found that, other than the horse manure, it consisted of food and packaging waste. The food waste I could compost in my double-decker, 108-cubic-foot composter. But what of the packages I bought at the supermarket? What of the companies that made the packaging? How much energy did it take to make the packaging? There is an endless stream of unanswered questions that relate to what we buy at the supermarket.

I started the New Consumer Institute to inform people around the world about how we can help the earth and our societies through our actions as consumers. From Hong Kong to Norway, we're actively sharing, learning, and acting in ways that will make the planet habitable and productive for future generations. We have no headquarters, no board of directors, and no budget. Through the *Conscious Consumer* newsletter, we communicate environmental and social responsibility issues. This book is but one result of our probe into consumerism.

This book is meant to enrich your knowledge base, and to encourage you to ask questions, but not to offer easy solutions. I'm not interested in guilt trips. With the kind of waste I create at home and in the car, I'm no paragon. I consider myself the emperor of guilt when it comes to waste, but I'm willing to be enlightened. I hope you are, too. Remember, Mother Earth is a fragile organism, we're part of her, and we must continue to learn how best to treat her.

Part 1

IT'S NOT EASY BEING GREEN

There's little question that after Earth Day's twentieth anniversary, being "green" attained a certain cachet. America has fallen in love with environmental consumerism. A Gallup survey commissioned by *Advertising Age* in 1990 found that nine out of ten respondents were willing to "make a special effort to buy products from companies trying to protect the environment." Those polled also said they would pay more for green products and even give up convenience to have them in their households. As a result, according to *The New York Times*, some 5,700 "green" products were launched in 1989 alone.

Similarly, a *New York Times*/CBS News poll revealed that 80 percent of those surveyed said that protecting the environment is so important that "requirements and standards cannot be too high, and continuing environmental improvements must be made regardless of cost."

Nearly every survey over the past three years has said virtually the same thing: Some 70 to 90 percent of Americans are willing to do their part for the environment. When you look at those results, it's easy to conclude that environmental awareness is high and that everybody wants to help the planet. But when they're actually in a store, will consumers pay more for earth-friendly products (or those labeled as such)?

A Roper Organization poll found that consumers would pay 6.6 percent more for such products. But as the Year of the Earth melted into a three-year recession, people put their pocketbooks before their environmental concerns. In 1992, the Consumer Network found that customers "don't understand why they should pay more for highly touted green benefits such as less packaging." Also in 1992, a survey by *The Wall Street Journal* found that consumers may no longer be willing to spend more for green products.

A survey conducted by the Hartman Group in California went even further. After conducting focus groups with consumers, they found that "price, quality, effectiveness, convenience and availability were the major barriers to buying green products." This may explain why, of the 70 percent of those expressing environmental concern, only 50 percent said they would make green purchases.

But if you *are* in the 50 percent ready and willing to buy green, it's not always so easy to decide just what the environmentally responsible choices are. This book is designed to help you do just that.

Chapter 1

Green Claims; Gray Areas

In answer to consumer demands and preferences, environmental claims have been showing up on more and more supermarket products. Despite the deluge of "green" products, the truth often is obscured. Companies launch messages on their packages. Environmental groups volley with another message through their publications and through the media. Yet another set of messages comes from Washington and statehouses. Whose messages can we believe? Which are helping and which are hurting?

For the more aggressive retailers, green marketing has become big business. For example, Loblaw's International Merchants, a Canadian supermarket chain with stores in New York, Michigan, and Missouri, sold $5 million worth of its green detergents, diapers, and other paper products. Nearly every major supermarket chain in the United States, Canada, and Europe has actively promoted its environmental efforts through shelf labeling, recycling programs, and private-label recycled goods.

But currently, there is little reliable, objective information on precisely what all those green claims mean. Congress and a host of state governments now have laws to regulate green claims, but they are no substitute for national legislation.

Government-sponsored seals of approval have sprung up in Germany, Canada, and Japan in recent years to note worthwhile green qualities in consumer products (recycled content, for example). Germany's Blue Angel program singled out green products that were rated better for the environment than similar products. Some 3,000 products have been awarded the seal over the past ten years. Germany even has a law that makes companies responsible for recycling the products they sell.

Canada's closely watched Environmental Choice program considers the scientific "life-cycle analysis" (LCA) of products. LCA is a nascent science that attempts to discover how a product impacts the environment from raw materials to manufacturing, transportation, and disposal. This "cradle to grave" approach will be the ultimate gauge in determining whether some products are less harmful to the earth than others.

The Federal Trade Commission (FTC) took a modest step forward in July 1992 by issuing guidelines on environmental terms widely abused by retailers and manufacturers. The guidelines, however, are strictly voluntary and don't carry any specific penalties if they're violated.

You can use the following guidelines to evaluate supermarket products:

• *General environmental benefits.* Unless they can be substantiated, broad environmental claims should be avoided or qualified.

• *Degradable, biodegradable, and photodegradable.* In general, unqualified degradability claims should be substantiated by evidence that the product will completely break down and return to nature. (This term has been used more cautiously after the Hefty Bag debacle.)

• *Compostable*. Unqualified compostable claims should be substantiated by evidence that all the materials in the product will break down into or otherwise become part of usuable compost. (This claim was used by Procter & Gamble for a brief time in 1991 in reference to their disposable diapers at a time when there were fewer than ten urban composting facilities in the United States. They stopped the claims after regulators intervened.)

• *Recyclable*. Claims about products with both recyclable and nonrecyclable components should be adequately qualified. Remember, if a product can't be recycled in your area, it's not recyclable. Putting recycling codes on products that aren't taken by most recycling facilities (e.g., vinyl and polypropylene) doesn't make them recyclable either.

• *Recycled content*. Claims of recycled content should be made only for materials that have been recovered or diverted from the solid-waste stream. "Preconsumer" waste is not as beneficial to the elimination of solid waste as "postconsumer" waste.

• *Source reduction*. Claims that a product or package has been reduced should be qualified. There must be some verifiable reductions of packaging, not comparisons to older packages of the same product.

• *Refillable*. The claim should not be made if it is up to consumers to find ways to refill the package. Nearly anything's refillable, but only if your store will refill it.

• *Ozone safe and ozone friendly*. Claims about the reduction of a product's ozone-depletion potential may be made if adequately substantiated. The Natural Resources Defense Council branded several products containing smog-causing 1,1,1-trichloroethane as misleading and filed a complaint with the FTC. The NRDC claimed that more than 140 products containing the chemical made green claims. Companies cited in the complaint included Borden, 3M, Blair Air Products, Nationwide Industries, Kiwi Brands, Alberto-Culver, Jerome Russell Cosmetics, and Zipatone. These companies have since changed their claims. This chemical and fluorocarbon-related chemicals (such as hydrofluorocarbons) are not good for the atmosphere. Representatives of eighty-seven countries have agreed to ban these chemicals. The best products use spray pumps.

Chapter 2

Biodegradability: It's All a Bunch of Garbage

If you go into a supermarket, you'll see any number of products claiming to be biodegradable or environmentally safe. The most popular of these are the cleaning agents. Dozens of items now claim to be biodegradable, but these claims often are not backed up by independent research and could be difficult to prove, since there are no official standards for biodegradability.

The EPA currently has no enforceable laws that define biodegradability. According to the classic, generic definition, a biodegradable substance is one that, when introduced into the environment, breaks down into elements or compounds that harmlessly disintegrate. Using that open-ended approach, nearly anything could be considered biodegradable—including plutonium and uranium, which break down over tens of thousands of years.

California has legislated strict standards for biodegradability and other environmental claims, but the law is tied up in court. Manufacturers are fighting the legislation because they think it's unfair and unrealistic. Other states are having similar skirmishes with industry.

What biodegradability means is fairly simple: a substance

ultimately breaks down into carbon dioxide, "basic miner-als," and water. In other words, when something biodegrades, no man-made chemicals are left. Natural substances such as vinegar, baking soda, and sodium borate (borax soap) biode-grade easily. But with the complex chemicals that comprise most consumer products, it's one of the most difficult claims to make. Scientific Certification Systems has certified only a few cleaning products as biodegradable. Among them are Blue Coral household cleaner, Enforcer septic tank cleaner, and EarthRite cleaners. Most of the products independently certified for biodegradability are cleaning products, because the chemical formulations are relatively simple and water-sol-uble (dissolved in water). In our research, we were skeptical of any product not independently certified; we wanted to make sure that a third party had tested these products.

The degradability question has even included "brown" paper-goods makers, who have aggressively labeled common items such as shopping bags "biodegradable." The National Resources Defense Council, among other environmental groups, has challenged these claims as well. The environmen-talists cite research that shows that even "natural" materials such as cellulose—the basic component of paper—do not de-grade in dark, dry landfill, where no microbial decomposition can take place. The environmental groups say that labeling products degradable misleads consumers into thinking that tossing something is better for the earth than recycling it.

Biodegradability is determined by what happens to a prod-uct when it ends up in a landfill. When you throw something away and your scavenger service picks it up, what happens to it? If it's nonrecyclable trash, it either gets incinerated (not popular in most populated areas) or gets buried in a landfill. Environmental scientists who have studied modern landfills doubt that much of anything can degrade in them given their lack of light, water, and bacterial activity, which are the necessary elements for natural degradation. Researchers have found thirty-year-old hot dogs in landfills that have mummified instead of decomposed. A landmark study by Dr. William Rathje of the University of Arizona confirmed this. He and his fellow "archaeological" researchers actually dug through a landfill to prove this fact of life.

Nevertheless, hundreds of marketers have labeled their products biodegradable. This prompted a group of attorneys general to sue Mobil (Hefty, Kordite bags) and others over their degradability claims. Since the Mobil bags (and others making the same claim) are largely *photo*degradable—that is, they are designed to break down under direct sunlight— they cannot degrade in a dark, dry landfill, environmental scientists claim. Moreover, what's left of the plastic polymers in the bags—if they degrade at all—poses another question: Is the residue toxic? While it may be years before that question is answered, that didn't stop a swarm of manufacturers from claiming their products were biodegradable. Today, only a handful of detergents can make that claim, because there's more testing to support their claims.

BIODEGRADABLE DOESN'T MEAN NONTOXIC

Claims of biodegradability often overshadow some serious health risks. For example, De-Solv-it multipurpose remover, made by Orange-Sol, Inc., of Gilbert, Arizona, makes a claim of being "biodegradable and non-carcinogenic." But De-Solv-it is still toxic (labeled "harmful or fatal if swallowed") and contains petroleum distillates. Although the chemicals in this product may eventually degrade, in its inert form, it is poisonous. The biodegradability claim does not mean it is not toxic.

Another odious part of the biodegradability craze is that very few of the products labeled biodegradable are also truly nontoxic, free of irritants, nonflammable, or noncarcinogenic. These health concerns may be even more important than the biodegradability claims since they involve household products that can be inhaled or come in contact with the skin. Many of those chemicals are believed to be "friendly" because they disinfect bathrooms, clean floors, and kill roaches. When hazardous household chemicals are ingested (or inhaled or touched), they can cause anything from kidney damage to nervous disorders. Some of them are all too familiar: Oven cleaner, bleach, ammonia, and paint solvents top the list of obvious nasties. Few people realize that laundry detergent, wood polish, dry cleaning fluid, and window cleaner also pose risks. Inhaled fumes or direct skin contact with these products may cause severe irritations.

All told, the list of hazardous home and garden products is extensive and intimidating. From our increased consciousness about hazardous chemicals we have learned that home-environment poisons and natural poisons are one and the same. The same highly toxic spot remover that is flushed down the drain goes into our water supply and is not degraded very well by nature—if at all. Bleach, or sodium hypochlorite, for example, can produce dioxins when introduced into the environment. Most petroleum-based products also are environmental poisons. Hence, the introduction of biodegradable household products.

The core of the biodegradability issue is to make products without chemicals known to be harmful to the environment. Although many of these products have recycled packaging and are "cruelty free" (not tested on animals), they are not necessarily biodegradable or free of toxic ingredients. Environmental impact is a matter of using the earth's resources wisely.

Chapter 3

The Power of a Label

Detailed green labeling will eventually appear on nearly everything you see in the supermarket. Because this labeling will allow you to "vote" with your pocketbook, you will have the power literally to force companies to clean up the way they do business. Just take a walk down the detergent aisle and read some labels; you'll see hundreds of examples of reduced and recycled packaging. If consumers hadn't wanted to see those changes, they wouldn't have been made. Profit follows the most particular customers. Over the past few years, customers have been particular about environmental issues. Let your supermarket chain and manufacturers know that you want detailed green labeling on their products. (Company telephone numbers for the supermarkets are in chapter 18; manufacturers' telephone numbers and addresses are in the back of the book.)

In the meantime, will the government regulate green claims? We are not holding our breath. An EPA spokesperson said that the agency is "in the process of finding out the utility of life-cycle analysis."

We've come a long way since 1990, when some 26 percent of new products made environmental claims, but 47 percent of those surveyed dismissed them as "mere gimmickry." But it will be decades before any public or private program has enough research behind it to say conclusively how a whole supermarketful of green products compare in terms of total environmental impact. That will require years of studies on everything from forest harvesting to the amount of energy consumed by the recycling process.

A BRIEF HISTORY OF BAD GREEN CLAIMS CAUGHT BY REGULATORS

The FTC's guidelines are good rules of thumb for you, but for manufacturers they are loosely defined suggestions. That's because the guidelines are voluntary and don't carry any specific penalties if they're violated. State and federal lawmakers have contributed various proposals and modest laws to regulate green claims, but few proposals will do the job on a national scale. To show how green-claims policing has evolved, you need to follow how the states and FTC have regulated product claims one company at a time. Following is summary of the actions. The companies mentioned have since changed their ways.

November 1992

A group of thirty-two attorneys general settled with General Electric over GE's energy-saving claims for its Energy Choice incandescent light bulbs. GE was ordered to pay them $165,000 and prohibited from claiming that the bulbs "save energy, reduce pollution, lowers consumers energy costs or otherwise benefits the environment. . . ."

July 27, 1992

Mobil Oil settled with the FTC and seven attorneys general over unsubstantiated claims of degradability of its Hefty line. The company stopped making the claims, because the bags do not degrade in landfill.

May 14, 1992

RMED International, maker of Tender Care disposable diapers, settled on consent agreement with the FTC over questionable "biodegradability" claims of their product. (See Mobil case, above.)

March 26, 1992

American Enviro Products, makers of Bunnies disposable diapers, settled over claims that diapers "will decompose and return to nature within 3–5 years [in a landfill]."

January 3, 1992

First Brands, maker of Glad trash bags, agreed to consent order over dubious claims that bags will "completely break down, decompose and return to nature in a short period of time."

August 30, 1991

Jerome Russell Cosmetics settled over claims that its products contained "ozone safe" chemicals. They did not.

July 29, 1991

Zipatone, makers of Spray Cement, settled charges that its product contained an "ecologically safe" substance, even though that chemical was a Class I (EPA) ozone-depleting substance.

August 27, 1990

The Von's Companies, a West Coast supermarket chain, settled over claims that its produce was free of pesticides.

WHY GREEN RATINGS AREN'T EASY: THE PAPER VS. PLASTIC DEBATE

The question here is whether plastic is less harmful to the earth than paper. The argument, however, isn't that simple. Disposability is but one of several factors involved. How much pollution is created by each manufacturing process? Which one uses the least amount of nonrenewable resources and energy? Paper, which is made from a "renewable" resource such as fast-growth pulp trees, is expensive to recycle, creates pollution when it's made—and recycled—and doesn't degrade in landfills any better than plastic does. In fact, paper is one of the principal components of landfills by volume (about one-third). It can also be argued that because of the way old-growth and rain forests are being mismanaged, trees are not renewable resources. If trees aren't harvested in a *sustainable* way, you can't argue that wood is a renewable resource.

Conversely, the plastic used in shopping bags is easily recycled, but it doesn't degrade much, either. Although there are some supermarket programs to recycle it, most of this kind of plastic ends up in landfills because most communities don't accept it for recycling. Markets for this plastic are young, and it poses sorting problems. It also consumes petroleum (a nonrenewable resource) and produces a host of toxins during the manufacturing process. Is plastic the villain, then? Scientists can't give you a definitive answer, because there haven't been enough studies that show exactly how much energy, raw materials, pollution, and other waste are by-products of each process. Some manufacturers reduce waste and pollution better than others. But to learn the full impact on the environment of each product we use, this kind of research must be done on a massive scale.

Two private groups have emerged to become "green security" police in the area of product claims. Scientific Certification Systems (SCS) in Oakland, California, has already certified more than 400 products for various environmental qualities and is expanding its program daily. It was founded by chemist Stanley Rhodes and is active internationally in developing LCA and environmental issues. For years SCS has also been working to reduce pesticide residues in food (through its Nutriclean division) and teach farmers how to grow crops with fewer pesticides. The group has sponsored free public conferences across the country and sits on the International Forest Stewardship Council.

Green Seal, established by Earth Day cofounder Denis Hayes (who has since left the program) in 1990, has just started its labeling program and hopes to become the accepted standard for green labeling. Norman Dean, president of Green Seal, said his group's standards were created after an extensive private and public comment period. Green Seal is using the giant insurance-industry testing concern Underwriters Laboratory to verify specific claims of the products receiving seals. Although business leaders are allowed to sit on the Green Seal board of directors, no directors may represent any consumer products company. Standards set by Green Seal will be reviewed every three years. An advisory committee of scientists and other experts works with an Environmental Standards Council to draft final standards and monitor the program.

At the time of publication, Green Seal had established thirty-five product standards and certified five products. The products are certified for recycled-paper content (CARE, Project Green, and AWARE bath and facial tissues) and made by Ashdun Industries of Englewood Cliffs, New Jersey. Green Seal certified the paper for 20 percent postconsumer waste. The group hopes to certify more products in the future and to begin labeling products with an Environmental Report Card in 1994.

To date, SCS has been focusing its efforts on certifying various packaging and content claims. They do so by inspecting factories and other aspects of manufacturing. They've certified, for example, that certain garbage bags contain recycled paper or plastic products made from postconsumer waste (PCW)—the stuff that you and I throw out. PCW is a term you'll hear a lot more about. When manufacturers use PCW in packaging, they're diverting refuse from our trash bins back into packaging. This is called "closed loop" recycling. Preconsumer waste, on the other hand, consists of trimmings and mill waste. It's material that probably wouldn't go to the landfill anyway. The difference between the two types of waste is important, yet few understand the distinction. According to an Environmental Research Associates poll, 75 percent of Americans claimed to know the meaning of "preconsumer waste" (waste that doesn't come from consumers). But in fact they didn't know. That's one of the things Green Seal and SCS will be monitoring in their attempts to monitor companies' claims. SCS, for example, has had a team of scientists testing produce for pesticide residues and moving farmers away from pesticides. Rather than set standards for manufacturers to meet, SCS checks plants to validate claims.

SCS has also formed an alliance with industry groups, manufacturers, environmental engineers, and private institutions to test and certify environmental claims. It recently teamed up with the Home Center Institute and the National Retail Hardware Association to independently review environmental claims on a wide variety of consumer products for some 15,000 stores across the country. The program stresses a partnership in verifying green claims on the manufacturing and retail levels. SCS has done a similar service for West Coast supermarket chains.

By working with retailers, SCS hopes ultimately to improve the environmental quality of merchandise and provide a standardized comparison-shopping guide for all certified products. The approach is similar to the Department of Agriculture program that provides research and information to farmers while inspecting and certifying meat and produce.

The idea behind the SCS program is to allow consumers to inspect a wide range of environmental claims and be able to compare similar products the way you would compare two melons. SCS is developing an Environmental Report Card that will show you a complete environmental dossier on each product. That way, you can compare similar products for their "greenness" and what kind of toxins are created in the manufacturing process. For example, a can of paint with an Environmental Report Card would tell how much carbon dioxide and smog-producing volatile organic compounds are released into the air when you use the paint.

LIFE-CYCLE ANALYSIS
MEANS INFORMED SHOPPING

With LCA, labels on supermarket products will tell you how much pollution the manufacturer generated in making the product, and the overall costs to the environment relative to an industry standard. Such labels will also indicate whether one product is better than another in terms of environmental impact. Will these factors affect your purchasing decisions?

LCA is such a powerful information tool that the very presence of the labeling will force manufacturers to clean up their operations. Fortunately, this science is widely accepted internationally. More than ever, scientists will be able to tell "who's been naughty or nice" based on how manufacturers *make* something—and not simply on what they claim.

In Europe, some $20 million has been spent on research into LCA. Great Britain, Switzerland, and Germany lead the pack in adopting LCA guidelines. Other groups eyeing LCA include the United Nations (Agenda 21), the European Economic Community, the International Standards Organization, and the U.S. EPA. Great Britain, for example, is using LCA to develop packaging guidelines. U.S.–based companies are also pursuing LCA. They include 3M, Coca-Cola, Scott Paper, Procter & Gamble, and Benckiser. The EPA has even issued rules on how to conduct proper LCA studies.

If governments and companies are interested in LCA, it's because consumers are the driving force for this information. A survey by Gerstman & Meyers found that 85 percent of those polled say there is "too little environmental information" on product labels. Some 72 percent want better environmental labeling because a scant 15 percent believe green claims.

There's little debate over the credibility and scarcity of green information on products. But what exactly do we want to know about a product? LCA will tell us how much a single product—and our use of it—hurts the earth. Engineers will measure and report gallons of water used, wood consumed, fossil fuels burned, pollutants emitted, and atmosphere-warming carbon dioxide released. Even better, we'll know from the label how it compared to similar products in an industry. Sometimes, when two identical products are made by two different manufacturers, one company pollutes much more than the other. This information will affect your product-buying decision.

For example, let's look at your refrigerator. Most older fridges are energy "hogs," consuming as much as 25 percent of the electricity in your home. Generally, the older the refrigerator, the more power it consumes. This is because their motors run constantly to keep your food at a constant temperature. These appliances are also designed inefficiently, with the heat-producing (compressors) components of the fridge located at the bottom of the unit. Heat rises, of course, constantly warming up what you're trying to keep cool. In addition, most refrigerators contain CFC coolants in the cooling coils and the foam insulation. These CFCs leak out over time and devour protective ozone molecules. But that's another issue. LCA includes what consumers do with products. If we use things beyond their peak operating efficiencies (cars, refrigerators), they tend to use more energy and pollute more. LCA will address these problems as well.

Let's try a comparison that LCA provides of a "standard" with a "state of the art" refrigerator bought in the Midwest.

The difference is dramatic. Here are some preliminary estimates prepared by SCS.

Environmental Burdens	Green Fridge	Standard Fridge
Water	3,527 gallons	6,188 gallons
Total energy used	165 mil. BTUs	289 mil. BTUs
Ozone-eating chemicals	0.5 lb.	1.5 lbs.
Carbon dioxide	48,270 lbs.	84,684 lbs.
Hazardous air pollution	173 lbs.	303 lbs.
Unclassified waste	3,132.72 lbs.	5,496 lbs.

You don't need a science degree to see that a refrigerator that pollutes twice as much as another one probably is hurting the earth. Here's another issue that isn't even in this label: You'll pay more to use the standard model. The EPA currently requires manufacturers of refrigerators and other major appliances to post stickers estimating how much energy they will use in a year. The greenest models always use less energy. In the process, they create less pollution from the mine to the landfill. But keep in mind that *every* product uses up resources in its manufacture and use, so there's no such thing as a perfect green product.

Part 2

EARTHLY CONCERNS IN THE SUPERMARKET

There are hundreds of things to consider when browsing through the supermarket. Most of them we can't measure because there's no consistently reliable way of getting inside a company's manufacturing process to see what's going on. We'd love to be able to tell you that a particular oatmeal was produced without using pesticides or a cosmetic wasn't tested on rabbits. Unless something's been verified or certified by an independent third-party agency or the government, we don't know if we can believe half of the claims being made. For most products, it's a matter of trust.

Chapter 4

Should I Be Concerned About Pesticides?

As with most key environmental issues, the presence of pesticides in fresh and packaged foods is vigorously debated. Pesticides are used in modern agriculture to ensure high crop yields and to reduce crop loss from insect attack. Other chemical tools used by farmers include fungicides, which kill molds and fungi, and herbicides, which kill weeds. While no one knows for sure how much of these chemicals end up in our food, several studies have indicated the presence of "residues" in fruits and vegetables. Some of these chemicals are believed to cause cancer and birth defects.

Under the Delaney Clause—an amendment to the Food, Drug and Cosmetic Act—it's illegal to use in foods any substances proven to cause cancer in laboratory animals. But industry groups such as the National Food Processors Association and the Fresh Fruit and Vegetable Association have fought the rule in court, claiming that it's too strict. The debate centers on how much residue is enough to trigger cancer. While environmentalists argue for "zero tolerance," a 1981 study by Richard Doll and Richard Peto found that environmental exposure may account for only 3 percent of all cancers. Major factors are smoking, high-fat diets, and too much alcohol consumption. Nevertheless, environmental groups such as the Natural Resources Defense Council claim that pesticide residues are a serious problem. The NRDC sampled produce from the United States and abroad and found that from 2 percent to eighty percent of their samples contained residues. The imported food samples typically contained more residues than did domestic products. An FDA study also found significant amounts of residues in produce.

The independent testing firm Nutriclean, for example, found the fungicide Captan in residues exceeding .05 parts per million in 74 samples. The chemical, which damages the human reproductive system, is used on fruits, vegetables, and nuts in quantities as high as 10 million pounds annually.

It pays for you to be cautious with produce since our government is lax in monitoring pesticide residues. The FDA is charged with testing domestic and imported produce, but it rarely takes action when it finds "adulterated" or tainted foods. The congressional Government Accounting Office (GAO) found that the FDA isn't dealing with "a long-term problem of importers distributing these [tainted] foods. . . . FDA rarely prosecutes such cases because of the practical difficulties of pursuing criminal prosecution."

If you read between the lines of the GAO report, it's clear that some of the pesticide-laden foods could be reaching grocery shelves. The GAO discovered that between 1988 and 1990, "about one-third of the imported food shipments that FDA found to be adulterated with illegal pesticide residues were not returned to Customs [Dept.] for supervised destruction or export." That means that the produce either rotted in a warehouse somewhere—or it was sold.

What does that mean to you as you shop? Since almost half of the produce sold during winter months is imported, you have to be aware of what you buy. The FDA can test only about 1 percent of the $16 billion in imported produce. In fact, no government agency could test even one-third of it. You also need to realize that most exporting countries don't have agencies like the FDA looking over their shoulder. As the GAO study showed, even if tainted produce makes it into the United States, it's unlikely that the FDA will do anything about it (barring new legislation), since it's not a law enforcement agency and the cost of prosecuting exporters is prohibitive. Besides, the FDA has limited resources. In 1990, the agency tested only 10,000 shipments out of 1.2 *million*.

Overall, you should temper your concern with the fact that only 4.3 percent of imported produce tested positive by the FDA for illegal pesticide residues. Unfortunately, the GAO noted, some 45 to 50 percent of that tainted produce actually reached supermarkets.

An even longer-term concern is the fact that overuse of pesticides by all producers poses a sustainability dilemma. Every year, more and more pesticides are used on crops around the world. The EPA, which registers pesticides in the United States, receives about 1,500 filings a year from companies manufacturing new substances. Of the existing 65,000 chemicals in use in industry, some 600 are known to adversely affect the human central nervous system.

Unfortunately, nature gives bugs the upper hand in defending against pesticides. They adapt to new poisons and continue to devour crops. This means that farmers are constantly looking for more lethal means to kill fungi, molds, blights, and insects. More pesticides mean more groundwater pollution; more river, estuary, and ocean pollution; and the resultant slaughter of aquatic plants and animals. Just ask a regional environmentalist about the death of Chesapeake Bay or any river system on the East Coast (or in any industrialized country, for that matter), and he or she can tell you grim tales that spring from pesticide runoff.

Yet another consideration is that pesticides are produced from petrochemicals and highly lethal chemicals. When released into the environment, these chemicals do everything from cause cancer to deplete the earth's protective ozone layer. The EPA recently banned the widely used pesticide methyl bromide, which is a prime ozone depleter. The manufacturing of pesticides also depletes nonrenewal resources such as petroleum.

Some hope lies in genetic engineering for pest-resistant strains of vegetables and fruits—if it proves safe for human consumption. Another school of thought examines "integrated pest management" and other natural means of fending off pests. Some of this technology is centuries old and is being used by organic farmers on a small scale. As with most issues in our economy, the cost of doing right by the earth is a paramount consideration. Organic produce costs about one-third more than conventional produce; organic farming tends to be more labor intensive and is done on expensive, smaller-acreage farms. Ironically, the broad use of pesticides keeps produce prices relatively low. Most industrial farmers consider only mass applications of economically viable alternatives. Considering the permanent damage to water and air that pesticides cause, though, it's time for government, farmers, and pesticide makers to include the total cost of pollution in their cost-benefit analyses. This isn't something you'll see reflected in the price of a head of lettuce, but it needs to be considered if we are fully to understand the earthly impact of our buying decisions. Progressive farmers and scientists are exploring ideas such as "low input sustainable agriculture" and "clean" food, which reduce the amount of chemicals used in farming. It's clear that another revolution will be needed in agriculture if we are to make it a sustainable industry.

WHAT YOU CAN DO

As long as the agriculture industry uses pesticides, there will be a problem with residues. It's not surprising that a Food Marketing Institute poll found that only 12 percent of consumers think their food is safe from pesticides. People are uneasy about the presence of so many chemicals in their environment—especially in their food. It's clear that the greatest threat of pesticide residues is to children, because they ingest much higher amounts of the chemicals relative to their body weight. To protect yourself and your family, thoroughly wash all produce you buy. If that doesn't allay your concerns, buy from producers who are independently certified for growing organic produce. If you can't find such products in your supermarket, try your local farmer's market. Urge your supermarket to carry certified organic produce. An even better alternative is to grow your own, using organic gardening techniques and integrated pest management. Perhaps the best resource on this subject is your local bookstore or *Organic Gardening* magazine, which is published by Rodale Press.

Also keep in mind that "organic" doesn't always mean your food is totally free of chemicals. Contact growers and your supermarket for more detailed information. The only way you can guarantee the purity of produce is to have your own garden's soil tested and grow it yourself.

Chapter 5

The Meat Question

A group led by activist Jeremy Rifkin recently launched a group called the Beyond Beef Campaign, which is pushing to reduce the amount of beef consumption worldwide. The group's basic premise is that cattle raising is environmentally harmful in a number of ways, so consumers should cut back on their beef consumption out of concern for the earth.

While we advocate taking a hard look at your diet, you need to know some facts. First, nearly *all* livestock production (for meat) is a drain on the earth's resources relative to production of grain. It should also be noted that meat is an important source of protein and can be mass produced and distributed easily, and the industry provides employment for millions.

However, livestock production may not be the greatest environmental villain. According to the World Watch Institute's *Taking Stock: Animal Farming and the Environment*, pork production "absorbs more grain than any other meat industry, followed by poultry production. Together they account for at least two-thirds of feed grain consumption. Dairy and beef cattle consume the remaining third."

The bottom line with meat production is that it consumes

massive amounts of resources without conferring maximum benefit as a food source. The meat that we produce is taking away resources from the quality of human life and biodiversity. Species are being lost forever when rain forests are cleared for cattle grazing. A cure for cancer might lie in those jungles.

In addition, eating fat-laden meats is a major factor in cardiovascular disease and cancer. Some other issues you need to consider when buying meat:

• Rain forests are depleted in developed countries to clear land for cattle grazing. Because cattle raising is seen as a more profitable activity, it's given precedence over the invaluable and irreplaceable resources of the tropics.

• Overgrazing by livestock causes erosion, depletion of vegetation, desertification, and destruction of habitat. The World Watch Institute claims that overgrazing has degraded 73 percent of the world's rangeland.

• Meat production is energy-intensive and consumes vast quantities of grain and water. Almost half of the energy used by agriculture in the United States is devoted to livestock and feed production.

• It is believed that livestock-generated methane is contributing to the "greenhouse effect," which is warming the earth's atmosphere.

WHAT YOU CAN DO ABOUT MEAT

If you can eat less meat, fine. To some extent, you can substitute a balanced diet of legumes, soy products, and whole grains. Not everybody can be a vegetarian, though. It can help the planet and the future of society if you take the costs of meat production into consideration when you plan your meals.

ANIMAL TESTING

For some consumers, animal testing is a major concern. Some companies use rabbits, hamsters, and other animals to see if their products will harm humans. Animal rights groups argue that this is inhumane treatment and urge consumers to boycott such companies. Of course, this is not a simple issue. It can also be argued that animal testing is necessary because companies don't have a choice; they're not in the business of harming people and can also treat animals humanely. You must decide for yourself. The group People for the Ethical Treatment of Animals has compiled a list of companies that do and don't practice animal testing. Contact PETA for copies of their list, or check the book *Save the Animals!* by Ingrid Newkirk, National Director of PETA, for more information.

Since we have no way of checking every company facility that does testing, we cannot know with certainty who's testing and who's not.

Chapter 6

Bottled Water

FDA RULES

The dual appeals of health and environmental concerns have muddied claims made by bottled water companies. The FDA recently issued (proposed) rules on claims that can be made by the $2 billion bottled water industry. Terms such as *mineral*, *spring*, *natural*, and *purified* were being used fast and loose. In 25 percent of the cases, the supposedly pure water was nothing more than tap water at the bottling plant, according to the FDA. Here are a few guidelines you should keep in mind:

• **Truthful labeling.** "If it's from a municipal water source, the water should be labeled," stated Dr. David Kessler, the commissioner of the FDA. You could be paying top dollar for tap water.

• **Mineral water definitions.** Bottled water must contain at least 250 parts per million in dissolved minerals to be called mineral water. Springwater must come from an underground source where water naturally flows to the surface—not from water mains.

• **Tap water standards.** Although the rules require that bottled water meet EPA standards for tap water, allowable lead levels in bottled water would be 5 parts per billion, lower than the 15 parts per billion standard set for municipal tap water.

If you want information on your community's water supply, contact your local village hall or federal Environmental Protection Agency office (see page 323).

Chapter 7

Understanding Food Labeling Claims

There's an interesting overlap between green claims and other aspects of food labeling. In an attempt to market to health-conscious consumers, manufacturers use an array of packaging and nutrition claims. Here are some things you need to be informed about:

• **Nutrition labels.** Manufacturers will be required to report standard servings and accurate amounts of fat, vitamins, etc., per serving by May 1994. The use of "fat free," "lite," and related terms will be strictly regulated. Before the new law, manufacturers used these terms spuriously. The law also requires that a daily diet be evaluated in terms of 2,000 calories—including intake of fat, carbohydrates, saturated fat, cholesterol, sugars, and dietary fiber.

• **Certified organic.** Under the Organic Foods Production Act of 1990, this term will be more tightly regulated. "Organic" means that the food has been certified by an independent firm for nonuse of synthetic fertilizers or pesticides. These foods are also processed without the use of chemical additives or preservatives. Check for third-party certification by Organic Crop Improvement Association (OCIA), Scientific Certification Systems (SCS), California Certified Organic Farmers (CCOF), and Organic Growers and Buyers Association (OGBA). While these products may not look as large and wholesome as their synthetically grown counterparts, they are virtually free of manmade chemicals and pesticides. Be aware, however, that just because something is certified organic, it isn't necessarily free of manmade chemicals. Lingering poisons such as DDT may still be in the soil (and in your food) because it takes decades for the chemical to go away. That may circumvent an organic farmer's best intentions.

• **Free range.** Commercial livestock and poultry that's sold for meat is often raised in cramped, filthy sheds with little light. These "factories" raise animals fast for slaughter. Many animal and consumer activists claim that "free range" animals, which are raised in larger, more sanitary facilities, are healthier for you in the long run because they live healthier, more natural lives.

• **Growth-hormone–free.** Growth hormones are used by some farmers to speed up the growth process. These chemicals produce 25 percent more fat in livestock such as beef, lamb, and dairy cows. This process, however, not only shortens the life span of the animals, it weakens their natural resistance to disease, which means farmers must use more antibiotics to treat them. Some of these chemicals end up in your food, although how much and the degree of the risk is yet to be determined.

• **Natural.** Although one of the least-regulated terms, when applied to meat, says the Department of Agriculture, the product was processed without chemicals and preservatives. When applied to other products, it gets vague. Loosely defined, it just means that fewer "unnatural" chemicals are in the product, although there's no rigid definition for how much processing makes something "natural." Be most wary of this claim.

• **Perfume-, dye-, and fragrance-free.** Often found on detergent packages, these chemicals are removed for those who are chemically sensitive or allergic to specific products. Why should this be a concern? The National Research Council estimates that 15 percent of U.S. citizens are now hypersensitive—that is, they develop some physical or allergic reaction—to chemicals found in common household products.

• **Unbleached, chlorine-free, unbromated.** Bread and grain products are often bleached white to enhance their appearance and to make the dough rise faster. Chemicals such as chlorine dioxide and benzoyl peroxide are used in the process. Chlorine-free detergents and paper products merely mean that chlorine compounds were not used in the bleaching process. Chlorine by-products that are emitted by paper mills have been linked with the suspected carcinogen dioxin (actually, a chemical family). Alternatives to chlorine bleaching include "natural brown" paper and "oxygen" bleaching.

Chapter 8

Shopping to Avoid
Household Toxins

There's a close link between what's good for the earth and what's good for you and your family. Many innocent-sounding cleaners and personal care products are quite dangerous if inhaled or ingested. Such products are considered "household hazardous wastes"—that is, they need special treatment in order not to pose a health threat.

The EPA estimates that the average U.S. household contains some fifty to one hundred pounds of hazardous waste. Although most of this waste is found in nasty things like paints, solvents, insecticides, and auto oil, there are some products in your medicine chest that require special attention. Many nail polish removers, hair sprays, and deodorants contain chemicals that pose health risks and create air pollution.

The health risks associated with home products range from skin sensitivity to carcinogens, which cause cancer. Most of these products have been studied extensively by government agencies and have been identified as to the possible health risks they might pose. You should note, however, that most of these chemicals pose the greatest risk if you use them over a long period of time and receive intense exposure. However, occasional use probably won't be a problem.

The environmental connection is that many household products contain volatile organic compounds (VOCs) that react with sunlight to produce that brown haze (aka "smog") that covers most urban areas. It's estimated that some 80 million people in the United States live in areas that don't meet federal air-quality standards. While most smog is due to vehicle exhaust, the EPA estimates that small businesses and consumers may account for 50 percent of VOC emissions. Some of those emissions are caused by household pesticides and disinfectants. The following charts list common categories of household chemicals and some suggested alternatives.

Smog-Causing Household Chemicals

Chemicals	Alternatives
Adhesives, glues	White glue
Air fresheners	Baking soda, white vinegar, herbal potpourri
Cleaners, ammonia	Lemon juice, vinegar, borax
Art supplies	Water-based paints, inks
Batteries	Rechargeables, manual items
Carpets	Natural fibers
Bleach	Nonchlorine bleach
Cleaners	Nontoxic cleaners
Deodorants	Baking soda
Disinfectants	Vinegar
Dry cleaning (fluid)	Washable fabrics
Fingernail polish	Dried henna
Paint strippers, solvents	Solvent-free strippers

Ammonia cleaners	Vinegar and water
Hair dyes (ammonia)	Henna rinse
Hair spray	Boil lemon juice, chill, put in spray bottle
Law care chemicals	Organic gardening
Metal polishes (acetone)	Baking soda and boiling water for silver; salt, flour and vinegar for brass; lemon juice and salt for copper
Mothballs	Cedar blocks, herbs
Paint	Nontoxic water-based paint
Perfumes, after-shaves	Natural oils
Pesticides	Organic pesticides, boric acid
Pet flea and tick treatment	Brewer's yeast, di-limonene pet shampoo
Rug/upholstery cleaners	Borax, baking soda
Spot removers	Borax, club soda
Toilet cleaners	Baking soda, lemon juice
Typewriter correction fluid	Correction tape

Source: Nancy Lilienthal, et al., *Tackling Toxins in Everyday Products: A Directory of Organizations,* Inform, Inc., New York, 1992. Used with permission.

Common Household Products and Possible Ill Health Effects

Chemical	Found in ...	Health Effects
Acetaldehyde	adhesives	A,C,E
Acetone	nail polish, polish remover	Ch,E

Acrylonitrile	fabrics	A,C,D,E,R
Ammonia	cleaners	A,Ch,E
Carbaryl	pesticides, pet prods.	A,Ch,E,N,R
Cadmium	ni-cad batteries	A,C,Ch,D,E,R
Chlorine	bleach, cleaners	A,Ch,E
Cresol	art supplies, cleaners	A,Ch,E
1,2-dichlorobenzene	carpets	C,Ch,D,E,M,R
DEHP 4	fabrics, hair spray	C,Ch,D,E,M,R
Ethylene glycol	deodorants, paint	Ch
Formaldehyde	glues, nail polish	C,Ch,E,M,R
Hydrochloric acid	toilet cleaners	A,Ch
Lead	hair dyes, batteries	D,N,R
Mercury	batteries	Ch,E,N,R
Methanol	paint strippers	N
Methyl chloroform/ Methylene chloride	paints, pesticides	C
Methyl ethyl ketone	adhesives, waxes, cleansers	Ch,D,N,R
Naphthalene	mothballs, pesticides	E
Butyl alcohol	after-shave, perfume	Ch
Paradichlorobenzene	mothballs, air fresheners	C,Ch,E
Perchloroethylene	dry cleaning fluid, spot removers	C,Ch,D,E,R
Phenols	art supplies, glues	A,D,E
Toluene	nail polish, strippers	D,E,M,R
1,1,1-trichloroethane	spot removers, glues	D,E,R
Vinyl chloride	plastics, clothes	C,Ch,D,M,R
Xylenes	glues, art supplies	Ch,D,E,R
Zinc	batteries	E

Key:
- A = Acute toxin that may cause harm through short exposure
- C = Cancer causing
- Ch = Chronic toxin that causes damage over years of exposure
- D = Developmental effects (birth defects, miscarriages)
- E = Environmental toxin that can harm wildlife
- M = Mutagen that causes gene damage
- N = Neurotoxin that harms the nervous system
- R = Reproductive effects that may affect fertility

Source: *Tackling Toxins in Everyday Products,* pp. 14–21. Reprinted with permission.

WHAT YOU CAN DO

1. If you think you've been poisoned by any substance in your house, call your doctor immediately. Note any exposures to household chemicals, and bring containers with you when seeking medical care. Children are even more susceptible to chemical poisoning because of their smaller size and body weight. In case of an emergency, call your local hospital's poison control center or emergency room.

2. Read labels. If you don't like the sound of any of the chemicals we've described, and if you discover them in your household products, don't use them. Consider the alternatives.

3. Call companies. Many companies supply toll-free numbers for product information. If no number is available, call the company's consumer affairs department.

Part 3

THE PACKAGING PROBLEM

Packaging is one of the main reasons why people may avoid certain products. "To most consumers, the environment means packaging," said Anthony Casale, president of Environmental Research Associates. Like eating in a restaurant in a foreign country, you need a little background before you start ordering. Following are the basics of packaging.

The Best Packaging Is Little or No Packaging

You can take your own shopping bags to the supermarket, buy food in bulk using reusable containers, or visit your local farmer's market once a week. You're not only diverting packaging from a landfill, you're saving the energy needed to make and transport the packaging from raw materials to the landfill. Even better, plant the largest garden your land can sustain.

Returnable, Reusable or Refillable Packaging Is Better

You used to be able to take your glass soft-drink bottles back to the store for a refill. Then bottlers discovered that selling their products in 2-liter PETE (polyethylene terepthalate) bottles allowed them to ship more with less energy—and the bottles were cheaper to produce. The bottles are recyclable but, unfortunately, not refillable. The same is true of plastic milk bottles. It would be nice if supermarkets offered a refilling service for bulk staples such as detergent, salt, sugar, and other basics. But start looking for them; you'll be seeing more of them in years to come. They're already popular in Western European countries. Like my mother and grandmother before me, I save margarine tubs to store leftovers and freezable foods. Another good thing to know is that most large supermarket chains take back plastic shopping bags for recycling. If they don't, you can bring your own bags or recycle the paper bags they supply. That's why the best answer to the paper-or-plastic controversy is really "neither."

Look for Source-Reduced or Minimal Packaging

Most products need some sort of packaging so that you can take them out of the supermarket. But it's better to use a package that contains less material. Again, this translates into less energy consumed in manufacture and transportation and less landfill waste.

Packaging Preference Order: Aluminum, Steel, Glass, Plastic, Paper, Mixed Materials

It's easy to buy something in glass, steel, aluminum, or PETE/HDPE plastics (the two most recyclable plastics). Just look at the container. In the case of plastics, look at the bottom of the container. It should be coded with a number within chasing arrows. The number indicates the type of plastic resin. Most recycling centers take the #1 plastic. The acceptability of the other plastics declines as you move from resins #2 to #7. Although the plastics industry is spending millions on starting recycling programs for all types of plastics, if your local recycling program doesn't take a certain type of plastic, let's face it, it's not recyclable. Paperboard (used in cartons) is generally made from recycled material but is rarely taken by recyclers. They're just not set up to handle it. Most recyclers also won't take magazines because of the high clay content in the paper coating. The chemicals in color inks aren't easily recycled and may contain toxic heavy metals. Ask your local recycler what they'll take and make a note of it.

Buy Products That Contain Recycled Material

If you can't do all of the above, this is the next best thing. While it can be said that the greenest container is no container at all, the best recycled container contains a high percentage of postconsumer content (the stuff you and I throw out). Many companies claim recycled content by using their own mill waste, which is preconsumer content. That doesn't help the landfill situation much, since such valuable scraps weren't likely to be thrown out anyway. Manufacturers are not required to use any postconsumer waste, nor are they required to disclose on their packaging the percentage of postconsumer waste used. Nevertheless, the most concerned companies put this information on the package or disclose it through their consumer hotlines.

Chapter 9

Solid Facts About Packaging

• We create about 4.3 pounds of garbage per person per day, or about 195 million tons for everyone in the United States, according to the EPA (1990 figures). By the year 2,000, the EPA expects 4.5 pounds per person per day, or 216 million tons per year.

• Packaging, including newspapers, is the largest single portion of municipal landfills, accounting for as much as one-third of the municipal solid-waste stream, according to the EPA. Of this waste "stream," a whopping 37.5 percent is paper; glass is 6.7 percent and plastics are 8.3 percent. The remaining 4 percent or so is aluminum, wood, and steel. Food and yard wastes make up the next largest piece of the landfill pie, accounting for about 18 percent of waste.

• Americans throw away 183 million disposable razors and 2.7 billion batteries each year, according to Alan Durning, author of *How Much Is Enough?* Worldwide, some 200 billion bottles, cans, plastic cartons, and paper and plastic cups are thrown out. That could explain why Americans spend some $225 per person on packaging every year—4 cents of every dollar spent on consumer goods.

• About 17 billion disposable diapers are bought in the

United States alone each year (as of 1991), with a child going through about 4,500 of them through his or her infancy. Although diapers take up only 0.5 percent to 1.8 percent of landfill space, they're neither degradable nor recyclable. Manufacturers are trying to improve the design, using some source-reduced, recycled, or recyclable materials, but they're still not environmentally friendly. Cloth diapers are reusable but use tremendous amounts of water, detergent, and fuel to clean them. Which is better? From any angle, diapers are a dirty, inconvenient business. Even the editor of *Garbage*, a fine environmental products magazine, admitted that she bought disposable diapers for her baby. The jury's out on this one.

• Convenience packaging is growing in popularity. For example, Tetra-Pak, the world's largest manufacturer of multilayer packaging, produced some 54 billion "drink box" cartons per year (as of 1989). These packages simply didn't exist twenty years ago. Although they don't require refrigeration and have a longer shelf life than conventional packaging, these packages are generally not recyclable. The packaging industry has started a few trial recycling centers for the drink boxes, but they're few and far between and not likely to be economically feasible.

• Single-use packaging consumes massive amounts of energy. Choose juices in recycled glass or cans and you save 15 percent of the energy needed to make the product from virgin raw materials. If you buy virgin plastic and recycle it, you're saving 92 to 98 percent of the energy needed to make the material from scratch. Reusing steel scrap (versus making steel from raw materials) reduces air pollution by 85 percent, water pollution by 76 percent, water by 40 percent, and mining wastes by 97 percent, according to the Steel Can Recycling Institute. If you consider production and disposal impact costs, "virgin" PVC (polyvinyl chloride, or "vinyl") and aluminum would be the most expensive packaging to produce, at $5,288 and $1,963 per ton respectively, according to the Tellus Institute. Reusing recycled materials saves the earth in a number of ways. The more you use recycled materials, the less pollution is released and the less energy is expended. According to an Arthur D. Little, Inc., study, the lowly two-piece steel tuna fish can is the most energy efficient.

It also takes tremendous amounts of energy to make, incinerate, and bury packaging. The United States is already the world's largest consumer of energy—about 26 percent—although we only have 5 percent of the world's population. Making, transporting, burning, and burying packaging consumes nonrenewable resources.

• Although Americans are recycling, we're still dumping garbage much faster. In 1960, we only recycled 7.2 percent of municipal solid waste. Now, we recycle about 17 percent of that garbage. However, despite the success of some recycling programs, there still are not enough markets for recyclables such as newspaper.

Chapter 10

What Is "Recyclable"?

Hundreds of manufacturers now place recycling codes on their plastic containers. These numbers correspond to resins that the industry widely recognizes. In our survey, we were disturbed that too many manufacturers expected consumers to believe that placing a recycling code on the bottom of a container was the same thing as making it recyclable. What's recyclable depends on who (locally) can and will recycle it. In truth, nearly anything can be recycled if you can find someone else to use it again. But the presence of a recycling code doesn't mean it can or will be recycled! For example, nearly all plastic containers had recycling codes, although only 2.2 of all plastics are actually recycled.

Read the chart below to see which products are being recycled the most. For our survey, we defined plastic recyclability as plastic containers coded either #1 or #2, because those contain the most widely recycled resins. If your local recycler doesn't take one or the other resin, please keep that in mind.

Plastics Recycling Rates

Code	Resin Abb.	% Recycled	Used in:
1	PETE	20.8 to 35.8	Pop bottles, peanut butter jars
2	HDPE	3.6	Milk, water, detergent bottles
3	Vinyl/PVC	0.1	Blister packs, shampoo, oil bottles
4	LDPE/ LLDPE	0.2	Lids, squeeze bottles, bread wrappers
5	PP	2.2	Syrup, ketchup, yogurt, margarine
6	PS	0.5	Coffee cups, meat trays, utensils
7	Other	NA	Various resins, mixtures, drink boxes

Note: All of the plastics resins can be recycled where facilities exist into other products such as soda bottles, carpet, lumber, pipes, trash cans, and garbage bags. The majority of recycling, however, involves soft-drink containers. If you want to choose a plastic for its recyclability, ask your local recycling program which resin it takes and buy accordingly.

Source: "Post-Consumer Plastics Recycling Rates," American Plastics Council 1990–1991.

Abbreviations: PETE = polyethylene terepthalate; HDPE = high-density polyethylene; PVC = polyvinyl chloride; LDPE = low-density/low polyethylene; PP = polypropylene; DS = polystyrene.

Recycling/Recovery Rates by Group

Material	Recovery Rate
Aluminum	38.1%
Automotive batteries	96.6%
Glass	19.9%
Paper	28.6%
Plastics	2.2%
Steel	15.4%
Tires	11.6%
Used motor oil	67%
Yard waste	4.2%

Note: These categories lump together all types of materials. Specific types of aluminum, paper, plastics, steel, and glass have higher recycling rates than the overall group. For example, more than 62.4 percent of aluminum cans are recycled and 33 percent of PETE beverage bottles. The glass soft-drink recycling rate is 26 percent. These rates do not reflect landfill waste by volume, either. For example, yard waste and paper account for the lion's share by volume in land-fills—accounting for 55 percent of landfill waste by volume, or more than 100 million tons of waste. All materials are re-cyclable to various degrees. Motor oil and batteries are highly recyclable because there's an organized network of profitable companies set up to do so. It is a different matter with plastics, paper, and yard waste, which are profitable in varying degrees.

Source: *Recycling Municipal Solid Waste Facts & Figures*, U.S. EPA, 1992.

SOURCE REDUCTION AND RECYCLED CONTENT

Manufacturers love the idea of source reduction. The more they reduce packaging materials, the less their products cost to make. That makes them more competitive because they can offer lower prices, sell more of their products, and increase profits.

Among the hundreds of companies we talked to, most didn't want to disclose much about their packaging development. In fact, most consumer hotlines did verbal double takes when we asked about recyclability and recycled content. A handful of "consumer specialists" even insisted that the two terms were interchangeable. They are not. Generally, the larger the company, the more detailed (and correct) packaging information was available.

As a rule, only the largest companies invest time and money in improving their packaging. Most small or mid-size companies rely on giant packaging producers such as Eastman Chemical, International Paper, and Dolco Packaging. Companies that employ source reduction have the blessing of the EPA, which deems the process one of its top priorities in reducing landfill waste.

Procter & Gamble and Unilever are highly vocal about what they're doing with packaging. As two of the world's leading consumer-goods conglomerates, they ought to be doing everything they can. For example, David Webb, chief executive officer of Unilever, proclaimed at the Pack Expo trade show in Chicago in late 1992, "By source reduction and lightweighting alone, we've eliminated 2.5 million pounds of plastic from our bottles each year." Unilever's Lever Brothers unit, which has a "packaging development center," is interested in reducing packaging wherever it can. As a world leader in detergents—such as a 50 percent reduction in packaging in its Ultra Snuggle fabric softener—Unilever can trim its operating and materials cost significantly. But when you're scanning the supermarket shelves, it's not easy to tell who's doing what—even if you read labels carefully, as we did.

Source reduction and lightweighting (reduction of the weight of packaging) are widely regarded by manufacturers as effective means of cutting costs, and much progress has been made in that area over the last decade or so. For example, PETE soda bottles have been reduced by 30 percent in the past twenty years; HDPE milk jugs by some 45 percent; and plastic grocery bags (LDPE) by 40 percent. Even glass bottles are 25 percent lighter than they were in 1984. Less packaging material not only reduces the burden on landfills, it means greater profits. We noted such source-reduction advances in our survey.

ConAgra, a giant food processor that runs a $1 billion-plus frozen foods division (Healthy Choice, Armour Dinner Classics, Banquet), gave us some specifics that typify what the larger companies are doing. Brian Hopkins, director of packaging for ConAgra Frozen Foods, noted that manufacturers are having problems getting enough plastic to use in their recycled containers and have to use other materials that won't raise the cost of the product. It's also difficult to use some materials because they might fade or break when exposed to heat or cold. Most frozen foods, he adds, need extra packaging (or wax/plastic coatings) because the freezing process buckles paper cartons.

Nevertheless, Hopkins points out that "the environmental movement is making food companies more sensitive about packaging. Source reduction almost always means cost [of production] reductions. But will consumers accept it?"

For example, ConAgra has reduced the paper content of its Banquet dinners by 15 percent and redesigned its Armour Dinner Classics by using a different kind of plastic and eliminating part of the package. One such packaging change means that ConAgra can eliminate the use of 6 million pounds of paper and save 20 percent of the packaging costs on a particular line. Like most companies, ConAgra won't disclose how much money it has saved through packaging changes. But it's clear that the savings make their products more profitable, otherwise they wouldn't consider them. Doubtless the greatest single reason why manufacturers use recycled paperboard for outer cartons is that it's cheaper than virgin material. They've been doing so since the turn of the century, although they're only just now capitalizing on the environmental cachet by putting green labels on packages.

The demand for recycled content in packaging is now being pushed by consumer concerns. Overall, two-thirds of the members of the trade group Grocery Manufacturers of America have told their suppliers to incorporate more recycled content in the materials they purchase. Some 75 percent of GMA members offer source-reduced packaging, recycle shipping containers, recycle plant materials, and reuse shipping pallets.

It makes good economic sense for packagers to use recycled material. It's a cheaper source than virgin, so they can lower the unit cost of their product and spend more on packaging design or marketing or boost their dividends to shareholders. For example, the Helene Curtis Corporation, maker of Salon Selectives hair care products, makes their bottles using an inner layer of recycled HDPE. As a result, some 6 million plastic milk cartons will be diverted from landfills.

As with all products, companies won't make recycled or recyclable products unless consumers are willing to pay for them en masse. We've included the addresses and telephone numbers in the back of this book of all the companies we surveyed. Let them know how you feel after you buy their recycled goods.

Don't depend on the manufacturer or the supermarket to tell you which products contain recycled material or the percentage of postconsumer waste in the packaging. Thousands of packages contain recycled materials and there's no way of telling. Aside from aluminum, steel, glass, paperboard, and plastic bottles, there's a wide variety of packages that are worth noting. Scientific Certification Systems (SCS) has inspected a number of manufacturers of plastic resin, paper, and glass to certify recycled content and percentage of postconsumer waste.

Although it's often difficult to tell which packager a manufacturer is using, if you spot the SCS logo in connection with a given product, you know that a third party has inspected the packaging process. It's like a "USDA inspected" or Good Housekeeping seal. Look for manufacturer symbols on the bottoms of bags, cartons, or boxes (if you can find them). When you use their packaging, you're endorsing their recycling efforts.

PACKAGERS CERTIFIED FOR RECYCLED CONTENT USE

Cardboard or Kraft (Brown) Paper (linerboard and boxes)

Gaylord Container
    Linerboard: 100% PCW
Longview Fibre

Kraft bag: at least 50% PCW

Menominee Paper/Belkraft

Natural linerboard: 70% postconsumer waste (PCW)

Bagstock: 72% PCW

Packaging Corporation of America

Egg cartons: 13% PCW

Stone Container

Good News kraft grocery sacks: at least 40 to 50% PCS

Visy Recycle

Brown bags: 50 to 100% PCW depending on bag size

Willamette Industries/Will-Cycle

Kraft paper: at least 40% PCW

Glass

Owens-Brockway

Amber glass (beer bottles): 42% PCW

Flint glass: 19% PCW

Glass: 27% PCW

Green glass: 47% PCW

Plastics

A&M Plastics

HDPE, LDPE, LLDPE resins: 100% PCW

Denton Plastics (Envirolac, Envirolon, Envirolex)

Various resins: 20% PCW

EnviroPlastics

Clear HDPE: at least 20% PCW

Envirothene

HDPE & PETE resins: 100% PCW

GEO Resources Recovery

HDPE and LDPE resins: 100% PCW

Green Bottle Company
    HDPE bottle: 94% PCW
HD Plastics
    HDPE, LDPE and PS: 100% PCW
Optiplast
    Merchandise and T-shirt bags: 30% PCW
Plasco Press/Bottle-Sack
    Plastic HDPE grocery bag: at least 30% PCW
Poly Pak America/Enviro-Sense and Enviro-Tuff
    Clear LDPE film: at least 25% PCW
Polytec Packaging Systems
    Merchandise and T-shirt bags: at least 10% HDPE and
    LDPE PCW
Roplast Industries/Fred Meyer
    Plastic merchandise bag: at least 15% LDPE and HDPE
Talco Plastic
    Various resins: 10 to 100% PCW
USA Polymer
    HDPE and LDPE plastic resin: 100% PCW
Vanguard Plastics
    Plastic grocery sack: 10% PCW
Wellman
    Recycled HDPE, polyester products, and PETE: 73 to
93% recycled resin (24 to 31% PCW)

Steel Cans

These tin plants produce cans with at least 10 percent postconsumer steel: Bethlehem, Dolasco, LTV, National (Granite City and Great Lakes), Stelco, USS Gary, Weirton, and Wheeling.

ASEPTIC PACKAGING: WHAT'S BEING DONE

The industry that makes the 3 billion drink boxes kids love so much is making an attempt to develop recycling of their products. It won't be easy, owing to the difficulty of recycling the boxes and the poor economics of doing so. Nevertheless, the Aseptic Packaging Council (APC) estimates that 1 million households are participating in curbside box recycling programs. Pilot recycling programs are set up in California, Connecticut, Florida, Illinois, Maryland, Massachusetts, Minnesota, New York, Ohio, Oregon, Pennsylvania, Rhode Island, Texas, Vermont, Virginia, Washington, and Wisconsin.

For more information, contact the APC at (202) 333-5900.

Chapter 11

Why All Packaging Can't Be Green

According to the Food and Drug Administration, packaging that comes in direct contact with food must not contain recycled plastics or paper, because of the possibility of poisoning from contaminated materials. However, there are a few exceptions to the rules. The FDA does permit (through a "nonobjection" ruling) Heinz to use a special multilayered PETE bottle for ketchup and Dolco packaging to distribute recycled polystyrene egg containers. Kraft is also using a recycled salad-dressing bottle. In addition to the FDA rules, many state laws make it difficult for a company that markets nationally and internationally to make one product that meets all state environmental and packaging requirements. Several manufacturers such as Reckitt & Colman—the makers of French's mustard—told us that they found it too difficult to label or change their packaging due to the confusion over state laws.

With a few exceptions, the vast majority of frozen foods, produce, milk, personal care items, bakery products, and over-the-counter remedies do not contain recycled material. Plastic- or wax-coated paper, multilayered plastic and foil, and special plastic and paper wraps all present the same problem: The technology doesn't yet exist to collect, clean, separate, and recycle these materials in a profitable fashion. That's why drink boxes pose such a dilemma. They're convenient and easily stored (saving refrigeration energy), but most of them end up in landfills. Manufacturers also told us that they couldn't obtain enough high-quality recycled paperboard stock for their packages. We can't verify this complaint, but we think it's plausible. That seems to be the story of American food packaging: too much packaging, too little green technology.

Environmental groups such as the Environmental Action Foundation are blunt about pilot recycling programs that have little chance of making money for the industry. "If we stop buying products in wasteful packaging, industry will have no choice but to stop manufacturing it," EAF's Solid Waste Alternatives Project states. EAF favors recycling and recycled-content laws, which are being fought vigorously by companies in states such as Massachusetts and California.

Nevertheless, industry too is experimenting with pilot programs to make their products more recyclable. For example, International Paper and Champion—two of the largest paper-packaging companies—are running pilot programs to recycle paper milk cartons in test locations in Memphis and New York. These cartons can only be recycled through a special process. To date, however, most areas are more likely to take the common HDPE (#2) plastic milk jugs for recycling. For any recycling program to succeed, it has to be supported by the community, recyclers, manufacturers, and consumers (who buy recycled products again). This is a true "revival" in a product's life cycle.

We'd all like to see 100 percent recycled content in nearly everything, but it's not always possible. Packagers can't always print well on recycled paper stock. There are also technical problems with the other materials. The higher the recycled content, the greater the problems. Recycled stock also may contain contaminants that blemish the final product. Surveys have shown that consumers prefer some food products in shiny white paper packages—or they won't buy it. Following are some other problems with packaging that consumers rarely hear about.

• **Not enough recycled supply.** Manufacturers need a consistent supply of recycled material. Steady supplies are only just developing for certain plastics. For some products—such as paperboard—there's been an oversupply.

• **Recycled paper stock doesn't meet quality standards.** A spokesman for the Non-Prescription Drug Manufacturers Association told us that it's difficult for manufacturers to print all of the required labeling (in small print) on the boxes of over-the-counter remedies. Much of the labeling is for health and safety reasons, is required by law, and must be clearly visible. It's hard to get top-quality printing on recycled stock.

• **Packaging must be 100 percent pure.** In the case of medicines, cosmetics, and food products, there can't be any possibility of contaminants from recycled material. There's only a handful of recycling processes that guarantee this. For products such as shampoos, the recycled packaging material must not chemically react with the product itself.

• **Products may be difficult to store or display without packaging.** So-called blister packs, which consist of a piece of plastic covering a product backed by foil or cardboard, are among the most common methods of packaging. At first glance, they may appear wasteful. Indeed, some products using this method are overpackaged. But blister packs enable retailers to hang small products on hooks, and they are especially useful for small items such as cosmetics and toiletries. Without blister packs, these items would be difficult or impossible to stack neatly. There is always room for source reduction in this area, though. We found numerous examples of overpackaging with unnecessary outer boxes and blister packs in the over-the-counter remedy aisle. When we asked an industry spokesman about what the industry was doing to address this problem, he noted that his group, the Non-Prescription Drug Manufacturers Association, has "formed an environmental and packaging task force, but hadn't met in a year due to lack of time."

• **Chemicals within the products are not recyclable.** These chemicals may include everything from adhesives that keep boxes together to pigments that color detergent-bottle caps. The easiest items to recycle are black and white, such as newspapers and clean plastic bottles. Until technology makes the sorting and separation process more efficient and cost effective, your local recycler won't take most colored paper.

• **Package must be tamper resistant.** Nearly every over-the-counter drug is packaged in a way that prevents tampering. This public safety measure came about after several cyanide poisoning deaths were reported several years ago when people innocently took some tainted pain-relief tablets. So, that extra, wasteful layer of package, foil, or paper is a necessary evil.

Chapter 12

What Industry Is Doing to Improve Packaging

In recent years, the leading consumer-product companies have taken some dramatic steps to improve packaging. Although these companies represent a minority of packaging concerns, they seem to be establishing a marketplace for greener packaging. Supermarkets, too, are active. According to the Food Marketing Institute, the trade group representing 1,600 large supermarket chains, "Grocers are asking food processors to reduce the amount of packaging materials and to make packaging more recyclable, and they are making similar changes in private-label packaging."

Generally, any company that does business in Europe or Canada is light-years ahead of companies that do business exclusively in the United States. That's because other countries have much stricter laws to reduce overall packaging. Europe has less space for landfills than we do, so they have to be tougher. Germany, for example, has a law that requires industry to take back, reuse, or recycle most packaging materials, large appliances, and autos, by 1995. Such an idea could work in the United States over a longer period of time.

Leading the charge on packaging in the United States is the Coalition of Northeastern Governors (CONEG), which is working directly with industry. CONEG has issued a challenge to companies to come up with ways of making packaging out of more recycled content, enhance its recyclability, and reduce or eliminate the use of heavy metals in inks. Companies such as Campbell Soup, Clorox, Gillette, Procter & Gamble, and Scott Paper have already accepted the CONEG challenge and are aggressively marketing source-reduced and recycled-content packaging. There's been some progress. The challenge was sent to 256 companies, and so far 33 companies have accepted. And fourteen states have passed CONEG's model legislation concerning heavy metals. Some have even started using soy-based ink for printing labels. This ink—made from soybean oil—doesn't produce pollutants such as smog-producing volatile organic compounds. It also uses a renewable resource that's grown in this country. Most other inks use petroleum distillates. However, like many of the other packaging issues being eyed by industry, the use of soy-based inks is not a panacea. The ink takes longer to dry and only works in certain applications.

Several states—such as Oregon and California—have also passed tough environmental laws in recent years that mandate either 25 percent recycled content in packaging or other options that will improve overall recycling. To industry, such measures seem draconian. To environmentalists, the laws aren't tough enough.

Manufacturers claim that their advances in packaging haven't received widespread attention. In terms of packaging reduction, there's been quiet progress over the past few years. It's rare to find any outer packaging or cardboard packing that *doesn't* contain recycled material. Cereal, cracker, and other paperboard food-product boxes that don't come in direct contact with food are extremely likely to contain recycled paper. Just look for the gray shade of the paper on the inside of the carton. That's generally the best way to tell if it's recycled. Paperboard cartons can contain up to 100 percent recycled material. While that's a step in the right direction, it's been going on for years because it's economical for manufacturers. Only recently have they begun to label their boxes "recycled." Since it's so easy to do and so many have done it for so long, it's hardly the most innovative green packaging. It's like automakers crowing about their cars having automatic transmissions. It's nice, but not a terribly new or difficult achievement. Hundreds of thousands of other packages contain recycled material, but probably won't label them as such.

- **Cans:** Aluminum cans contain up to 60 percent recycled content; steel cans up to 50 percent. Next to paperboard these are among the most recycled of all materials.
- **Glass bottles:** Glass containers contain up to 35 percent "Cullet" from crushed bottles is easily and efficiently recycled.
- **Plastic bottles:** Some bottles contain up to 25 percent recycled content depending on the part of the country and the local availability of recycled plastic resin. Other plastic containers such as garbage cans or trash bags may contain up to 100 percent.

Sources: Aluminum Assn., Steel Can Recycling Institute Glass Packaging Institute, Society of Plastics Industries.

PACKAGING ADVANCES

- **Coca-Cola's recycling effort.** Coca-Cola cans and bottles are recyclable. The 2-liter bottles are made of PETE plastic, which can be brought to your local recycling center. The company claims that in 1988, it recycled 175 million pounds of the plastic into things such as sleeping bags, wallboard, and strapping. If you call the company's toll-free consumer line (1-800-438-2653), they will send you information on recycling. Although the kit is mostly brochures from other organizations, it's a start in learning about the recycling process.

• **Film packaging.** The Japanese film manufacturer Fuji claims to use recycled paper packaging for its film products. Eastman Kodak also has entered into a recycling effort for its disposable cameras, processing chemicals, and packaging. Kodak said it will recycle its canisters from 110- and 126-mm film (no word on 35-mm). Last year, more than 600 million units of 35-mm film were sold, so these programs will be helpful.

• **Heinz "catches up" to green packaging trend.** The company is using a new kind of plastic packaging for its ketchup line that "addresses a critical challenge to plastics packaging—the diversion of materials from overcrowded landfills." The new plastics packaging is recyclable PETE, the most recycled plastic. Check to see, however, if it's recycled in your community.

• **Kraft's Velveeta box.** Kraft General Foods is including a reusable plastic box for its Velveeta cheese (can be used to store more Velveeta). They've also downsized and lightweighted a host of products.

• **Unilever/Lever Brothers.** The world's largest consumer-goods company says it has source-reduced nearly all of its detergent products. Ultra Snuggle uses 50 percent less packaging; Snuggles singles uses 35 percent less packaging.

• **Mobil to recycle plastic bags from grocery stores.** The petrochemical giant has started a national recycling effort to recycle plastic grocery bags. Each year, supermarket chains use about 12 billion of the bags. Mobil is the second-largest manufacturer of the bags, behind Sonoco Products, which has its own recycling program.

• **Procter & Gamble.** The consumer-goods giant said it's highlighting recycled packaging of its Tide, Cheer, Era, Dash, and Downy (64-ounce) bottles. These containers will be composed of "at least 25 percent recycled HDPE plastic. The refills will contain at least 50 percent recycled content." P&G said it will also buy up 10 percent of the nation's supply of recycled milk jugs.

• **Sanyo's "RechargAcell" batteries.** This innovative product actually solves two problems. First, these rechargeable batteries tackle the disposability of heavy-metal products into landfills. Second, Sanyo provides the packaging in the form of a postage-paid "Mailback Recycle System" to send back the batteries when they are spent.

• **Uncle Ben's rice box.** The company eliminated an inner liner to reduce packaging waste.

• **Webster Industries.** Maker of Good Sense and Handi-Bags trash bags, this company claims its bags are "the first branded trash bags made with 80 percent to 90 percent recycled content."

PACKAGING MISSTEPS

Despite all the money invested in dressing up corporate environmental records, the prime motivation in packaging is profit. Sometimes the environment and effective packaging form a happy union. Sometimes there's a bitter divorce. A case in point was the detergent industry's experiment with "bag in the box" designs in 1990–91. The boxes were a classic example of source reduction, dramatically reducing the amount of packaging. Corporations such as Unilever were enthusiastic about the design because it meant that they could offer more product in less package and thereby reduce their costs by a factor of millions (exactly how much, they never reveal, for competitive reasons). The package was also 100 percent recyclable and used 75 percent less plastic. But something *didn't* happen. Consumers walked away from the packages in favor of standard HDPE bottles. Perhaps it was the convenience factor.

Similarly, Procter & Gamble marketed refill pouches for six laundry brands, then scrapped them after consumers abandoned them for rigid bottles. Undaunted by failures, manufacturers experiment with green packaging one brand at a time in an effort to boost and retain market share. For example, Jergens/Kao is experimenting with the refill package for its Advanced Therapy line. Similar to most refill pouches, the packages are said to use 70 percent less material. Kodak's L&F Products is also trying refill pouches for its Direct and Resolve cleaners. These pouches use less plastic, but there's one drawback—they are unrecyclable, because they're a multilayered plastic. Is this a better packaging solution? Only if the total amount of waste going to a landfill is lower and the refill pouches are less resource- and energy-intensive to make. On a scientific level, it could take years before it becomes clear if these products are better.

One option would be to offer refills of soaps and detergents from in-store dispensers, thus eliminating the refill packages. Such an alternative exists on a small scale through Body Shop health and beauty boutiques. It may not be practical on a large scale, but how will we know unless we try?

BAD PACKAGING

Cosmetics Lead the Pack

As a rule, all the cosmetic products we surveyed were over-packaged. Examples include nail polish bottles inside plastic-sealed cards, hair coloring bottles in boxes, and skin-lotion bottles inside boxes. Nearly every manufacturer was guilty.

Wastemaker Products

U.S. Representative Frank Pallone, Jr. (D-NJ), and Clean Water Action, Environmental Action Foundation, and U.S. Public Interest Research Group teamed together to form a "short list" of companies making green claims while also making products that are wasteful or that otherwise contribute to pollution. The following products were cited.

• **Oscar Mayer's Lunchables.** Single portions of lunch meat, cheese, and crackers that are packaged for quick disposal. The packages can't be recycled. The company, owned by Philip Morris, still markets the product. Oscar Mayer did not return our calls.

• **Frito-Lay Kid Size Variety Pack.** There's no need for this collection of small snack packages when you can buy the larger packages and put them in reusable containers.

• **Nissin Foods Cup 'o Noodles.** A single-use Styrofoam cup is encased in plastic shrink wrap and cardboard.

• **Starkist Charlie's Tuna Lunch Kit.** The can and mixing bowl are recyclable, but the rest is disposable. The parent company, Heinz, insisted that this kit represents advances in source reduction.

• **American Home Foods Chef Boyardee Microwave Teenage Mutant Ninja Turtles.** A combination of plastic cups with Styrofoam shells and foil tops make this a recycling albatross. When we tried to get a statement from American Home Foods about their environmental policy, they faxed us a bland, uninformative brochure.

• **Campbell Microwave Soup.** Another microwave convenience product. Stick with their canned products.

• **Doubletree Foods (Dial) Light Balance Lunch Bucket.** This microwavable product is typical of overpackaged, nonrecyclable convenience items. A plastic LDPE (generally nonrecyclable) lid crowns a #7 (combination of nonrecyclable plastics) container with an aluminum pull top. Covering the container is a nonrecyclable polystyrene foam shell. The only thing recyclable in this package is the small lid. Ninety percent of the package is designed to be thrown out.

IS PACKAGING THE REAL PROBLEM?

Of course, the blame for polluting the earth does not fall only on product manufacturers. They are making something that ultimately we consume and never reuse. We're part of the problem. We're also part of the solution.

We love convenience. We indulge in overpackaged ready-to-serve meals, push-button appliances, instant breakfasts—the list goes on. We don't have time to make everything from scratch. In my house, a home-cooked meal is a real luxury. But we pay a price for this convenience. The more "convenient" a product is, the more energy and materials were consumed in producing and packaging it. And every time we go to the supermarket, order out, or dine in a restaurant, we are consuming fossil fuel, a nonrenewable resource. Our vehicles burn this fuel, which in turn creates carbon dioxide, carbon monoxide, and a host of other chemicals that contribute to global warming and smog.

Our car culture alone costs the earth dearly. For every gallon of gasoline burned, 19 pounds of carbon dioxide are released into the atmosphere. That's without getting into all the other nasty chemicals released. The internal combustion engine is the single largest contributor to air pollution. A 1987 University of California study found that between 7,000 and 30,000 people die each year from auto air pollution.

The problem is most profound in the United States. Nathan Gardels, editor of *New Perspectives Quarterly*, pointed out that "the average U.S. family affects the environment 40 times more than a family in India and a hundred times more than a family in Kenya." How can we reconcile modern life with a consciousness of what it's doing to our earth, our quality of life, and our future on the planet? How many people do you know who can shuttle kids back and forth to extracurricular events and bring home six bags of groceries on the back of a bicycle?

Consider, for example, chlorofluorocarbons (CFCs), the infamous ozone-eaters that scientists believe elevate skin cancer rates and cause crop damage. Do you think that buying hair spray labeled "ozone friendly" is going to enable you to use less sunscreen? For one thing, most CFCs were eliminated from aerosol products years ago. Your refrigerator and auto air conditioner pose a greater threat to the atmosphere. DuPont, the world's largest producer of CFCs, has vowed eventually to stop production of the chemical, but that doesn't mean there's a decent alternative waiting in the wings. What should we consumers do in the meantime?

Part 4

SHOP GREEN, *LIVE* GREEN

You already know the first step: If you have a local recycling program, use it! By the year 2,000, Americans will be dumping 200 million tons of solid waste annually. Not only are our landfills filling up and closing at an alarming pace, but disposal rates are climbing dramatically. The bottom line is that each year, the "average" U.S. household generates more than a ton of garbage. Since 1980, more than 3,000 landfills have closed, and the remaining 5,500 will be shut over the next few years. Obviously, something must change.

America recycles only about 17 percent of its garbage now, and incinerates about 10 percent. A radical solution is in order, to prevent disposal costs from rivaling property tax bills. But where are we going to put it all? The first howl of any community—rural or metropolitan—is, "Not in my backyard!" There is a widespread perception that landfills leach toxic wastes into water supplies. The same belief persists for more efficient incinerators and waste-to-energy plants. In fact, most large metropolitan areas are trucking their garbage to less-populated areas of neighboring states. For example, the Chicago area's waste is ending up in southern Wisconsin; northern New Jersey's refuse goes to Pennsylvania. Is that any way to treat a neighbor?

Garbage disposal, like recycling, is a public service and a business. As William Rathje and Cullen Murphy point out in *RUBBISH! The Archaeology of Garbage* (HarperCollins, 1992), "Recycling gets done not because it's a good thing, it gets done because it's a profitable thing, and profitability depends upon demand for recyclable materials." The researchers found that certain valuable and highly recycled materials such as aluminum and glass are being found less frequently in landfills—one of the success stories of recycling.

The fact that we've created so much waste and have run out of cheap places to put it will force a wave of research, planning, political organizing, and action on every level. It's the classic kind of emotional and "pocketbook" issue that can decide local elections. The bottom line is that poor waste management is a form of societal self-destruction. Unless it's reversed, we could be inundated with the refuse of our neglect. We *can* recycle more and encourage the use of recycled products and recyclable materials. The EPA set a goal of 25 percent national recycling by the end of 1992. We recycled only about 17 percent as of 1990. We have a long way to go.

FIFTY WAYS TO BECOME A GREEN SHOPPER

1. Make sure you have an energy-efficient way of getting to the supermarket. If you can take a bike or public transit, do so.

2. If you have a car, make sure it's tuned up and the tires are properly inflated. Patronize service stations that recycle oil, antifreeze, coolant, and other fluids.

3. Plan your trips to consolidate driving. Go when the store and roads are least congested (weeknights). You'll spend less time in traffic and burn less fuel.

4. Bring your own shopping bags. Return the plastic or paper bags you've accumulated. Most major chains will recycle the plastic bag through special programs. If your store doesn't have such a program, ask the manager to start one.

5. Plan your meals, and bring a list. Don't shop when you're hungry. This will prevent you from buying things you don't want, and throwing away even more food and packaging.

6. "Precycle"—that is, buy products in recyclable containers. Aluminum, glass, and steel are better than most plastics for recyclability. Make sure that what you buy is recycled locally. Remember, "recyclable" is more than a chasing-arrows logo (see Part 3, The Packaging Problem). And "recycled content" (in paper or plastic) doesn't mean recyclable. If you don't know where to recycle, call the National Recycling Coalition at (202) 625-6406 or (800) 937-1226 or (800) 243-5790.

7. Reduce your use of "convenience" foods. These include "shelf stable," "microwave ready," and frozen foods. If you buy fresh ingredients, you'll be taking home—and throwing away—less product packaging. You'll also be eating better.

8. Read labels. Know what you're buying in terms of nutrition and recyclability. Although glass and steel containers may not be labeled, they are more recyclable than many plastic containers labeled with the recycling logo. A package that's recyclable is better than one that contains recycled material.

9. Buy refillable or reusable packaging. Margarine tubs and jelly jars are good reusable containers. They are ideal for freezing and leftovers.

10. Buy the largest size you can. You'll save money and use less packaging in the long run.

11. Buy in bulk. Again, you'll save money and use less packaging. With the expansion of warehouse clubs and "hypermarts," nearly every metropolitan area offers bulk buying. If you're really ambitious, form a cooperative with your friends, family, and neighbors.

12. Buy aluminum foil wraps instead of plastic or wax paper. They can be recycled easily if you clean them off.

13. Avoid purely disposable items. A reusable dish rag is better than a paper towel, an electric razor is better than a disposable one, and metal flatware is better than plastic.

14. Buy rechargeable batteries and a recharger. They are slightly more expensive, but you'll save hundreds of dollars over the years. Also consider rechargeable flashlights and toys. Send the batteries back to the manufacturer when they're used up.

15. If you have a question about a company or its product, call them or write them a letter. Many companies print toll-free numbers and addresses on their product labels. See the resources section at the back of the book for an extensive list of company phone numbers.

16. Don't buy packaged produce if you can avoid it. You'll eliminate having to throw out more packaging material.

17. Buy energy-efficient light bulbs (with the proper fixtures) and appliances. You'll save on utility bills and reduce air pollution.

18. Patronize farmer's markets. You'll get fresher produce, reduce some transportation pollution (by eliminating the middleman), and possibly get a better price.

19. Buy products that are certified for biodegradability or recycled content. That way, you'll know that an independent third party (such as SCS or Green Seal) has verified a company's claim.

20. Buy products packaged in recycled paperboard boxes and cartons. You can identify them by looking inside the box or peeling back the boxtop. Recycled board is newspaper gray and speckled. Not all such boxes are labeled "recycled."

21. Buy recycled paper products. Most are labeled. Choose the products with the highest postconsumer-waste content.

22. Don't buy produce or cheeses that are packaged or prepared. You'll pay more and have more packaging to throw away. Produce by the multipound bag is cheaper than buying one pound at a time.

23. Plan meals so that you'll use all the food you buy. Every week, Americans throw out about 15 percent of the food they buy.

24. Use coupons for the products you normally buy, but don't buy just because you feel a need to use the coupon. You may be buying something that's overpackaged.

25. Make your own salad dressings and condiments (nearly every cookbook has several recipes). Store them in reusable containers and you won't have to throw out new packages.

26. Avoid shopping at convenience stores: You'll buy more, pay more for it, and be saddled with even more throwaways.

27. Buy private-label goods or generics, preferably on sale. You'll save more money because less of the product's price reflects advertising and packaging.

28. Bake your own bread. This is a great way to avoid those virtually nonrecycled bread wrappers. There are recipes and bread-making kits in your market's baking goods aisle.

29. Bake your own cakes, cookies, and desserts. Since the advent of the two-income, always-on-the-go family, few people have time to bake desserts. But this is a great way to avoid excess packaging and shopping trips. If you must, buy the prepared recipes already on the shelves.

30. Return your bottles and cans for deposit. This is better than buying nonrecycled containers. Many supermarkets now have vending machines that will refund money for cans.

31. Bring your bottled water containers back to the store to be refilled (if this service is available). Some large chains have machines that will refill your bottles and jugs.

32. Don't buy "multipacks." Most common with snack foods and drinks, these shrink-wrapped packages have several packages within them. For example, it's better to buy one big bag of potato chips and put them in reusable containers (for lunches), or a large glass bottle of fruit juice and pour it into lunchbox bottles. Here again, you're reducing your use of packaging—and saving money.

33. Don't buy prepackaged lunch meats. They're more highly processed and packaged. Buy your lunch meats at the deli counter once a week.

34. Avoid presliced cheeses or "single servings." You'll get a fresher, more wholesome, and less packaged product at your supermarket's deli counter. If your supermarket doesn't have one, consider buying small pieces of turkey, chicken, and sausage and cooking them once, then slicing them for several days thereafter. Aged cheeses have a shelf life of about one week; poultry lasts two to three days.

35. Consider smoked and dried foods. They last longer,

use less packaging, and may contain fewer preservatives. Salamis and dried fruits (prunes, apricots) are great lunch foods.

36. Consider combined products. For example, it's common to find shampoo with conditioner or hand soap with moisturizer. But don't pay more for it.

37. If you buy alcoholic beverages, remember to recycle the aluminum and glass containers.

38. Make your own baby food. Babies eat what they like, as long as it's mashed up. Use your blender or food processor to make fresh mashed vegetables or fruits. That way, you'll avoid a lot of packaging and provide fresher foods (whose ingredients are known to you) to your children.

39. Check containers for expiration dates. If you plan to keep something beyond its expiration date, you'll probably end up throwing it out. This is a special problem with short-lived dairy products, most of which come in unrecyclable containers.

40. Buy juices in concentrate form. This is one form of source-reduced packaging. You make your juices in your own reusable container, so you're throwing out only one small package versus several big ones. The variety of frozen juice concentrates is staggering these days. Also think of concentrates as substitutes for any juice in a carton or drink box. Keep your juices cold in a large pitcher or dispenser in your refrigerator and dispense at meals or into lunchbox bottles.

41. Make your own juices, and eliminate packaging entirely. Anything in the produce section can be made into a fresh juice with a good food processor or juicer machine. Even better, the old-fashioned conical, glass juicers give you some exercise.

42. Grow your own herbs and spices. Garden stores all

carry "window kits" to grow spices. Even apartment dwellers can do this. You'll save money and be amazed at the difference between a fresh and a packaged spice. You can even buy pregrown spices to grow in your garden. We grew some lemon basil and curry and brought them inside after Jack Frost descended. Many spices serve as natural pesticides (garlic, rosemary).

43. Can and freeze your home-grown produce. You'll avoid new disposable packaging, reuse packaging, and enjoy the fruits (and vegetables) of your labor. You will also have complete control over pesticide use, fertilizer application, distribution, and packaging. Gardening and home canning/ freezing are among the most energy- and resource-efficient food systems yet invented.

44. Instead of buying packaged vitamins, eat a balanced diet consisting of whole grains, green vegetables, fresh fruits, and fish. Nutritionists say that you don't need vitamin supplements if you eat a balanced diet.

45. Don't idle your car in front of the supermarket to make your walk shorter if you can wheel the cart to your car. You'll save on gas and pollution and get additional exercise.

46. Use plastic film and detergent containers for whatnots and kids' craft projects.

47. Detergent bottles make great receptacles for at-home oil or antifreeze changes. Take the used fluids to your local service station for recycling. Most major chains will accept it.

48. If your supermarket doesn't accept seldom-recycled items such as foil, cooking oil, shrink wrap, or other plastics, ask them to do so as a community service.

49. Shop at chains that provide drug, photo, and other

nonsupermarket services (such as banking). You'll avoid extra trips and the resultant energy use and pollution.

50. Ask if your supermarket donates leftover and damaged packaged foods to the homeless and local food banks. Urge them to start if they don't already do so.

Part 5

THE GREEN SURVEY

Chapter 13

How We Conducted the Survey

This guide rates 220 companies and more than 2,000 products. In doing so, we made quite a few trips to the supermarket. We read every label we could. We even bought products to get beyond outer packaging. While we wanted to know everything we could about a product, we had to rely on (1) what the package told us, and (2) what the company told us. Since we didn't have access to every plant, supplier, and distributor, it was impossible to verify company claims. Where possible, we relied on Scientific Certification Systems (SCS) to audit recycled content, biodegradability, and related green claims.

We gathered information on companies through annual reports, consumer affairs literature, and SEC documents and investment newsletters. In the case of the companies with the largest number of products, we contacted them by letter and phone. With some companies, we made as many as six phone calls in an attempt to get the information we needed. Only a handful did not respond to our survey: Dr Pepper/7-Up, Lake Pharmaceuticals, Maybelline, PET, Reckitt & Colman, Revlon, Sally Hanson, and SC Johnson and Son.

We evaluated companies and products for our survey based on the following:

• **Environmental policy and actions.** First, we called any toll-free consumer hotline printed on packaging. If there wasn't a toll-free number, we called the company's consumer affairs department or corporate communications office. If that didn't work, we wrote letters to consumer affairs departments or chief executives. If it was a large and highly visible company, we called corporate communications departments directly—some as many as seven times. Most large companies had consumer hotlines. We focused on major, nationally distributed brands. We always asked if a company had a written environmental policy statement and could cite specific actions taken to help the environment. It should be noted that we did not receive a response to any of our letters to chief executives.

• **Packaging.** We read labels to determine if the product (1) contained recycled material, (2) was recyclable, and (3) was widely recycled based on recycling rates and the type of material. We noted if a company claimed something was recyclable that really wasn't. We also asked consumer hotlines and corporate communications departments to provide us with lists of products that contain the recycled or recyclable material. If our questions were answered on those items, we asked for any additional steps the company was taking to reduce packaging disposability (such as source reduction). Unless certified by a third party such as Scientific Certification Systems, in most cases you'll have to take the word of the company as to recycled content, the percentage of postconsumer waste, and whether something is more preconsumer than postconsumer in content. We noted whether either PETE or HDPE resins were used in plastic bottles. If they were, they were identified as "recyclable." Although the overall recycling rates for these plastics are not high, since they are the two most recycled resins, that's an encouraging sign. We ignored claims of recyclability if containers were coded "vinyl," "low-density polyethylene," "polystyrene," or "mixed materials," since these resins aren't recycled in sufficient quantities to be considered recyclable. We also didn't consider paperboard recyclable, because the National Recycling Coalition told us that most recycling centers won't take it (mostly due to the inks and clay content). But check with *your* local recycler to be sure.

• **Overall environmental enhancements.** The most enlightened companies were making international top-to-bottom efforts to green their operations. That included everything from reducing plant emissions to office recycling. Few consumer hotlines could tell us this information, however. We scanned annual reports, investment newsletters, SEC documents, EPA toxic-emissions surveys, company statements, magazine and newspaper articles, and books for this information. We think it's important that a company conducts its business in an environmentally responsible manner. You endorse a company's behavior by buying its products.

• **Focus on national brands and companies.** We called every major chain in an attempt to include private-label products, but they didn't have the relevant information. If you're willing to do some homework, ask your local supermarket who makes their private-label goods and if they contain any recycled content or are recyclable. Chances are, a large, national company makes these products.

We grouped our survey tables according to wide product categories, then by company. We wanted to show you how a company performed along product groupings and brands.

We didn't include every product a company makes, nor did we include every brand. The survey is designed to give you a sample of some of the more important product changes on a national level. We mentioned more products in a particular line if it had a special quality such as a highly recycled material, source reduction, or SCS certification.

For detailed summaries of specific product categories, read Chapter 15. To find specific products, check by category, then by company.

SURVEY SUMMARY

219 Manufacturers Surveyed

117 reported environmental policies/statements
40 firms submitted to independent environmental audits
33 provided no environmental information through hotlines
5 had consumer representatives who confused "recycled" with "recyclable"
35 products were independently certified for biodegradability

2,000 Products Surveyed

115 products independently certified by SCS for environmental attributes
26 using recycled content in packaging
12 independently certified for recycled paper content

THE EFACT RATING SYSTEM OF
"CONSCIOUS" COMPANIES

When rating a company, we considered a number of variables. The following details what we at the New Consumer Institute call our EFACT system, which stands for Environmental and Financial Action Transformation. We chose this phrase because of the companies that are in the process of transforming themselves into the best possible environmental citizens. That is, their ideal state is a profitable balance between sustainability and resource management. We use a 20-point scoring method to indicate how well they do according to a number of criteria. Because the system is tough yet fair, few companies stood out; none received a perfect score. Most were merely acceptable. It was also difficult to rate privately held companies and most smaller companies due to a lack of available information.

One of the problems in rating companies is that all companies pollute in some way. Even if all of the employees work at home using computer networks, their homes emit carbon dioxide when the heat goes on and leak ozone-eating chlorofluorocarbons (CFCs) when their refrigerators or air conditioners leak coolant. Of course, on the other extreme, there are the top polluters named by the EPA in its "Toxic Release Inventory" (TRI), which reports some 4.8 billion pounds of pollutants released by 10,800 U.S. manufacturers. Environmental groups have used those figures to assemble reports on the leading polluters, further mobilizing public opinion against these companies to clean up.

Although a widely used measure for industrial pollution, the TRI is highly flawed. Of the 70,000 estimated chemicals produced by industry, the EPA tracks only some 300 toxic chemicals. According to the environmental group INFORM, the TRI excludes some key cancer-causing chemicals (carcinogens) and other suspected carcinogens. On top of that shortcoming, the EPA changed the reporting rules in recent years so that some companies were able to show vast improvements in pollution emissions through a bureaucratic loophole. According to Citizen Action, this rule change allowed most of the companies surveyed to show drops in pollution from 1989 to 1990, although the actual pollution levels did not change. It's also troublesome that the EPA has to take the word of the companies on their toxic emissions. It would be nearly impossible to audit every single plant. Some of the companies make products you're familiar with: DuPont makes Nylon, Teflon, and thousands of other products; 3M makes Scotch Tape and Post-it Notes; Monsanto makes Nutrasweet artificial sweetener and Round-up weedkiller (all are trademarked products). Although these companies are listed because they are heavy manufacturers, you should note that all have pledged to reduce their emissions and are members of a special voluntary EPA program to do so (see below).

TOP 10 INDUSTRIAL POLLUTERS

DuPont (nylon®, CFCs, Dacron polyester®)
American Cyanamid (drugs, chemicals)
Monsanto (Nutrasweet®, Round-up®)
RTZ America (mining concern)
Freeport McMoRan (chemicals)
Renco Group (industrial concern)
ASARCO (mining)
3M (Scotch® Tape, Scotchguard®)

GM (autos, trucks)
BP America (gasoline, petroleum products)

Source: EPA "Toxic Release Inventory" (1990 Total Releases of Toxic Chemicals)

EFACT RATING CRITERIA

We carefully surveyed and reviewed the following:

• **Environmental policy statements.** It was surprising to us that not every company had an environmental policy statement. This is merely a written set of objectives a company adopts on environmental citizenship. Some companies—e.g., 3M, Quaker Oats, HJ Heinz, and DuPont—have sophisticated policies that cover nearly every phase of their operations. Others haven't even bothered to put together one page. We see the environmental policy statement as a starting point, a verbal step toward action. —**2 points**

• **Environmental management action.** A step beyond a policy statement, this means that a company has implemented initial but modest programs to improve its environmental citizenship. Action in this area includes office recycling, packaging-waste reduction, contributing to environmental groups, use of recycled materials, etc. If a company allowed SCS to audit its manufacturing process, they were awarded an extra 2 points. —**4 points**

• **Environmental management programs and investments.** These are large-scale programs that involve significant expenditures (proportional to a company's profits) to implement. Since capital expenditures were required, we also looked for these programs to produce measurable savings on an industrial scale. We noted these enhancements where reported. We'd like to see more access to this information, but until there's true outside environmental auditing, we'll have to take each company's word for it. Measurable improvements in product packaging—e.g., source reduction or changing to more recyclable materials—were also considered. For this category, we checked the participants of the EPA's 33/50 pollution reduction program, which entails anything from installing antipollution devices in plants to recovering raw materials. We subtracted 4 points if the company was on the TRI Top 100 list of polluters. —**4 points**

• **Energy efficiency programs.** In addition to pollution control improvements, any company can improve its energy consumption, which can range from installing compact fluorescent light bulbs to computer monitoring of electricity usage. Companies that enact these programs can save big and reduce their consumption of nonrenewable resources such as oil and coal. We included participants in the EPA's Green Lights energy-saving program for these points. Each of the more than 300 companies will be able to cut its lighting bills by more than 60 percent over the next five years, which reduces fossil fuel consumption, pollution, and global-warming–related impact. —**2 points**

• **Corporate responsibility and citizenship.** This is a broad category of corporate behavior that covers labor and community relations, charitable donations, community program sponsorship, and sustainable agriculture efforts. We reviewed the holdings of the leading socially responsible mutual funds to see what professional money managers choose through their sophisticated research systems. —**2 points**

• **Socially enhancing factors.** We grouped together many of the check points commonly used by socially responsible investors. Companies lost 2 points if they produced nuclear or defense armaments; produced and/or sold tobacco products; had South African investments; or ignored fair-employment practices in Northern Ireland (the MacBride Principles). They gained 2 points if they stayed clear of these areas or any other socially irresponsible activities such as false advertising, safety violations, or government contracting violations. We downgraded Nestlé, American Home Products, GE, Philip Morris, and Hormel in these categories even though they scored higher in others. —2 points (plus or minus)

• CERES signatory. Companies could have picked up 4 points for signing up with CERES. However, with the exception of Ben & Jerry's Homemade, none on our list of supermarket-related manufacturers or retailers did. We weighted this category highly because of the accountability clause. —4 points

• Quality product and consumer information. We used independent consumer group ratings and our own survey of more than 250 customer service hotlines and letter responses. We checked effectiveness of consumer hotline specialists, including quantity and quality of information they provided over the phone and in response to written inquiries to consumer or corporate communications departments. If companies were deceptive, misleading, or blatantly lacking in their customer communications efforts, they lost 2 points. There's a direct link between companies that serviced their customers, provided quality products, and made an attempt to become greener companies. —2 points

The Greenest Consumer Companies: A Sampling

Key:

20 = perfect;
18 = superior;
16 = excellent;
14 = very good;
12 = noteworthy, but needs improvement;
10 = improving, but needs attention to special issues;
 8 = below average;
 6 = troubled;
 4 = a major problem;
 2 = reprehensible

Outstanding Companies	Points
Ben & Jerry's Homemade	18
Celestial Seasonings	18
Merck	16

Honorable Mentions (leaders in their industries)

General Mills	14
Kellogg	14
Rubbermaid	14
Unilever/Lever Bros.	14
(Chesebrough-Pond's, Lipton, Lever Bros., VDB Foods)	
Cadbury-Schweppes	12
Campbell Soup	12

CPC/Best Foods	12
Clorox	12
Colgate-Palmolive	12
Coca-Cola	12
ConAgra	12
Church & Dwight	12
Helene Curtis	12
Dial	12
Gillette	12
HJ Heinz	12
Johnson & Johnson	12
Pepsico	12
Procter & Gamble	12
Quaker Oats	12
Warner-Lambert	12
Webster Industries	12

(Special considerations made for environmental programs)

Hershey Foods	12
Bristol-Myers Squibb	12
Dow Chemical	12
Statler Paper	12
Fox River	12
Eastman Kodak	12
Smuckers	12
3M	12
Reynolds Aluminum	12
Mead Paper	12
Wal-Mart	12

The Grayest Consumer Companies

Kraft/General Foods-Philip Morris	10
Nestlé	10
RJR Nabisco	10
Borden	8
Hormel	8
Monsanto	8
American Home Products	8
DuPont	8
GE	8
American Cyanamid	6

Notes: Merck scored highly on the list for quality management on every level even though it makes only one pure consumer product—Mylanta—a joint venture with Johnson & Johnson. Although they are relatively small companies, Ben & Jerry's Homemade and Celestial Seasonings did well because they work on every level to ensure environmental soundness. Celestial Seasonings goes so far as to work with suppliers to promote sustainable agriculture. Wal-Mart should be praised for its environmental efforts, although they have in the past endorsed many products before their environmental effectiveness was established, have declined to consider some shareholder proxy actions, and have had controversies surrounding its Buy America program. Some major polluters such as 3M and Procter & Gamble made the list despite their being on the EPA's list of Top 100 polluters. They've made considerable efforts to correct their pollution problems. The companies that made our "gray" list are either top polluters or dubious corporate citizens. Although Philip Morris should be commended for its charitable contributions and the work of its Kraft General Foods and Miller Brewing divisions, it still makes billions from cigarettes—and the cancer deaths that come with them. That's why they're considered a gray company. Dow, Monsanto, Eastman Kodak, and DuPont have all announced major pollution reduction and recycling programs. We refrained from listing companies that indirectly produced consumer products because consumers usually don't have direct contact with these companies. These lists also represent the companies that were making the most visible efforts in particular areas. We don't have access to all corporate activities. We conducted all of our research using publicly available documents.

HOW OTHER COMPANIES FARED

Most companies did not have to do much to score an average 10. A company was either downgraded or was pretty lackluster to score below that. The ratings for the rest of the companies mentioned in this book are in the survey tables in Chapter 16.

Chapter 14

What We Found

In investigating these 220 companies, we found a wide variety of policies, actions, and responses. It's difficult to generalize what companies were trying to do, but we uncovered a few underlying themes.

First, we noted that companies that do business in Canada or Europe, where laws are much stricter, knew exactly what we were talking about and could give us detailed responses to our questions. International marketers like Nestlé, Procter & Gamble, Heinz, Quaker Oats, Lever Brothers, and Eastman Kodak had not only done their homework on what the issues were, they had working environmental committees, had taken dozens of positive steps, and were prepared to do more.

Second, we found that the more recognizable the brand name, the more the company did to "green" its image. Modern corporations will do anything to protect and expand the power of their brand names. They don't want anything to tarnish the image of these profitable products and cultural icons. Coca-Cola, Pepsi, Starkist tuna, and Heinz ketchup, to name a few, are marketed all over the planet. The last thing these companies want is for consumers to associate these products with dirtying the planet. Can you imagine what would happen to Disney's many well-managed businesses if people thought Mickey Mouse was a litterbug? Or Charlie the Tuna was involved in drowning dolphins?

Third, we discovered that bigger is not necessarily better when it comes to the environment. Some large companies such as Abbott Labs (Selsun Blue) and Reckitt & Colman (French's mustards) didn't answer our questions on environmental policy, which was one of our criteria in assigning our EFACT rating to a company's overall environmental strategy. Small companies such as Ben & Jerry's Homemade (ice cream) and Celestial Seasonings had better environmental programs than did some of the multibillion-dollar conglomerates we contacted.

Chapter 15

Walking the Aisles: Product Category Analysis and Summaries

ALCOHOLIC BEVERAGES

We didn't look too closely at products in this category since most alcoholic beverages are packaged either in aluminum or in glass, both of which contain higher-than-average recycled content. Companies such as Seagram's stated that they've been reducing the size of their packaging. Anheuser-Busch is trumpeting its extensive recycling program and corporate Buy Recycled campaign. G. Heilman detailed several in-plant energy and resource conservation measures, while Coors also highlighted its plant operations. Philip Morris's Miller Brewing unit highlighted activities with environmental groups such as the Nature Conservancy. Each company has spent millions on public relations supporting such efforts.

GREEN CHOICES

- Beverages in aluminum cans (if you recycle them)
- Beverages in glass bottles (if you recycle them)

BABY PRODUCTS

In the baby products aisle, you have some of the most recyclable packaging in steel formula cans and the least in disposable diapers.

Disposable diapers continue to pose a dilemma. While the major manufacturers claim to have partially recyclable components (plastics and papers, when separated) and source reduction, the diaper is still an environmental pariah. After all, it's designed to be disposable. Source reduction claims were rampant in the wake of Procter & Gamble's failed attempt to sell the "compostability" of diapers. The company is still funding pilot projects for composting across the country. It's too early to say whether this technology of grinding up, cooking, and turning diaper waste into fertilizer on a large scale is economical or practical. The FTC and state attorneys general settled several actions against diaper makers two years ago to remove compostability and degradability claims. The jury's still out on whether disposables consume less energy, resources, and landfill space than cotton diapers that are washed by diaper services (which use heavy amounts of detergent, water, gas, and electricity).

Other disposable baby products include the increasingly popular "wipes" designed for convenience and one-time use. Scott's Baby Fresh and Washabye Baby products had a redeeming feature, though, in that they were packaged in reusable containers made of #2 HDPE plastic. Other baby products in HDPE include Johnson & Johnson's Baby Powder, Schering-Plough's Mexana powder, and Colgate-Palmolive's Baby Magic powder.

Only a handful of companies make infant formula—Abbott Labs/Ross (Similac, Isomil), American Home Products (Nursoy, SMA, Promil), Bristol-Myers Squibb/Mead Johnson (Enfamil, Sobec), and Nestlé/Carnation (Good Start). Fortunately, these products are packaged in either aluminum or steel cans, which are among the most recycled materials. It should be noted that, as this book goes to press, Nestlé and American Home Products are the object of an international boycott over their distribution of infant formula in Third World countries. When mixed with untreated local water, the formula spreads often-fatal disease to children.

GREEN CHOICES

- Formula in steel cans
- Baby products in reusable containers (if you have a use for them)
- Baby powders, oils in HDPE (#2)
- Baby food in glass jars (if you recycle them)

OVERPACKAGED OR RARELY RECYCLED MATERIALS

- Gerber's Pedialyte (#5 plastic), blister-pack accessories
- Johnson & Johnson's baby shampoo (#3), Colgate's Baby Magic shampoo (#3)
- Disposable diapers

BAKERY GOODS

At first glance, this industry seems to waste very little. Most bread packages are a single, low-density plastic bag with little other packaging. Although the bag is generally un-recyclable, slowly but surely more recycling centers are starting to take them. Most boxes that do not touch food contain some recycled material. Nabisco, Sunshine, and Keebler use recycled paperboard. If some process could be developed to incorporate sterile recycled material into inner packaging, we'd like to see it on the market (see Condiments). Even more troublesome are cake and cookie boxes with plastic "windows," which make them even less recyclable. Since people want to see the product they're buying, we don't see any big changes here. "The problem is, we didn't have a lot to reduce in the first place," a spokesperson for the American Bakers Association told us.

GREEN CHOICES

- One-piece packages (plastic bread wrappers, etc.)
- Home-baked bread, cookies, cakes

BATTERIES

If there's a theme to modern batteries over the past three years, it's "get the mercury out." As a highly toxic heavy metal, mercury is perceived as a major environmental threat. Although it's doubtful that the major source of mercury pollution in the environment is from batteries leaching in landfills—it comes primarily from industrial processes—major battery makers are producing their premium batteries without it. Eveready, Duracell, Sanyo/GE, and Rayovac all market an alkaline "no mercury added" battery. However, according to an Eveready representative, the batteries contain "trace" amounts of mercury that occur naturally. Actually, mercury isn't critical to a battery's performance. Conventional carbon-zinc batteries contain no mercury at all.

The real issue with batteries is their disposability. We recommend using rechargeable batteries (which unfortunately contain even more heavy metals like cadmium) and suggest that you send them back to the manufacturers for recycling. The Sanyo/GE line allows you to do this through a clever package/mailer. Rechargeable batteries, though, are only part of the solution. If they're thrown out, they deposit toxic heavy metals in landfills. The EPA estimates that rechargeable batteries accounted for about half the 1,800 tons of cadmium in the waste stream in 1986. That's a drop in the bucket compared to the 200,000 tons of lead in the waste stream.

GREEN CHOICES

- Rechargeable batteries that can be returned to manufacturer (GE/Sanyo)

CANDIES, CHIPS, POPCORNS, SNACKS

Candy wrappers are highly disposable and unrecyclable. They can't contain recycled material, either, due to food safety laws. But that doesn't mean that manufacturers can't clean up their operations through recycling and environmental management. Helen Gordon, the president of Tootsie Roll Industries, called us back personally to detail some company programs. Wrigley and M&M Mars also have environmental programs in place. Nestlé, which makes everything from

Butterfingers to Crunch bars, promptly responded with a list of environmental activities. We'd like to see all candymakers work toward more recyclable packaging, but that's a difficult matter given the cost of the product, health regulations, and the short shelf life of the products.

The most information we could get was from Warner-Lambert, the maker of Certs, Dentyne and Trident. The outer packaging of their candy line was 50 percent PCW paper.

Snack foods are usually packaged in the most disposable, unrecyclable ways. The bags are neither made from recycled content nor are recyclable. Nevertheless, companies such as Frito-Lay (Pepsico) have in place extensive plant programs to recover and reduce waste. The company also acknowledged reducing volume in its Lays and Ruffles bags. The second-largest producer of potato starch in the United States, the company recovers almost 20 million pounds of starch per year and resells it to other manufacturers. The program has enabled the company to reduce its waste water discharges by 35 percent, the company told the EPA. The other big players in the business—Borden and Keebler—provided us with little information, although their packaging employs some source reduction.

In popcorn, it's hard to recommend the microwave versions, since they are designed to be used once and thrown out. We were pleased to see ConAgra's Orville Reddenbacher offer their product in a recyclable PETE bottle.

GREEN CHOICES

- Eagle or Fisher nuts in steel cans or glass jars
- AH/Jiffy Pop in aluminum tray

OVERPACKAGED PRODUCTS

- Del Monte's pudding cups
- ConAgra/Hunt's Snack Packs
- General Foods/Jell-O variety pack
- Chip variety packs (Frito-Lay)
- Procter & Gamble's Pringles (unrecyclable metal and paper)
- M&M Mars' Pretzel Combos (metal and paper)
- Nabisco/Planter's peanut and snack cans (metal and paper)

CEREALS, BREAKFAST FOODS

It's a universal industry practice to use recycled paperboard in cereal boxes. However, the latest generation of labeling emblazons this fact as if it happened overnight. The typical amount of postconsumer waste is 35 percent, which is noted by most manufacturers.

What we really wanted to know about the largest players in this business—General Mills, Kellogg, and Ralston Purina—was whether they encouraged or practiced sustainable agriculture. That means reduced pesticide use, topsoil preservation, and efficient water management. This is one of the most critical environmental issues in agriculture. If the earth is to support 10 billion people in the twenty-first century, we need to find a way to grow crops without destroying water supplies and topsoil. According to Wes Jackson, president of the Land Institute, "We could very well exhaust our soils trying to feed 10 or 20 billion people." Unfortunately, big companies feel that consumers will be bored or intimidated by the subject of sustainable agriculture. We'd like to see more about it on the ample cereal box labels and on the coffee cans of Maxwell House (Kraft General Foods/Philip Morris) and the tea containers of Lipton (Unilever) and Nestea (Nestlé). These companies combined probably have more impact on world agriculture than do the thousand largest private family farms in America. It also was bothersome that most of the cereals have little nutritional value, especially the most exploitive ones tied in with television shows and movies. These products contain so many "empty" calories, you can almost hear an echo when you tap the boxes.

The company environmental records of General Mills, Quaker Oats, and Kellogg were above average. Quaker Oats is an active internal recycler that diverts "more than 50 million pounds of steel, aluminum, cardboard, and food waste from the landfill and sent to recyclers [in one year]." The company also purchases more than 100 million pounds of recycled paperboard for its packaging and printed its environmental policy in its 1991 annual report. Except for a change in its traditional Quaker Oats oatmeal box from cardboard to plastic, the company seems to practice what it preaches. An *outstanding* company was Celestial Seasonings, a tiny company in Boulder, Colorado, known for its herbal teas and Earthwise cleaning products and garbage bags. They not only featured oxygen-bleached tea bags without "string tabs," but detailed several positions on "composting nonutilized tea, corporate integrated pest management, and a grassroots environmental committee." More interesting was Celestial Seasonings' involvement in international sustainable agriculture programs and "cross-fertilization of ideas between different indigenous peoples."

Source reduction was commonly found in cereal-box liners and in coffee cans. As containers go, it's difficult to beat the standard steel coffee cans for recycled content, recyclability, and reusability.

GREEN CHOICES

- Coffee, tea, or cocoa packaged in steel or glass
- Tea bags without the string and tab

OVERPACKAGED PRODUCT

- KGF/Maxwell House single filter packs (as opposed to regular grounds you measure yourself)

CONDIMENTS

For manufacturers and consumers, the massive shift to plastic bottles in recent years has been both a blessing and a curse. Plastic bottles are light, unbreakable, and squeezable (allowing the consumer to waste less product). But the technology that makes the bottles lighter also makes them less recyclable. There was a time when you could only buy ketchup, mustard, pickles, and salad dressing in glass bottles, which are commonly recycled. Now your selection is limited by the invasion of PETE bottles (marked with the #1 plastic resin code at the bottom of the containers), which are recyclable but not nearly as widely as glass. Kraft and Heinz have even found a way to incorporate some recycled material in their bottles, which is a step in the right direction. Unless you have young children or just prefer the plastic, perhaps glass is your best choice in this category. Many labels now include a message to recycle glass, which may contain some recycled material.

GREEN CHOICES

- Condiment packaged in steel (large size only), glass, or PETE
- Kraft's recycled PETE salad dressing bottle
- Heinz's recycled PETE ketchup bottle

PACKAGES THAT NEED TO BE MADE MORE RECYCLABLE

- Stick margarine boxes
- Nearly all dairy condiments coded #5 plastic
- ConAgra/Hunt's Ketchup (#7 plastic, virtually unrecycled)
- Nabisco Brands/Del Monte Ketchup (#7)
- Reckitt & Colman/French's Classic Yellow Mustard (#4 plastic, rarely recycled)
- VDB-Unilever/Imperial margarine (#5 plastic, rarely recycled)
- Land O' Lakes Spread with Cream (#5)
- Kraft/Log Cabin syrup (#5)
- Heinz Weight Watchers syrup (#5)
- Quaker Oats Aunt Jemima (#5)
- VDB/Unilever Soft Fleischmann's margarine (#5)
- Kraft/Parkay Squeeze (not coded for recycling)
- Heinz's Starkist Charlie's Lunchkit
- Kraft/Oscar Mayer's Lunchables

COOKIES, CRACKERS

Here again it's common to see outer boxes made of 35

percent postconsumer recycled material and labeled as such. But that's merely a start. Plastic polystyrene and low-density polyethylene wrappers and packages are almost never taken by local recyclers. Some cookie cartons have dividers, paper slots, and additional bags. Nabisco and Pepperidge Farm have some of the simplest packaging, which is preferable to the multiple layers of unrecyclable material.

Pepperidge Farm, the premium cookie maker owned by Campbell Soup, has an above-average environmental record and employs mostly paper packaging (some recycled). Keebler, in contrast, employs mostly plastic packaging. With the exception of the wax-paper liners used in most cracker boxes, Nabisco products appeared to utilize the most economical packages. As perhaps the most dominant player in the business, they should.

GREEN CHOICES

- Any single box versus a "soft" plastic/paper package
- Home-baked cookies or cakes

CLEANING PRODUCTS

This is one of our largest categories because so much has been done to alter the size and composition of packages in recent years. All detergents used to be packaged the same way—in cardboard boxes. Now you can find three different kinds of plastics used in addition to paperboard. Since this is such a competitive business, the companies doing battle will do all they can to attract a loyal customer. The goliaths in this business—Procter & Gamble, Colgate-Palmolive, and

Lever—are rated highly in our company surveys for environmental responsibility. Detergents have more environmental messages per package than perhaps any other product line. Some of the messages include recycling codes, source reduction, concentrated formulas, and recycled boxes. There's no clear leader in this category, however, since we didn't see any independent audits of these companies' industrial operations. However, we can tell you that nearly every detergent box contains recycled paperboard and nearly every bottle is made of #2 HDPE plastic, the second-most recycled plastic. Only the Church & Dwight (Arm & Hammer) line informed us how much postconsumer waste was used in their packaging.

One of the most dramatic developments in the detergent aisle is the offering of "superconcentrated" detergents. These products come in smaller boxes and allow you to use less detergent per washing load. Even the scoops are said to be recyclable. All of the major detergent makers were promoting these pricier products heavily and trumpeting the reduced-packaging claim. As of early 1993, these new products claimed about 55 percent of all detergent sales, according to Information Resources. Whether they will reduce the amount of packaging going to the landfill remains to be seen.

With a few exceptions, most dishwashing liquids are packaged in #1 PETE plastic, the most recycled plastic. Colgate's Palmolive dishwashing-liquid bottle is a genuine highlight. Not only is the bottle one of the few PETE plastic bottles made of 20 percent postconsumer material, but the entire back label of the bottle outlines Colgate's environmental message. It's strong on recycling, in addition to being biodegradable and phosphate-free. We saw a plethora of no-phosphate and biodegradable claims, although most detergents have been that way for years. We're leery of the biodegradable claim unless it has been independently certified. In our survey, the only products SCS certified for biodegradability were: Benckiser's EarthRite line; Blue Coral's Clear Magic line; Descale-It's products; Enforcer's Drain Care and Septic Treatment; 20/10's windshield cleaner; and Roebic septic products.

One of the most informative consumer hotlines in this group is Dow Chemical's Dow Brands division (Fantastic, Yes, Glass Plus, Ziploc). Although a relatively small factor in this market (compared to Procter & Gamble, Colgate, and Lever), Dow combines information on packaging and company environmental programs. Although still a major polluter and producer of highly toxic chemicals, Dow makes most of its containers from #2 HDPE and is instrumental in developing recycling technologies and programs for polystyrene and polyethylene. As a major producer of both chemicals, they have a large financial stake in these programs.

Some problem claims were observed on AJ Funk's Sparkle Glass Cleaner's sticker claim that its vinyl bottle was recyclable. Vinyl, while technically recyclable, is rarely taken by recyclers. SC Johnson's Windex Pro-Strength, Reckitt & Colman's Easy-Off, and Blue Coral's Shower Power also come in vinyl bottles. We found another inconsistency in the form of Eastman Kodak/L&F Products' Resolve and Direct refills. While these plastic SmartPack containers use 25 percent less plastic than the original bottles, they are not recyclable, the manufacturer told us. Nevertheless, despite these problems, L&F has the greatest number of bottles packaged in recycled PETE, probably owing to the fact that L&F's parent company—Eastman Kodak—was a major producer of PETE. We also noted a few "CFC-free" claims (mostly by SC Johnson), which are irrelevant since nearly all consumer aerosols are required by law to be free from CFCs. And lack of CFCs doesn't mean there are no other harmful effects on the environment.

All told, the cleaning aisle continues to be a rich source of experimentation in packaging. We hope that since the competition is fierce, environmentalism will continue to be a part of the effort to market packaging. It's also important that the megaproducers of detergents and cleaners enhance their efforts to use recycled resin in PETE, HDPE, and vinyl bottles and increase the postconsumer content in their boxes. Let them know how you feel. Almost all cleaning products display toll-free customer service numbers on their labels (see the resources section for a complete list).

GREEN CHOICES

- Benckiser's EarthRite line (40 percent PCW HDPE bottles, SCS–certified biodegradable)
- Planet Product's line (25 percent PCW HDPE, SCS–certified biodegradable)
- Church & Dwight's Arm & Hammer baking soda (recycled box, benign product)
- L&F Lysol brand products in recycled PETE
- Refillable products (provided you recycle original containers) by Lever, Procter & Gamble, and L&F
- Procter & Gamble's Ultra Downy (100 percent recycled HDPE)

OVERPACKAGED PRODUCTS

- All plastic air fresheners, including Airwick, Glade, and Renuzit lines

- SC Johnson Wax's Plug-ins, Glade Country Pottery, and Pledge Busters (not recyclable)
- L&F's Love My Carpet and Lysol Touch-up Wipes
- All toilet bowl cleaners in two-part cans (all contain highly caustic and poisonous compounds)

PRODUCTS THAT NEED TRULY RECYCLABLE PACKAGING

- Colgate-Palmolive's 42-oz. Ajax, Palmolive, and Sensiskin liquid detergents (#3 PVC, not recycled)
- DowBrands' 28-oz. Pine Power (#3)
- Reckitt & Colman's 22-oz. Woolite

DAIRY PRODUCTS AND DESSERTS

Here we found no examples of recycled packaging, which is understandable due to federal health laws. However, we did find numerous examples of source reduction in packaging, although none of it was noted in labeling. Dean Foods, a major national producer of cottage cheese, yogurt, ice cream, and dips, reported that it had reduced the volume of those product packages by 10 percent, according to a company spokesman. The company has also "lightweighted" its milk bottles by 10 percent and claims to have "the lightest milk bottles in the business."

The dairy business is a difficult one to track since most dairy products such as milk and butter are produced regionally. With the exception of companies such as Kraft General Foods, Ben & Jerry's Homemade, Land O' Lakes, and Dean Foods, few companies market dairy products nationally. That's due mostly to the nature of the business. Dairy products typically have a short shelf life, need refrigeration, and do not transport well over long distances.

We found several examples of source reduction when we were able to talk to packaging executives. It's safe to say that nearly every manufacturer was incorporating source reduction in some way. As with most other paperboard packaging, we also found a high percentage of (minimum) 35 percent PCW paperboard.

While most dairy product packaging is not recyclable, most plastic milk bottles are. The switch from glass to paper to plastic has been an interesting battle over the years. Plastic and paper win on the safety front, but neither is as recyclable as glass. Paper is especially difficult due to the wax coating. A few pilot programs have been put in place, but it's an expensive process. Plastic jugs, made of #2 HDPE, are recycled in most large programs and are being remade into things like garbage bags and park benches. Although environmentalists prefer a "closed loop" process where the product is recycled into the original product, HDPE resin is gaining in demand among plastics companies.

GREEN CHOICES

- Dairy products in glass or in clear HDPE
- Ready-made frosting in reusable HDPE (Duncan Hines, Betty Crocker, Pillsbury)

OVERPACKAGED PRODUCTS

- Dean Ice Cream bars
- Dole Fruit Juice bars

- M&M/Dove, Snickers, Milky Way bars
- Nestlé's Crunch bars
- Heinz/Weight Watchers bars

FILM PRODUCTS

The "big three" in retail amateur film have spent tidy sums promoting their recycling efforts. Eastman Kodak, which used to dominate the business, now has healthy competition from Fuji Film USA and Polaroid.

Kodak caught flak several years ago when it introduced its disposable Funsaver camera. Responding quickly to the public relations fallout, it instituted a recycling program for the camera. It also packages all of its 35-mm film in recycled-paper boxes, recycles developing chemicals, and has an international environmental program. It should be noted that Eastman invented a way to recycle PETE and is working on a process to make materials with 100 percent recycled PETE by 1995. This is a classic example of a plastic producer defending its product and market share by developing recycling technologies. This socially beneficial relationship is fostered by pure capitalism.

Fuji, in contrast, has a long history of recycling, having established an antipollution committee in 1965. The giant Japanese conglomerate also recycles its QuickSnaps disposable camera and makes its film boxes from recycled paper. Fuji also replaced its plastic 35-mm film canisters with moisture-proof paper. Similarly, Polaroid has a recycling program, although its product tends to contain a lot of disposable waste, due to the technical nature of instant photography. The company features an excellent consumer hotline, however. These days, all major film producers and processers recycle darkroom chemicals and silver from film. Ask if your local film processor does the same.

GARBAGE BAGS
(KITCHEN, LAWN AND LEAF, TRASH, PAPER)

Despite the fact that these products were the sacrificial lambs (in the eyes of the industry) for environmentalists and watchdog regulators over green claims, the major manufacturers have done surprisingly little to enhance their products—or their images. Yet, some of the smallest plastics companies in the business have responded with bags made of recycled plastic. As we noted earlier, Mobil (Hefty, Kordite), Glad (Baggies) and Carlisle (Ruffies) were forced to drop claims that their bags were "degradable" (nothing happened in landfills, of course) after the FTC and state attorneys general sued them. Although some of the remnants of that short-lived frenzy are still on supermarket shelves, the companies are quietly pushing claims of source reduction.

Mobil, for example, told us that source reduction was the biggest virtue of its Hefty and Kordite lines. The bags have been "lightweighted 20 percent to 30 percent over the last three years with the thickness of the bags going from 1.3 mil (one-thousandth of an inch) to under 1 mil," a company spokesman said. Unfortunately, though, the line employs no postconsumer content (some preconsumer/plant waste is used). Mobil claims it can't obtain enough of the postconsumer resin. First Brands' Glad was in a similar situation, claiming no postconsumer content, but making bold and inflated claims on its packaging that by reducing the amount of plastic in its bags it would "reduce landfill waste by 2 percent." Both First Brands and Mobil have been active on the national and community levels in recycling programs, which, we trust, will result in high volumes of recovered plastic for them to incorporate into their products.

The greenest company in the garbage bag business is Webster Industries, a $150 million company in Peabody, Massachusetts. Compared to the $64 billion-plus Mobil, Webster is a drop in the ocean, but it manages to produce a 100 percent recycled (24 percent to 30 percent PCW) bag in its SCS-certified Renew line. The company claims to recycle more than 100 million pounds of plastic in making its bags. It also sells a source-reduced or "ultracondensed" product (also 30 percent PCW) that they claim is one-quarter to one-third thinner than conventional bags while suffering no loss of strength.

Other small- to medium-sized companies had rival offerings. Strout Plastics markets a Mr. Neat Bags Again line with 15 percent PCW; Argon Industries a 10 percent PCW bag; Poly-America a Husky line with 20 percent PCW; Carlisle Plastics a source-reduced, 15 percent Re-cycle, Ruffies Eco-Choice, and Sure Strength lines; Petosky Plastics a 10 percent PCW line; and Brawny Plastics a source-reduced recycled line. Highly rated Celestial Seasonings also marketed a source-reduced Ecologic line.

GREEN CHOICES

- Webster's Renew line (30 percent PCW)
- North American Plastics' Harmony and Recycle 1 (30 percent PCW)
- Strout Kleensite (15 percent PCW)

LIGHT BULBS

There's real promise in this group. Over the past three years, every major bulb maker (there are only a handful) introduced a line of compact fluorescent (CF) light bulbs that save up to 75 percent of the energy used by incandescent bulbs. While costing more, they also last for years. General Electric, GTE/Sylvania, and Philips' Earth Light were the leaders.

Generally, the CF bulbs are the real energy savers. These products are great values, can cut your energy bills, and can reduce air pollution and global warming. For example, one (unverified) claim is that a single 23-watt compact fluorescent can prevent up to 1,072 pounds of global-warming carbon dioxide from entering the atmosphere (from fossil-fuel–burning power plants), 7.8 pounds of acid-rain–causing sulfur dioxide, and 4.1 pounds of smog-producing nitrogen dioxide. More important, the bulbs can save up to $67 (per bulb) in utility costs over the life of the bulb—which is at least 10,000 hours.

The incandescent bulbs that make energy-saving claims save minuscule amounts of electricity, so we didn't list them. In fact, GE was cited by a group of state attorneys general over energy-saving claims on the incandescents in its Energy Saver line. The company has since settled the charges.

Be careful when evaluating these products, though. While compact fluorescents generally save energy and cost less over the long run, they may not produce as much light as incandescents. You may need special fixtures and shades to gain maximal output. Just screwing them into a conventional table lamp may net 90 percent *less* light if not accompanied by a special shade.

Fluorescent Bulb Replacement Guide

Compact Fluorescent	Rated Life	Replaces	Incandescent Life
26 watts	10,000 hours	90 watts	2,500 hours
20 watts	8,000 hours	75 watts	750 hours
15 watts	8,000 hours	60 watts	1,000 hours

Source: General Electric Lighting. Uncertified estimates used for purposes of example only.

MISCELLANEOUS

This potpourri includes everything from recycled rubber mats and "soaker" garden hoses (made from recycled car tires) to recycling bins. We also include aluminum wraps, paints, paint removers, nontoxic pest control agents, and some recycled containers. Nearly all of these products have a high recycled content, and you can find them in most of the modern supermarkets. We actually bought soaker hoses, paints, and auto supplies in our local supermarket, which is not large by today's standards. Of course, "hypermarts" and warehouse clubs carry a much wider variety of this kind of merchandise.

OVER-THE-COUNTER REMEDIES
(PAINKILLERS, COLD REMEDIES,
NONPRESCRIPTION DRUGS)

With the exception of Bristol-Myers Squibb, Upjohn, and Lilly, company responses to our survey in this area were uniformly poor. Not only were our written queries largely unanswered or inadequate, but the consumer hotlines we called had little or no information on recycled packaging or environmental policies. We had to call Bristol-Myers Squibb's headquarters to obtain their rather comprehensive environmental policy. (Their hotline, in contrast, had no information.) The same was true of the consumer affairs departments of American Cyanamid (Fibercon), SmithKline Beecham (Contac), Mentholatum, Nostrilla, RPR (Maalox), Whitehall/AH Robins/American Home Products (Dristan, Robitussin), Block Drug (Polident), Miles (Alka-Seltzer), Sandoz (Triaminic), Ciba (Doan's pills), Schering-Plough (Solarcaine), Pfizer (Ben-Gay), and Warner-Lambert (Rolaids). Ironically, the companies with the fewest products in the consumer arena—Eli Lilly (mostly pharmaceuticals), Burroughs Wellcome (Sudafed, Actifed, Neosporin), and Upjohn (Cortaid, Kaopectate, Motrin)—provided the most complete information on their environmental efforts.

Granted, most over-the-counter companies said they couldn't use recycled packaging on their inner packages due to health laws. And they complained that they couldn't find enough high-quality recycled paper to clearly print all of the government-mandated health-related information on their packages. They even noted that they needed the extra packaging just to print the required information. We can accept most of that, except for the problem with finding enough high-quality recycled paperboard. Nearly every analgesic (painkillers) was packaged in both an unrecyclable bottle and box. Not one manufacturer disclosed whether it had eliminated the use of heavy metals in their inks or used water-based inks. The most positive sign we noted in the home-remedy section was the presence of #1 PETE cough syrup bottles (Sandoz, Warner-Lambert). This safety tradeoff replaces the traditional glass bottles with a less recycled product. Most measuring caps, however, were unnecessary and made from the unrecycled #5 polypropylene resin. If a way could be found to get all the health-related information onto a single bottle, that would eliminate most boxes. There's room for much improvement here.

One telling sign about the "greenness" of the industry emerged when we contacted the Non-Prescription Drug Manufacturers Association (NDMA) in Washington for an overview of the industry's environmental programs. Like most trade groups, the NDMA monitors and lobbies for laws that impact the industry and provides public relations for its members. But Bill Bradley, the director of technical affairs for the NDMA, told us only that "we've seen some [environmental] trends in the industry that seem to be taking place, but there really hasn't been a lot going on." Bradley noted that the group had formed a task force on recycling and environmental issues, but it hadn't met in a year "due to lack of time."

We were able to obtain some information from Warner-Lambert through John Lime, their vice president of environmental affairs. He cited a number of the company's activities, including their $100 million effort to develop a truly biodegradable plastic called Novon. Additionally, the company's Effergrip, Sinutab, and Efferdent products are packaged in boxes made of at least 50 percent postconsumer paperboard. The company is also a participant in the EPA's Green Lights energy-saving program and is experimenting with alternative fuels and plastics. Lime added that his company tried to remove the brown outer wrap from its flagship product Listerine, but relented when market share dropped. In that case, there was some perceived value in having the excess packaging.

Bristol-Myers Squibb provided us with an exhaustive package of environmental actions on every level. So did Merck, Upjohn, and Lilly. Written information from the other drug companies was paltry. Ciba Consumer Pharmaceuticals sent us a letter consisting of three paragraphs, two of which expressed "appreciation and thanks for your interest." American Home Products (Whitehall/AH Robins) sent us a brochure stating in generic language that the company will "adhere to all environmental protection standards and regulations which may be applicable." No specifics, just boilerplate legal jargon that any company can produce with minimal effort. Burroughs-Wellcome sent us a five-paragraph letter containing sparse detail, but at least enclosed some coupons for their products. Sterling Health sent us a short letter and a one-page environmental statement.

It was unacceptable to us that the consumer hotlines of four of the largest companies in the business—Bristol-Myers Squibb, Warner-Lambert, SmithKline Beecham, and Schering-Plough—had *no* available information on environmental activities. We pursued them all the way up to corporate levels and found the following: Schering-Plough is using "nonmetallic printing inks, is assembling an environmental task force, and is making bottles from recyclable plastic," but the company spokesman would not provide any written information or elaborate further. Despite a letter and several calls,

Schering-Plough's consumer affairs department sent us only a three-paragraph letter that stated: "We are pleased to inform you that we have recently formed a special committee for improved environmental packaging and hope to implement this immediately." Although Warner-Lambert didn't have any written environmental information either, their environmental department at least provided a long (verbal) list of environmentally responsible activities. Bristol-Myers Squibb was clearly the most active company on the green front and had generous materials to prove it. If their consumer hotline gave out this information, we wouldn't take issue with the $11 billion concern.

Compared to the cleaning products group—things that you do not ingest and that do directly affect your health—the over-the-counter group has a long way to go.

GREEN CHOICES

- Least packaged items (i.e., cough syrup bottles without the outer box)
- Any remedies packaged in glass or PETE (cough syrups, mouthwash)

PAPER PRODUCTS
(DISPOSABLE NAPKINS, TOWELS, BATH TISSUES, PLATES, STATIONERY, GREETING CARDS, OFFICE SUPPLIES)

If you're looking for great strides in any one product group, this is the one. Produced by an industry that's been recycling for decades, it seems that paper goods have "come out of the closet" with recycled claims. We found a bounty of old products that were labeled as recycled and entirely new product lines that incorporated recycled content. Recycled products were most prevalent in stationery and office supplies, where recycled content can easily be added to low-cost products such as notebooks, file folders, and binders without any noticeable drop in quality. Considering that nearly all of these products are disposable—and recyclable—this is an ideal use for the recycled-paper market, which has suffered due to lack of consumer and business demand.

As with so many other groups, the largest companies in the business were the least active in offering recycled products. The biggest papermakers—Kimberly-Clark (Kleenex, Huggies), James River (Northern tissues), Georgia Pacific (Coronet, Sparkle), and Procter & Gamble (Pampers, Charmin, White Cloud)—had no complete lines of recycled-paper goods. James River and Georgia Pacific said that their lines contained some recycled content, but they couldn't specify how much or the proportion of postconsumer waste. When we asked why this was the case, we couldn't get a straight answer. There's certainly enough paper out there to keep their mills busy for decades.

In contrast, much smaller companies with considerably less distribution and marketing power had complete lines of recycled goods. Some good examples were American Tissue, Fort Howard, Statler/Tree Free, Pope & Talbot, Cascades Industries, Morcon, Marcal, and Webster. These SCS-certified companies featured 10 to 80 percent PCW paper.

Stationery and other office-products companies also offered a wide selection of recycled goods. Mead, Dutton LeBus, Esselte Pendaflex, Georgia Pacific, Stuart Hall, and Safco sold everything from mailers with recycled plastic to Ms. Piggy pads (Mead). It was hard *not* to find dozens of recycled products in the stationery/office supplies aisle. Generally, the bigger the store, the better the selection. For nearly all of these products, there was no reason not to incorporate recycled materials.

Greeting-card lines from Hallmark and American Greetings featured recycled content in varying degrees, although not as much as we'd like for a disposable product.

GREEN CHOICES

- Paper products with the highest recycled PCW content. See Chapter 16 for a complete list. Some SCS-certified examples include American Tissue's private-label line (80 percent PCW), Cascades (80 percent PCW), Webster's Renew (40 percent PCW)
- Mead's Muppets theme line (100 percent PCW), theme books
- Hallmark's Christmas Naturals line (90 percent reduced packaging)
- Esselte Pendaflex 3-ring binders (93 percent PCW)

PERSONAL CARE (COSMETICS, DEODORANTS, FRAGRANCES, MOUTHWASHES, SKIN-CARE PRODUCTS, TOILETRIES, SHAMPOOS, TOOTHPASTES, DISPOSABLE DIAPERS)

There were plenty of examples of overpackaging in this group. Although we had little quarrel with shampoos and skin-care products, cosmetics and deodorants were a mine field of wasteful packaging. A typical example was the two- or three-piece (unrecycled) outer carton that displayed an unrecyclable bottle or roll-on dispenser. Some manufacturers such as Bristol-Myers Squibb (Ban) decided to liberate their roll-ons as stand-alones, but these multiplastic containers are not recyclable. Relative to the amount of paper sitting in landfills, we doubt if roll-on containers pose much of a waste problem in terms of volume. But it's clear that quite a bit of cosmetics packaging can be eliminated without compromising health concerns. How important is the removal of the outer carton on all toiletries? Helene Curtis, for example, estimates that by removing the carton on its line of Suave and Degree brands, they will save more than 1,500 tons of paperboard a year.

One encouraging development was Bristol-Myers Squibb's use of recycled paperboard in its Ban outer containers. Although we'd like to see this "shell" eliminated, this is a good first step.

The mouthwashes were the least offensive (no pun intended) of the personal-care products. With the exception of Bausch & Lomb's Clear mouthwash, all the plastic mouthwash bottles we saw were packaged in #1 PETE. Of course, as we noted before, most of these mouthwashes used to be packaged in highly recyclable glass, but since breakage is a big factor with these products, we think the trade-off is justified.

In toothpastes, our wish list includes removing the largely unnecessary outer boxes, although in most cases that would make it difficult to shelve, owing to the shape of most toothpaste tubes. Colgate-Palmolive addressed this problem recently with a "stand-up tube," which is a wide tube with a cylindrical base. The design is actually an answer to an earlier source-reduced "pump" design launched by Procter & Gamble's Crest (Neat Squeeze) several years ago. Colgate claims that its tube weighs 20 percent less than conventional laminated tubes and 70 percent less than pumps. It doesn't appear that either product is any more recyclable than the conventional tubes, but they use less material. If these products prove successful, you may see more of them. Boxes labeled 35 percent postconsumer paperboard include Church & Dwight's Dental Care; Chesebrough-Pond's/Unilever's Aim, Pepsodent, and Close-up; and Colgate-Palmolive's Baking Soda, Peak, and Ultra-Brite.

Hair-care products were relatively straightforward. With few exceptions, most bottles were made of #2 HDPE plastic, the second-most-recycled resin. Again, this is safer than glass packaging, although it diminishes the recyclability of the product. Some shampoo bottles, however, contain nearly unrecycled #3 vinyl. Mennen's Baby Magic shampoo was one such example. One standout is Helene Curtis's Salon Selectives line, which uses 25 percent postconsumer trilayered #2 HDPE. The company estimates that the packaging will consume 800,000 pounds of recycled plastic per year, or 6 million milk containers. Chesebrough Pond's Aquanet bottle employs some recycled content, as does Bristol-Myers's Clairol Logic line (25 percent). Procter & Gamble heralds its Vidal Sassoon Airspray line, because it is both refillable and nonaerosol. Its Pantene and Shamtu brands make similar claims. The most glaring dilemma with hair products is the use of hydrocarbon propellants (butane, isobutane, propane), which are both flammable and create smog. If you can choose a pump product, do so.

Mostly due to product size, cosmetics manufacturers rely on blister packs to hang their products on racks or line them up on shelves. While blister packs represent overpackaging, they appear to be a practical solution for retailers. One idea we'd like to see catch on is the independent chain Body Shop's idea for selling personal-care products in refillable containers that you bring back to the store. Although we doubt that supermarkets will want to get into this kind of business, it offers a solution to the glut of overpackaging that most cosmetic products create.

One bright spot was Sara Lee's L'Eggs product line, which has replaced its characteristic plastic egg container with paperboard.

It should be noted that most of the cosmetics companies (except for Cosmair/L'Oreal and Procter & Gamble's Max Factor/Cover Girl) did not respond to our survey, despite repeated efforts. The no-shows were Revlon, Smith-Kline Beecham, Lake Pharmaceuticals, Maybelline, Sally Hanson, WOC Products, and Carter-Wallace. We received short, unsatisfactory verbal statements from Procter & Gamble (Max Factor/Cover Girl) and Chesebrough-Pond's (Aziza, Faberge, Prince Matchabelli) that told us little. For an industry that makes billions on appearances, we found nothing to indicate that any major cosmetics house was coloring their operations green.

GREEN CHOICES

- Helene Curtis's Salon Selectives (recycled HDPE)
- Nonaerosol pump sprays (all), Procter & Gamble's Airspray
- Johnson & Johnson's Band-Aids in reusable steel cans

OVERPACKAGED PRODUCTS

- SmithKline Beecham's Aquafresh toothpaste
- Unilever's Faberge/Brut (bottle and box)

- Westwood's Keri
- Warner-Lambert's Listerine (original wrapped bottle)
- Revlon's Mitchum deodorant
- Gillette's Soft n' Dri, Dry Idea

PRODUCTS IN NEARLY UNRECYCLED MATERIALS (#3 PVC)
(NOT COMMONLY RECYCLED, THOUGH RECYCLING
IS TECHNICALLY POSSIBLE)

- Alberto-Culver's Alberto VO5 shampoo
- Bausch & Lomb's Clear Choice mouthwash
- Unilever's Vaseline Petroleum Jelly
- Johnson & Johnson Baby Shampoo
- Helene Curtis's Finesse
- Johnson & Johnson's ACT mouthwash

DEODORANTS WITHOUT OUTER CARTONS

- Carter-Wallace's Arrid Xtra Dry
- Unilever's Faberge/Brut, Speed Stick
- Helene Curtis's Degree, Suave
- Procter & Gamble's Old Spice, Sure, Secret

PET FOODS, SUPPLIES

The pet food industry is one of the most efficient recyclers of food waste in the world. Pet food consists mainly of things that the meat-processing industry would otherwise throw out. Dogs and cats love the stuff that most people can't stomach. With the exception of boxed or bagged products, pet foods can be found in aluminum or steel cans, which are widely recycled and contain recycled content.

A few large companies dominate this business. Heinz, which makes 9-Lives cat food, has initiated a water conservation program at one of its large plants. M&M Mars, which owns Kal-Kan, also operates recycling programs. Nestlé (Friskies, Mighty Dog) features recycled paperboard and aluminum cans. However, most Purina products (dog and cat chows) come in unrecyclable bags. It should be noted that Nestlé's Friskies line is one of the largest to offer aluminum cans. Heinz's Vets, Skippy, and 9 Lives come in steel cans, as do Grand Metropolitan's Alpo and Nestlé's Mighty Dog. Hartz Mountain chose not to respond to our survey.

GREEN CHOICES

- Foods in aluminum and steel cans (Friskies, 9 Lives, Skippy, Vets, Mighty Dog, Alpo, Ken-L-Ration)
- Ralston Purina's Nature's Course (some proceeds donated to Earth Day USA)

PACKAGING/DISPOSAL PROBLEMS

- All kitty litters (contain nondegradable clays)
- Happy Cat (#3 PVC container)
- Pet foods in multiple-layer wax-paper coated bags

PROCESSED/CONVENIENCE-PACKAGED FOODS (MICROWAVABLE, OVEN-READY, FROZEN)

We really had to dig to discover anything new in this category. The most promising developments were things you could neither see nor note on the label. The biggest story for these products was source reduction—or lack of it. The largest manufacturers—ConAgra, Campbell, Dial, and Nestlé—told us they had reduced the amount of materials in their packaging. But for every example of source reduction, we found six examples of overpackaging that made us question the commitment of the industry to cutting overall packaging waste.

The worst offenders were in the convenience or microwave-ready aisle. Since pure metals generally can't be microwaved, that nixed the recyclability of most of these containers. What we found were multiple-material packages that could only be thrown out. Dial's Doubletree microwave foods are a case in point. The containers are part aluminum, part polystyrene, and part polyethylene. As a whole, these containers are a recycling nightmare. Separately, at least the polyethylene and aluminum have some chance with recyclers. The problem with complex packages, which are designed to withstand heat, cold, and bacteria, is that it's uneconomical for recyclers to tear them apart to get at the valuable materials. Kraft's source-reduced Budget Gourmet was the least offensive line in this category, although not recyclable. Products by Hormel, Armour and Healthy Choice (ConAgra), Campbell and Dial (Doubletree) aren't going to win any awards for recyclability, either. Gone are the days when the foil-topped aluminum tray dominated the "TV dinner" business. With the advent of cable television, video, and the microwave, people in a hurry have many more choices. However, not one of these alternatives is better than the old TV dinner for recyclability.

With the exception of single-package products such as Heinz's Ore-Ida line or anything in cans or glass, this category is a disaster for the environment. Most of these packages will end up in the landfill. We encourage you to contact manufacturers to work on technologies to make these products more recyclable—or to buy fresh foods and cook them yourself.

Canned goods (steel and aluminum) appear to be the strongest alternative in this category, although we noted them sparsely. To our knowledge, the major tuna brands don't use drift nets that catch and drown dolphins. Heinz's Starkist division has additionally started water conservation and waste management programs worldwide. Hormel's standard Spam can and smaller meals come in aluminum and steel. Campbell's Swanson chunk meats were in aluminum, as were ConAgra's Armour foods in 7.5-ounce cans. All companies using aluminum reported source reduction by reducing package weights. Campbell, for example, reduced weights in nonbeverage cans by 20 percent.

The reason why aluminum and steel cans remain the best choice in this category is that they probably contain recycled material and are easily recycled. Nabisco's Del Monte, for example, uses steel cans that contain up to 30 percent recycled steel; its aluminum cans contain up to 50 percent recycled content. Nestlé's Libby's, Contadina, Buitoni, Carnation, and Crosse & Blackwell brands contain from 54 percent (aluminum) to 20 percent (boxes) recycled content.

PET, Inc. (Progresso, Underwood, Old El Paso, Van De Kamp's), didn't respond to our letter and repeated calls.

GREEN CHOICES

- Fresh produce
- Microwavable foods with PETE inner tray (Le Menu, Healthy Choice). This is a reluctant choice, but the best this group has to offer.
- Frozen foods in a single bag (least packaging)

OVERPACKAGED PRODUCTS

- All microwavable french fries
- All microwavable multimaterial containers (Libby's, Hormel, Chef Boyardee)

SOFT DRINKS

There's very little of note in this group. The entire industry offers source-reduced PETE bottles with little recycled content. Aluminum cans contain recycled content, but it's nearly impossible to say how much because of the variety of sources for aluminum. Since more than 60 percent of aluminum is recycled, it's likely that you'll find some recycled content in aluminum cans. As such, aluminum cans are the greenest choice in this category, followed by steel, glass, and PETE (the most recycled plastic). Due to their popularity and light shipping weight, nearly all beverage makers are marketing aseptic "drink boxes," which are not recycled in most places (except where there are pilot programs). See the list below for more recycled alternatives.

The "big two" companies (Coke and Pepsi) were active in promoting recycling on corporate, national, and community levels. They also are attempting to incorporate more recycled resin into their bottles. Both companies have a 25 percent recycled 2-liter PETE bottle in limited distribution. There are even labeling messages encouraging recycling. Dr Pepper/7-Up did not respond to our survey. Overall, we believe the companies can do even more to create markets for their plastic bottles, which have all but replaced the refillable/returnable glass versions.

GREEN CHOICES

- Any beverage in aluminum, steel, or glass (nearly every major brand) that you recycle after use
- Drink box alternatives in aluminum, steel, or glass (5.5 oz.–6 oz. cans)
  Campbell's V8 and tomato juices (aluminum, glass)
  Coca-Cola's Hi-C (glass)
  Dole juices (aluminum)
  Nestlé/Libby's Juicy juices (aluminum)
  Quaker Oats' Gatorade (glass)
  Mott's Cadbury juices (aluminum, glass)
  Nestea (glass)
  Ocean Spray juices (glass)
  Procter & Gamble's Hawaiian Punch (aluminum, steel)
  Snapple juices (glass)
  Sunsweet Prune juice (aluminum and glass)
  Tropicana juices (glass)
  Veryfine juices (glass)
  Welch's juices (glass)

Chapter 16

The Survey Results

Our survey is based on information generally believed to be reliable, but it is not guaranteed for accuracy. Most information was obtained from product packaging and company inquiries. Except for the SCS-certified claims, all claims are nonaudited and subject to review. No product rating should be considered an endorsement or scientific evaluation in any way. All information is subject to change.

All items in **bold print** are considered to have the best environmental merits in the group, due mostly to packaging concerns. We didn't mention every product packaged in recycled paperboard, aluminum, or glass, which contain recycled materials. Products noted are to show you a sampling of a brand or product line.

Generally, we favored products packaged in aluminum, steel, and glass, and highlighed them if there was a choice between them and plastic or paper. We also found that because of the relatively high recycling rates of these materials, there was a high probability of finding recycled content in these packages. Since aluminum is recycled at more than a 60 percent rate nationwide, chances are that each aluminum can you buy contains some recycled material. With steel and glass, the rates are from 25 to 35 percent. Although no manufacturer would guarantee recycled content for all of its products, some provided minimum-recycled-content rates. With products packaged in paperboard, the standard guaranteed recycled content was 35 percent, although paperboard packages certainly contain much more. Although these packages can be recycled, they rarely are, due to high clay content, inks, and the low quality of the paper, according to the National Recycling Coalition. As a result, we didn't rate these packages as recyclable. In nearly every case, though, most paperboard was previously recycled, as long as it was an outer package that didn't come in contact with food.

We also noted claims of source reduction for entire lines of packaging. Aluminum and plastic packages have been reduced significantly over the past decade. Also, any package containing plastic film has been lightweighted or made with a thinner layer of plastic.

TOP-OF-THE-PAGE ABBREVIATIONS

RP = Recycled packaging (part. = partial, or % indicated). If 100%, the PCW content is noted in "notes," where available.

Rb = Recyclable, based on the most recycled materials of aluminum, steel, glass, and PETE and HDPE plastic resins. Paperboard is not considered widely recycled by the National Recycling Coalition, although it may contain recycled fibers.

SR = Source-reduced packaging. Based largely on company statements as to reduced use of overall material in packaging.

SC = Scientific Certification Systems scientific audit/certification. The product claims have been independently certified by this third party through plant audits and inspections. This is the best available method of double-checking the truth of green claims. SCS is expected to begin labeling products with Environmental Report Cards in 1994.

EFR = EFACT rating. The rating of the company's overall environmental management, operation, and record as assigned by the New Consumer Institute. It's based on pollution records, energy-saving programs, environmental policy/management, and socially responsible factors (see Chapter 13).

1 = worst possible record; 8 = below average; 10 = improving, but needs attention to special issues; 12 = noteworthy; 14 = very good; 16 = excellent; 18 = superior; 20 = highest rating. These objective ratings are based on the best available public information and are subject to change as more information becomes available. Not all companies were rated, especially if they were not U.S.–based or were private or small.

Notes: This section elaborates on type of packaging material such as glass, recycled paperboard (rec. paper.), and percentage of highly desirable postconsumer waste (PCW). Also mentioned are "no-CFCs," a weak claim that doesn't rule out the presence of smog-producing hydrocarbon propellants. Where indicated, we note nonaerosol products that employ simple pumps. Other noteworthy claims include "no mercury added" for alkaline batteries; "energy-saving" for light bulbs; "pr" for partially recycled; "rec. con. or pac." for unspecified recycled content; and "PB" for peanut butter. We also noted use of vegetable or soy inks, nontoxic qualities, reusability, and biodegradability. Aluminum, glass, and steel may be listed as containing recycled content because of the overall high recycling rate of these materials. Percentage of recycled material varies widely depending on the source of the packaging. We did not mention manufacturer claims of "safe for incineration or landfills," because we didn't receive adequate scientific definitions of those terms from the companies.

HDPE = High-density polyethylene, the second-most-recycled plastic resin, which is found in milk, detergent, and shampoo bottles.

IC = Ice cream.

OP = Outer packaging only.

Paper = Paperboard cartons or packages.

PCW = Postconsumer waste content, which refers to the minimum amount of consumer-generated waste reused in the outer packaging only.

PETE = Polyethylene terepthalate, the most recycled plastic, found in soft-drink bottles and condiments containers.

Rec. con. = Unspecified recycled content.

Red. pac. = Reduced packaging.

Rem. = Removable.

COMPANY ABBREVIATIONS

Ab – Abbott Laboratories
AB – Anheuser-Busch
AD – Avery Dennison
AG – American Greetings
AH – American Home
    Products
AT – American Tissue
AV – Astro-Valcour
BM – Bristol-Myers Squibb
Bn – Benckiser
Bo – Borden
BW – Burroughs Wellcome
CA – ConAgra
Ca – Canfield's
CB – Curtice Burns
Cf – Confab
CC – CPC International/
    Best's
CD – Church & Dwight
Cd – Cadbury-Schweppes
Ch – Chesebrough Pond's/
    Unilever
CI – Cascades Industries
Cl – Clorox
Cm – Campbell Soup
Co – Coca-Cola
CP – Colgate-Palmolive
Cp – Carlisle Plastics
CS – Celestial Seasonings

CT – Chicago Transparent
    Plastics
Db – DowBrands
DF – Dean Foods
DP – DynaPak
Dl – Dial
DS – Dr Pepper/7-Up
Dt – Dutton-LeBus
Ek – Ekco Housewares
EK – Eastman Kodak
EP – Esselte Pendaflex
Ev – Eveready/Ralston
    Purina
FB – First Brands
FH – Fort Howard
GE – General Electric
GH – G Heileman
Gi – Gillette
Gl – General Mills
GM – Grand Metropolitan
GP – Georgia Pacific
GT – GTE/Sylvania
HC – Helene Curtis
HM – Hallmark
Ho – Hormel
Hs – Hershey
HZ – Heinz
JJ – Johnson & Johnson
JR – James River

Ke – Keebler/United Biscuit
KC – Kimberly-Clark
KG – Kraft General Foods/Philip Morris
Kl – Kellogg
LB – Lever Brothers/Unilever
LU – Lipton/Unilever
Ma – Manco
MD – Marion Merrell Dow
Md – Mead
Mn – Morcon
NA – North American Plastic
Ne – Nestlé USA
PA – PolyAmerica
Pe – Pepsico
PG – Procter & Gamble
Pl – Playtex
PT – Pope & Talbot
QO – Quaker Oats
Rb – Rubbermaid
Re – Reynolds
RN – RJR Nabisco
RP – Rhone Poulenc Rorer
Sf – Safco
SC – SC Johnson (Wax) & Son
Sc – Scott Paper
SK – SmithKline Beecham
SL – Sara Lee

Sn – Sunshine-Salerno
3M – Minnesota Mining & Manufacturing
VL – Van den Bergh Foods/Unilever
Wb – Webster Industries
WL – Warner-Lambert
Wr – Wrigley

BABY PRODUCTS Company/Product	RP	Rb	SR	SC	EFR	Notes
Ab/Ross Isomil form.	n	y	n	n	10	steel can
Ab/Ross Similac	n	y	n	n	10	steel can
AH/Wyeth Nursoy form.	n	y	n	n	8	steel can
AH/Wyeth SMA form.	n	y	n	n	8	steel can
BM/MeadJohn Enfamil	n	y	n	n	12	steel can
BM/MeadJohn Sobec	n	y	n	n	12	steel can
BM/Nutramigen	y part.	y	n	n	12	alum.
CP/Baby Magic bath	n	y	n	n	12	HDPE
CP/Baby Magic lotion	n	y	n	n	12	HDPE
Gerber formula	y part.	y	n	n	10	glass
Gerber baby food	y part.	y	n	n	10	glass
JJ/bath	n	y	n	n	12	HDPE
JJ/lotion	n	y	n	n	12	HDPE
JJ/powder	n	y	n	n	12	HDPE
JJ/Pooh shampoo	n	y	n	n	12	HDPE
JJ/shampoo	n	y	n	n	12	HDPE
KC/Huggies	y part.	n	y	n	10	rec. handle
KC/Pullups	n	n	y	n	10	red. pac.
Ne/Carnation GStart	y part.	y	y	n	10	alum.
PG/Luvs diapers	n	n	y	n	12	40% less pac.
PG/Pampers diapers	n	n	y	n	12	40% less pac.
RP/Beechnut bfood	y part.	n	y	n	10	glass
Sc/Baby Fresh	n	y	n	n	10	reusable

Sc/Washabye baby	n	y	n	n	10	reusable
BATTERIES **Company/Product**	**RP**	**Rb**	**SR**	**SC**	**EFR**	**Notes**
Duracell AA	y	n	n	n	10	no merc. add.
Duracell C	y	n	n	n	10	no merc. add.
Duracell D	y	n	n	n	10	no merc. add.
Duracell 9V	y	n	n	n	10	no merc. add.
Eveready Energizer AA	y	n	y	n	10	no merc. add 35% PCW pac.
Ev/En C	y	n	y	n	10	no merc. add.
Ev/En D	y	n	y	n	10	no merc. add.
Ev/En AAA	y	n	y	n	10	no merc. add.
Ev/En 9V	y	n	y	n	10	no merc. add.
Ev/Super heavy duty	y	n	y	n	10	no merc. add.
Ev/En hearing aid pz	y	n	y	n	10	no merc. add.
Rayovac AA	-	n	n	n	10	no merc. add.
Rayovac C	-	n	n	n	10	no merc. add.
Rayovac D	-	n	n	n	10	no merc. add.
Rayovac 9V	-	n	n	n	10	no merc. add.
Sanyo/GE AA	-	n	n	n	-	no merc. add.
Sanyo/GE C	-	n	n	n	-	no merc. add.
Sanyo/GE D	-	n	n	n	-	no merc. add.
Sanyo/GE 9 volt	-	n	n	n	-	no merc. add.
Sanyo/GE AA recharge.	-	y	y	n	-	returnable
S/GE recharge. C, D	-	y	y	n	-	returnable

BREAKFAST FOODS Company/Product	RP	Rb	SR	SC	EFR	Notes
CA/Swift's Prem. saus.	n	n	y	n	12	red. pac.
CA/SP Sizzlean	n	n	y	n	12	red. pac.
Gm/Basic Four	y	n	y	n	14	35% PCW box, 12% red. liner
Gm/Cheerios	y	n	y	n	14	35% PCW box, 12% red. liner
Gm/Cinn. Toast crunch	y	n	y	n	14	35% PCW box, 12% red. liner
Gl/Cocoa Puffs	y	n	y	n	14	35% PCW box, 12% red. liner
Gl/Count Chocula	y	n	y	n	14	35% PCW box, 12% red. liner
Gl/Fiber One	y	n	y	n	14	35% PCW box, 12% red. liner
Gl/Franken Berry	y	n	y	n	14	35% PCW box, 12% red. liner
Gl/Golden Grahams	y	n	y	n	14	35% PCW box, 12% red. liner
Gl/Kix	y	n	y	n	14	35% PCW box, 12% red. liner
Gl/Lucky Charms	y	n	y	n	14	35% PCW box, 12% red. liner
Gl/Oatmeal crisp	y	n	y	n	14	35% PCW box, 12% red. liner
Gl/Raisin Nut Bran	y	n	y	n	14	35% PCW box, 12% red. liner

Gl/Total	y	n	y	n	14	35% PCW box, 12% red. liner
Gl/Trix	y	n	y	n	14	35% PCW box, 12% red. liner
Gl/Wheaties	y	n	y	n	14	35% PCW box, 12% red. liner
Gl/Betty C. granola	y	n	n	n	14	35% PCW box, 12% red. liner
Gl/Nature Valley gb	y	n	n	n	14	35% PCW box, 12% red. liner
Kl/All Bran	y	n	y	n	14	35% PCW box, 12% red. liner
Kl/Common Sense	y	n	y	n	14	35% PCW box, 12% red. liner
Kl/Corn Flakes	y	n	y	n	14	35% PCW box, 12% red. liner
Kl/Corn Pops	y	n	y	n	14	35% PCW box, 12% red. liner
Kl/Cracklin Oat Bran	y	n	y	n	14	35% PCW box, 12% red. liner
Kl/Crispix	y	n	y	n	14	35% PCW box, 12% red. liner
Kl/Frosted Bran	y	n	y	n	14	35% PCW box, 12% red. liner
Kl/Frosted flakes	y	n	y	n	14	35% PCW box, 12% red. liner
Kl/Frosted miniwheats	y	n	y	n	14	35% PCW box, 12% red. liner

Kl/Fruitful bran	y	n	y	n	14	35% PCW box, 12% red. liner
Kl/Honey & Nut crunch	y	n	y	n	14	35% PCW box, 12% red. liner
Kl/Just Right	y	n	y	n	14	35% PCW box, 12% red. liner
Kl/Krispies (all)	y	n	y	n	14	35% PCW box, 12% red. liner
Kl/Low-fat granola	y	n	y	n	14	35% PCW box, 12% red. liner
Kl/Mini buns	y	n	y	n	14	35% PCW box, 12% red. liner
Kl/Mueslix	y	n	y	n	14	35% PCW box, 12% red. liner
Kl/Nutragrain	y	n	y	n	14	35% PCW box, 12% red. liner
Kl/Raisin bran	y	n	y	n	14	35% PCW box, 12% red. liner
Kl/Smacks	y	n	y	n	14	35% PCW box, 12% red. liner
Kl/Special K	y	n	y	n	14	35% PCW box, 12% red. liner
Kl/Squares (all)	y	n	y	n	14	35% PCW box, 12% red. liner
Kl/Nutragrain bars	y	n	n	n	14	35% PCW box, 12% red. liner
Kl/Pop tarts	y	n	n	n	14	35% PCW box, 12% red. liner

KG/Post cereals	y	n	n	n	10	35% PCW box, 12% red. liner
KG/Tang jars	y part	y	y	n	10	25% rec. glass
Ne/Carnation bars	y	n	n	n	10	35% PCW paper.
RP/Addams Family	y	n	n	n	10	35% PCW paper.
RP/Batman Returns	y	n	n	n	10	35% PCW paper.
RP/Chex (all)	y	n	n	n	10	35% PCW paper.
RP/Cookie Crisp	y	n	n	n	10	35% PCW paper.
RP/High Fiber hot	y	n	n	n	10	35% PCW paper.
RP/Honey Almond Del.	y	n	n	n	10	35% PCW paper.
RP/Muesli (all)	y	n	n	n	10	35% PCW paper.
RP/Sunflakes	y	n	n	n	10	35% PCW paper.
RP/Teenage Mutant NT	y	n	n	n	10	35% PCW paper.
RP/Urkel Os	y	n	n	n	10	35% PCW paper.
RP/Wonder Brand (all)	y	n	n	n	10	35% PCW paper.
RN/Fruit wheats	y	n	n	n	10	35% PCW paper.
RN/100% bran	y	n	n	n	10	35% PCW paper.
RN/Shredded wheat	y	n	n	n	10	35% PCW paper.
RN/Frosted wheat sq.	y	n	n	n	10	35% PCW paper.
RN/Shred. wheatnbran	y	n	n	n	10	35% PCW paper.
RN/Spoon Size sw	y	n	n	n	10	35% PCW paper.
RN/Team	y	n	n	n	10	35% PCW paper.
QO/Captain Crunch	y	n	n	n	12	35% PCW paper.
QO/Cinnamon & raisin	y	n	n	n	12	35% PCW paper.
QO/Crunch berries	y	n	n	n	12	35% PCW paper.
QO/Crunchy corn bran	y	n	n	n	12	35% PCW paper.

QO/Granola bars	y	n	n	n	12	35% PCW paper.
QO/Instant oatmeal	y	n	n	n	12	35% PCW paper.
QO/Life	y	n	n	n	12	35% PCW paper.
QO/Oat bran	y	n	n	n	12	35% PCW paper.
QO/Oat Squares	y	n	n	n	12	35% PCW paper.
QO/Oat Sq. cinn.	y	n	n	n	12	35% PCW paper.
QO/Peanut butter cr.	y	n	n	n	12	35% PCW paper.
QO/Puffed Wheat	y	n	n	n	12	35% PCW paper.
QO/Puffed Rice	y	n	n	n	12	35% PCW paper.
SL/Jimmy Dean saus.	n	n	y	n	12	red. pac.
SL/Jimmy Dean light	n	n	y	n	12	red. pac.
SL/JD prem. bacon	n	n	y	n	12	red. pac.
SL/Sara Lee danish	n	n	y	n	12	red. pac.
CLEANING PRODUCTS Company/Product	**RP**	**Rb**	**SR**	**SC**	**EFR**	**Notes**
Bn/Calgon Res. rem.	n	y	n	n	-	HDPE
Bn/ScrubFree	n	y	n	n	-	HDPE
CD/Arm & Hammer bakings	y	n	n	n	12	35% PCW
CD/AH allfab bleach	y	n	n	n	12	35% PCW
CD/AH air freshspray	n	n	n	n	12	no hydro.
CD/AH Light fresh cd	y	n	n	n	12	35% PCW
CD/AH Pet Fresh cd	y	n	n	n	12	35% PCW
CD/AH Potpourri cd	y	n	n	n	12	35% PCW
CD/AH fabricsoft	y	n	n	n	12	rec. box

CD/AH Super washsoda	y	n	n	n	12	35% PCW
Cl/Liquid Plumr	n	y	n	n	12	HDPE
Cl/Tilex	n	y	n	n	12	HDPE
CP/Ajax liquid	n	y	n	n	12	20%–50% PETE
CP/Ajax can	y	n	n	n	12	50% PCW alum.
CP/Crystal White Oc	n	y	n	n	12	HDPE
CP/Palmolive auto	n	y	n	n	12	HDPE
CP/Dermassage liq.	y	y	n	n	12	20%–50% PET
CP/Ajax all-purpose	n	y	n	n	12	HDPE
CP/Murphy oil soap	n	y	n	n	12	HDPE
CP/Palmolive liq.	y	y	n	n	12	20%–50% PET
Bn/Earthrite allp	40% PCW	y	n	y	-	biodegradable
Bn/Er floor	40% PCW	y	n	y	-	biodegradable
Bn/Er countertop	40% PCW	y	n	y	-	biodegradable
Bn/Er dish liq.	40% PCW	y	n	y	-	biodegradable
Bn/Earthrite glass	40% PCW	y	n	y	-	biodegradable
Bn/Er liq. laundry	40% PCW	y	n	y	-	biodegradable
Bn/Er toilet clean	40% PCW	y	n	y	-	biodegradable
Bn/Er tub & tile	40% PCW	y	n	y	-	biodegradable

Descale-it bath clean	n	n	n	y	-	biodegradable
Descale-it Lime-eater	n	n	n	y	-	biodegradable
Dl/Brillo pad	y	n	n	n	12	100% rec. steel
3M Scotchbrite pad	y	n	n	n	12	100% rec. PETE
CS/Earthwise apcon	y	y	n	n	18	biodegradable
CS/Earthwise bath	y	y	n	n	18	biodegradable
CS/Earthwise dish	y	y	n	n	18	biodegradable
CS/Earthwise floor	y	y	n	n	18	biodegradable
CS/Earthwise laundry	y	y	n	n	18	biodegradable
LB/all liquid	y	y	n	n	14	35% PCW HDPE
LB/All Free clear	n	y	n	n	14	HDPE
LB/Dove dish liq.	n	y	n	n	14	HDPE
LB/Snuggle singles	y	n	n	n	14	35% PCW box
LB/Ultra all	y	n	y	n	14	35% PCW paper., 100% rec. scoop red. pac.
LB/Ultra Rinso	y	n	y	n	14	35% PCW paper., 100% rec. scoop red. pac.
LB/Ultra Surf	y	n	y	n	14	35% PCW paper., 100% rec. scoop red. pac.
LB/Wisk PowerScoop	y	n	y	n	14	35% PCW paper., 100% rec. scoop red. pac.
LB/Ultra Snuggle	n	y	y	n	14	HDPE
LB/Final touch ref.	n	n	y	n	14	refill.

LB/Snuggle refill	n	n	y	n	14	refill.
LB/Lever 2000 soap	n	n	y	n	14	red. pac.
LB/Sunlight dish.	n	y	y	n	14	HDPE
LF/Formbys paint rem.	y	y	n	n	12	25% rec. steel
LF/Formbys prwash	y	y	n	n	12	25% rec. steel
LF/Formbys aer. pr.	y	y	n	n	12	25% rec. steel
LF/Red Devil enamel	y	y	n	n	12	25% rec. steel
LF/Red Devil rsolut.	y	y	n	n	12	25% rec. steel
LF/Red Devil ptrem.	y	y	n	n	12	25% rec. steel
LF/Thompsons c&eprot.	n	y	n	n	12	HDPE
LF/Minwax ant. oil	y	y	n	n	12	25% rec. steel
LF/Minwax fin. wax	y	y	n	n	12	25% rec. steel
LF/Minwax wood fin.	y	y	n	n	12	25% rec. steel
LF/Minwax af refinish	y	y	n	n	12	25% rec. steel
CD/Arm & Hammer/ Ultra Fresh laundry box	y	n	y	n	12	Concentrated rec. box
CD/Arm & Hammer/ Ultra Fresh bottle	n	y	n	n	12	Concentrated rec. box
CP/Ajax Ultra 1/2 cup	y	n	y	n	12	rec. scoops
CP/Ajax 1 cup box	y	n	n	n	12	55% PCW paper.
CP/Ajax liq. 32 & 64 oz.	y	y	n	n	12	25% PCW HDPE
CP/Cold Power box	y	n	n	n	12	55% PCW paper.
CP/Fab Ultra 32 oz.	y	y	n	n	12	25% PCW HDPE
CP/Fab Ultra 64 oz.	y	n	y	n	12	25% PCW HDPE
CP/Fab 1 cup	y	n	n	n	12	55% PCW paper.
CP/Fab Ultra liq.	y	y	n	n	12	25% PCW HDPE

CP/Fresh Start	y	n	n	n	12	100% PCW
CP/Fresh Start bottle	y	y	n	n	12	25% PCW
CP/Punch 1 cup	y	n	n	n	12	55% PCW paper.
CP/Super Suds 1 cup	y	n	n	n	12	55% PCW
Dl/Borateem box	y	n	n	n	12	rec. cartons
Dl/Dutch	y	n	n	n	12	rec. cartons
Dl/Purex Classic	y	n	n	n	12	rec. cartons
Dl/Purex Ultra	y	n	y	n	12	20% less pac.
Dl/Sta Puf fab. soft.	n	-	y	n	12	75% less pac.
Dl/Toss n' Soft fab. soft.	y	n	n	n	12	rec. cartons
Dl/20 Mule Team Borax	y	n	n	n	12	rec. cartons
Dl/Sno-bol toilet	n	y	n	n	12	HDPE
EK/LF D-Con	y	n	n	n	12	30% PCW paper.
Miles/SOS pads	y	y	n	n	10	35% PCW box
PG/Ariel Ultra (box)	y	n	y	n	12	30% less pac.
PG/Bold Ultra (box)	y	n	y	n	12	30% less pac.
PG/Cheer Ultra	y	n	y	n	12	30% less pac.
PG/Cheer Free Ultra	y	n	y	n	12	30% less pac.
PG/Dash Ultra (box)	y	n	y	n	12	30% less pac.
PG/Downy Ultra (bottle)	y	y	y	n	12	100% PCW HDPE, 35% less pac.
PG/Dreft Ultra (box)	y	n	y	n	12	concentrated
PG/Gain Ultra (box)	y	n	y	n	12	concentrated
PG/Ivory Snow Ultra	y	n	y	n	12	concentrated

PG/Tide w/bleach Ultra (box)	y	n	y	n	12	concentrated
PG/Tide Ultra (box)	y	n	y	n	12	concentrated
PG/Tide Free Ultra	y	n	y	n	12	concentrated
PG/Bold liquid	y	y	n	n	12	25% rec. HDPE
PG/Cheer liquid	y	y	n	n	12	25% rec. HDPE
PG/Dash liquid	y	y	n	n	12	25% rec. HDPE
PG/Era liquid	y	y	n	n	12	25% rec. HDPE
PG/Tide liquid	y	y	n	n	12	25% rec. HDPE
PG/Bold refill	y 50%	n	n	n	12	25% rec. HDPE
PG/Cheer refill	y 50%	n	y	n	12	40% less pac.
PG/Cheer Free refill	y 50%	n	y	n	12	40% less pac.
PG/Dash refill	y 50%	n	y	n	12	40% less pac.
PG/Era refill	y 50%	n	y	n	12	40% less pac.
PG/Solo refill	y 50%	n	y	n	12	40% less pac.
PG/Tide refill	n	n	y	n	12	40% less pac.
PG/Tide Free refill	n	n	y	n	12	40% less pac.
PG/Tide w/bleach ref.	n	n	y	n	12	40% less pac.
PG/Bounce fab. soft.	y	n	n	n	12	35% PCW box
PG/Joy dish. liq.	n	y	n	n	12	HDPE
PG/MrClean lemon	n	y	n	n	12	HDPE
PG/SpicnSpan Cinch	n	y	n	n	12	HDPE
PG/SpicnSpan pine	y	y	n	n	12	rec. PETE
PG/SpicnSpan Cinch	n	y	n	n	12	HDPE
SC/Behold furniture	n	n	n	n	-	CFC free
SC/Brite	n	y	n	n	-	HDPE

SC/Endust	n	n	n	n	-	CFC free
SC/Drano drain clean.	y	n	n	n	-	CFC free
SC/Liquid Drano	y	n	n	n	-	HDPE
SC/Glade country pot	y	n	n	n	-	rec. box
SC/Mr Muscle oven	n	n	n	n	-	CFC free
SC/Pledge pump	n	y	n	n	-	HDPE
SC/Pledge wood rich	n	n	n	n	-	no CFCs
SC/Raid liq. ant kill	n	y	n	n	-	HDPE
SC/Shout stain rem.	n	y	n	n	-	HDPE
SC/Vanish	y	n	n	n	-	rec. box
SC/Windex	n	y	n	n	-	HDPE
SC/Windex aerosol	y	n	n	n	-	steel can
Scott's Liq. Gold wood cl	n	n	n	n	10	CO_2 propel.
SLG Touch of Scent	y	y	n	n	10	CO_2 propel
SLG glass cleaner	n	n	n	n	10	rec. caps
SLG Touch of Scent/Too	y	y	n	n	10	rec. caps
Sunshine/Simple Green	n	n	n	n	-	biodegradable
Blue Coral/Clear Magic Auto Cleaner	n	n	n	y	-	biodegradable
BC/CM Household	n	n	n	y	-	biodegradable
BC/CM Industrial	n	n	n	y	-	biodegradable
Cl/Clorox 2 box	y	n	n	y	10	81% PCW paper.
Cl/1 gallon bleach plastic bottle	y	y	y	n	10	20% PCW HDPE, not wide. av.

Cl/Formula 409	y part.	y	n	n	10	HDPE blend
Cl/Pine Sol	y	y	n	n	10	PETE
CL/Soft Scrub	y part.	y	n	n	10	HDPE blend
Cl/Soft Scrub bleach	y part.	y	n	n	10	HDPE blend
Enforcer/drain clean	n	n	n	y	-	biodegradable
Enforcer/septic	n	n	n	y	-	biodegradable
EK/L&F Minwax wood con.	y	y	n	n	12	25% rec. steel
EK/Minwax Tung Oil	y	y	n	n	12	25% rec. steel
EK/Minwax Watco oil	y	y	n	n	12	25% rec. steel
EK/Formby's refin.	y	y	n	n	12	25% rec. steel
KC/Eco 2000 degreaser	n	n	n	y	-	biodegradable
Planet/Cleaners (all)	y	y	y	y	-	biodegradable 25% PCW HDPE
Roebic/K-37 septic	n	n	n	y	-	biodegradable
Roebic/K-47 cesspool	n	n	n	y	-	biodegradable
Roebic/K-57 septic	n	n	n	y	-	biodegradable
Roebic/K-67 drain	n	n	n	y	-	biodegradable
20/10 windshield	n	n	n	y	-	biodegradable
Dowbrands/bath. clean.	y	y	n	n	12	25% PCW HDPE
Db/Fantastic	n	y	n	n	12	HDPE
Db/Glass Plus	n	y	n	n	12	HDPE
Db/Grease Relief	n	y	n	n	12	HDPE
Db/Janitor in a Drum	n	y	n	n	12	HDPE
Db/Pine Magic	n	y	n	n	12	HDPE

Db/Pine Power	n	y	n	n	12	HDPE
Db/Spray n'Wash	n	y	n	n	12	HDPE
Db/Tuffact	n	y	n	n	12	HDPE
Db/Vivid non-chlor.	n	y	n	n	12	HDPE
Db/Wood Plus	n	y	n	n	12	HDPE
Db/Yes	n	y	n	n	12	HDPE
Dl/Bo-Peep ammonia	n	y	n	n	12	HDPE
EK/L&F Direct Refill	n	n	y	n	12	75% less pac.
LF/Lysol pine tubtile	n	y	n	n	12	HDPE
LF/Lysol disinfect.	y	y	n	n	12	100% rec. PETE
LF/Lysol spray cans	y	y	n	n	12	25% rec. steel
LF/Lysol Touchups	y	n	n	n	12	35% PCW box
LF/Glassmates	n	y	n	n	12	HDPE
LF/Pine Action	n	y	n	n	12	HDPE
LF/MopnGlo	n	y	n	n	12	25% PCW HDPE
LF/Perk floor	n	y	n	n	12	HDPE
LF/Resolve	n	n	y	n	12	25% less pac.
LF/Resolve smartpack	n	n	y	n	12	75% less pac.
LF/Resolve upholstery	y	y	n	n	12	25% PCW HDPE
LF/Resolve can	y	y	n	n	12	25% rec. steel
LF/Rid-X box	y	n	n	n	12	25% PCW box
COFFEES, COCOAS, TEAS Product/Company	**RP**	**Rb**	**SR**	**SC**	**EFR**	**Notes**
CS/Country Peach tea	y	n	y	n	18	35% PCW paper.
CS/Harvest Spice	y	n	y	n	18	35% PCW paper.

CS/Iced Delight	y	n	y	n	18	35% PCW paper.
CS/Mandarin Orange	y	n	y	n	18	35% PCW paper.
CS/Peppermint	y	n	y	n	18	35% PCW paper.
CS/Raspberry Patch	y	n	y	n	18	35% PCW paper.
CS/Strawberry Fields	y	n	y	n	18	35% PCW paper.
CS/Wild Blackberry	y	n	y	n	18	35% PCW paper.
CS/Zinger series	y	n	y	n	18	35% PCW paper.
CA/Swiss Miss	y	n	n	n	12	35% PCW paper.
CA/Swiss Miss light	y	n	n	n	12	35% PCW paper.
KG/Brim	y	y	n	n	10	15% rec. glass
KG/Cappio	y	y	n	n	10	15% rec. glass
KG/Chock Full o' Nuts	y	y	y	n	10	steel
KG/Internationals	y	y	y	n	10	steel
KG/Max. House capp.	y	n	n	n	10	rec. paper
KG/Max. House can	y	y	y	n	10	steel can
KG/Maxwell House	y	y	y	n	10	25% rec. glass
KG/Max. House F. roast	y	y	y	n	10	steel can
KG/Max. House sp. blend	y	y	y	n	10	steel can
KG/Postum	y	y	y	n	10	steel can
KG/Sanka	y	y	y	n	10	steel
KG/Sanka	y	y	y	n	10	glass
LU/Lipton tea	y	n	n	n	14	35% PCW paper.
LU/Lipton decaf.	y	n	y	n	14	35% PCW paper.
LU/Lipton herbal	y	n	y	n	14	35% PCW paper.

LU/Special blend	y	n	y	n	14	35% PCW paper.
LU/Iced tea bottle	y	y	y	n	14	glass
LU/Iced decaf.	y	y	y	n	14	glass
LU/Iced sugar-free	y	y	y	n	14	glass
LU/Iced lemon	y	y	y	n	14	glass
Ne/Carn. Coffeemate	y	y	y	n	10	glass
Ne/Carn. choc. milk	y	n	n	n	10	rec. paper
Ne/Hills Brothers	y	y	y	n	10	steel
Ne/Hills Bros. instant	y	y	y	n	10	glass
Ne/MJB	y	y	y	n	10	steel
Ne/Nescafé	y	y	y	n	10	glass
Ne/Nestea can	y	y	y	n	10	steel
Ne/Nestea bottle	y	y	y	n	10	glass
Ne/Taster's Choice	y	y	y	n	10	glass
PG/Folger's	y	y	y	n	12	steel
PG/Folger's crystals	y	y	y	n	12	steel
PG/Folger's ins. 12 oz.	n	y	y	n	12	PETE
PG/Folger's vacuum	n	n	y	n	12	foil
PG/Folger's instant	y	y	y	n	12	glass
Sandoz/Ovaltine clas.	y	y	y	n	10	glass
Sandoz/Ovaltine orig.	y	y	y	n	10	glass
CONDIMENTS Company/Product	**RP**	**Rb**	**SR**	**SC**	**EFR**	**Notes**
AH/Gulden's mustard	y part.	y	n	n	8	glass
AH/Gulden's mustard	n	y	n	n	8	PETE
Cm/Bbq sauce	y part.	y	n	n	12	glass

Cm/Maries salad dr.	y part.	y	n	n	12	glass
Cm/Open Pit bbq sauce	y part.	y	n	n	12	glass
Cm/Prego sauces	y part.	y	n	n	12	glass
Cm/Vlasic pickles	y part.	y	n	n	12	glass
Cm/Pep. Farm gravy	y part.	y	n	n	12	glass
CB/Brooks chili sauce	y part.	y	n	n	-	glass
CB/Rich & Tangy ketch.	y part.	y	n	n	-	glass
CA/Peter Pn. PB sfree	n	y	n	n	12	PETE
CA/Peter Pn. PB whip	n	y	n	n	12	PETE
CA/Wesson oil	n	y	n	n	12	PETE
CA/Wesson Canola	n	y	n	n	12	PETE
CA/Wesson light	n	y	n	n	12	PETE
CA/Wesson corn	n	y	n	n	12	PETE
CC/Argo corn starch	y	n	n	n	12	rec. paper.
CC/Hellman's Mayo.	y	y	n	n	12	20% rec. con.
CC/H. Mayo 64, 128 oz.	n	y	n	n	12	HDPE
CC/Mayo 8, 128 oz.	y part.	y	n	n	12	steel
CC/Karo syrp. 16, 32 oz.	y part.	y	n	n	12	20% rec. glass
CC/K syrp. 64, 128 oz.	n	y	n	n	12	HDPE
CC/Knorr sauce 15 oz.	y part.	y	n	n	12	20% rec. glass

CC/Knorr sauce 13 oz.	y part.	y	n	n	12	20% rec. glass
CC/Knorr sauce cans	y part.	y	n	n	12	steel
CC/Mazola oil 16, 48 oz.	n	y	n	n	12	PETE
CC/Mazola oil 128 oz.	n	y	n	n	12	HDPE
CC/Mazola no-stick	n	n	n	n	12	no CFCs
CC/M margarine exlt.	n	y	n	n	12	HDPE
CC/M mar. diet	n	y	n	n	12	rec. paper.
CC/M mar. unsalted	n	y	n	n	12	rec. paper.
CC/Skippy PB 6 oz.	y part.	y	n	n	12	20% rec.
CC/Skippy 5 lb.	y part.	n	n	n	12	30% rec.
CC/SPB 12, 18, 28, 40 oz.	n	y	n	n	12	PETE
CC/SPB roast hny. nt.	n	y	n	n	12	PETE
CC/Mueller's pasta	n	y	n	n	12	rec. paper.
CC/Devonsheer	n	y	n	n	12	rec. paper.
CC/Old London	n	y	n	n	12	rec. paper.
CC/Brownberry	n	y	n	n	12	rec. paper.
CC/Arnold	n	y	n	n	12	rec. paper
Cl/HidValleyRnch sd.	n	y	n	n	12	PETE
Cl/HidValleyRnch sd.	y part.	y	n	n	12	glass
Cl/KC Masterpce bbq	y part.	y	n	n	12	glass
Cl/Kingsford bbq	y part.	y	n	n	12	glass
Heinz/chili sauce	y	y	n	n	12	glass
Hz/cocktail sauce	y	y	n	n	12	glass

Hz/57 sauce	y	y	n	n	12	glass
Hz/hot sauce	y	y	n	n	12	glass
Hz/lite sauce	y	y	n	n	12	glass
Hz/horseradish	y	y	n	n	12	glass
Hz/Ketchup	y part.	y	y	n	12	PETE
Hz/Vinegar	y part.	y	n	n	12	glass
Hz/Vinegar	n	y	n	n	12	HDPE
Hz/Weight Wrs. fatfr	y part.	y	n	n	12	glass
Hz/Weight Wrs. sweet	n	y	n	n	12	HDPE
Hershey/choc. syrup	n	y	y	n	12	HDPE
Hs/strawberry syrup	y part.	y	n	n	12	glass
Hs/Reese's PB	n	y	n	n	12	PETE
KG/Cool Whip 8 oz.	n	y	y	n	10	reusable
KG/Mayo	y part.	y	y	n	10	glass
KG/Mayo 48 oz.	n	y	y	n	10	PETE
KG/Miracle Whip. 48 oz.	n	y	y	n	10	PETE
KG/Miracle Whip Lt.	n	y	y	n	10	PETE
KG/Miracle Whip Free	n	y	y	n	10	PETE
KG/Salad dress. 16 oz.	n	y	y	n	10	PETE
KG/Salad dress. 24 oz.	y 25%	y	y	n	10	PETE
KG/Salad dress. free	n	y	y	n	10	PETE
KG/Stove Top Stuff.	y	n	n	n	10	rec. paper.
KG/Parkay margarine	n	y	y	n	10	HDPE reuse.
KG/Seven Seas s.d.	y part.	y	n	n	10	glass

KG/Seven Seas s.d.	n	y	y	n	10	PETE
LU/Lawry's Seasons	n	y	y	n	4	PETE
LU/Lipton Recipe sp.	y	ń	n	n	4	rec. paper.
LU/Wishbone salad dr.	y part.	y	n	n	4	glass
LU/Wishbone s.d. 16 oz.	n	y	y	n	4	PETE
Cd/Motts apple sauce	y part.	y	n	n	12	rec. glass
Ne/Contadina sauces	y part.	y	n	n	10	25% rec. con.
Ne/Libby's spreadable	y part.	y	n	n	10	54% rec. alum.
Ne/Libby's pumpkin	y part.	y	n	n	10	25% rec. con.
Ne/Buitoni sauces	y part.	y	n	n	10	30% rec.
Ne/Buitoni clam sauce	y part.	y	n	n	10	25% rec.
Ne/La Lechera cmilk	y part.	y	n	n	10	25% rec.
Ne/evaporated milk	y part.	y	n	n	10	25% rec.
Ne/CrosseBlackwll sc	y part.	y	n	n	10	30% rec.
Ne/CB shrimp sauce	y part.	y	n	n	10	30% rec.
Ne/CB jellies & marm.	y part.	y	n	n	10	30% rec.
Ne/CB brandied hs	y part.	y	n	n	10	30% rec.
Ne/CB mincemeat	y part.	y	n	n	10	30% rec.
Ne/CB worcestershire	y part.	y	n	n	10	30% rec.
Ne/Maggi seasoning	y part.	y	n	n	10	30% rec.
Ne/Maggi bullion	y part.	y	n	n	10	30% rec.
Ne/Maggi chili sau.	y part.	y	n	n	10	30% rec.
Newman's Own salad d.	y part.	y	n	n	-	rec. glass

Plochmans mustd. 24 oz.	n	y	n	n	-	PETE
Plochmans boldnspicy	n	y	n	n	-	PETE
Plochmans Dijon	y part.	y	n	n	-	glass
Plochmans Koscko	y part.	y	n	n	-	glass
Plochmans stone grnd.	y part.	y	n	n	-	glass
PG/Crisco oil	n	y	y	n	12	28% less pac.
PG/Crisco	n	y	y	n	12	PETE
PG/Jif	n	y	y	n	12	PETE
PG/Jif nosalt	n	y	y	n	12	PETE
RC/French's mustd. 24 oz.	y part.	y	n	n	10	glass
RC/F Dijon	y part.	y	n	n	10	glass
RN/A1 steak sauce	y part.	y	n	n	10	glass
RN/Grey Poupon must.	y part.	y	n	n	10	glass
RN/Fleischmann's soft	n	y	n	n	10	HDPE
Smuckers jams & jellies	y part.	y	y	n	12	glass
VL/CantBelieveBut.	n	y	y	n	4	HDPE
VL/Ms. Butterworth's	y part.	y	y	n	4	glass
VL/Promise margarine	n	y	y	n	4	glass
VL/Shedd's Spread m.	n	y	y	n	4	HDPE
FLAVORS, SPICES						
Ho/Real Bacon bits	y	y	n	n	8	glass
Ho/Real bac. pieces	y	y	n	n	8	glass

KG/BettyCrocker bac.	y	y	n	n	10	glass
McCormick/Bac'n	n	y	n	n	10	PETE
MC/Spices 3.5 oz.	n	y	n	n	10	PETE
MC/Spices 15 oz.	n	y	n	n	10	PETE
MC/Spices bottles	y	y	n	n	10	glass
MC/Extracts 2 oz.	y	y	n	n	10	glass
MC/Flavors 2.75 oz.	y	y	n	n	10	glass
COOKIES & CRACKERS Company/Product	**RP**	**Rb**	**SR**	**SC**	**EFR**	**Notes**
Cm/Pepperidge Farm	y	n	y	n	12	rec. boxes
Keebler/Chips Deluxe	y	n	y	n	10	35% PCW box
Ke/Club	y	n	y	n	10	35% PCW box
Ke/Elfkins	y	n	y	n	10	35% PCW box
Ke/Golden Vanilla	y	n	y	n	10	35% PCW box
Ke/Graham	y	n	y	n	10	35% PCW box
Ke/Honey graham	y	n	y	n	10	35% PCW box
Ke/Ln. Crisp	y	n	y	n	10	35% PCW box
Ke/Mini Middles	y	n	y	n	10	35% PCW box
Ke/Pecan Sandies	y	n	y	n	10	35% PCW box
Ke/Sweet Spots	y	n	y	n	10	35% PCW box
Ke/Zesta saltine	y	n	y	n	10	35% PCW box
Ke/Zesta lowsalt	y	n	y	n	10	35% PCW box
Ke/Zesta unsalted	y	n	y	n	10	35% PCW box
Ke/Zesta wheat	y	n	y	n	10	35% PCW box
RN/Barnum's Animals	y	n	y	n	10	35% PCW

RN/Bugs Bunny graham	y	n	y	n	10	35% PCW
RN/Chips Ahoy (mini)	y	n	y	n	10	35% PCW
RN/Chips	y	n	y	n	10	35% PCW
RN/Grahams	y	n	y	n	10	35% PCW
RN/Honey Maid	y	n	y	n	10	35% PCW
RN/Lorna Doone	y	n	y	n	10	35% PCW
RN/Mini chips ahoy	y	n	y	n	10	35% PCW
RN/Mini Oreo	y	n	y	n	10	35% PCW
RN/Nilla Vanilla	y	n	y	n	10	35% PCW
RN/Nutter Butterbits	y	n	y	n	10	35% PCW
RN/Premium Saltines	y	n	y	n	10	35% PCW
RN/Premium fatfree	y	n	y	n	10	35% PCW box
RN/Premium lowsalt	y	n	y	n	10	35% PCW box
RN/Premium multigrn.	y	n	y	n	10	35% PCW box
RN/Premium unsalted	y	n	y	n	10	35% PCW box
RN/Ritz	y	n	y	n	10	35% PCW box
RN/Ritz lowsalt	y	n	y	n	10	35% PCW box
RN/Ritz unsalted	y	n	y	n	10	35% PCW box
RN/Ritz wheat	y	n	y	n	10	35% PCW box
RN/Teddy Grahams	y	n	y	n	10	35% PCW box
RN/TG Bearwich	y	n	y	n	10	35% PCW box
RN/Snackwells	y	n	y	n	10	35% PCW box
RN/Amer. Classic	y	n	y	n	10	35% PCW box
RN/AC crack wheat	y	n	y	n	10	35% PCW box
RN/AC dairy butter	y	n	y	n	10	35% PCW box

RN/AC golden sesame	y	n	y	n	10	35% PCW box
RN/AC minced onion	y	n	y	n	10	35% PCW box
RN/AC toasted poppy	y	n	y	n	10	35% PCW box
RN/Better Cheddars	y	n	y	n	10	35% PCW box
RN/BC lowsalt	y	n	y	n	10	35% PCW box
RN/Cheddar Wedges	y	n	y	n	10	35% PCW box
RN/Cheese Tidbit	y	n	y	n	10	35% PCW box
RN/ChickenBiskit	y	n	y	n	10	35% PCW box
RN/Crown Pilot	y	n	y	n	10	35% PCW box
RN/DipinaChip	y	n	y	n	10	35% PCW box
RN/Garden Crisps	y	n	y	n	10	35% PCW box
RN/Harvest Crisp 5 gr.	y	n	y	n	10	35% PCW box
RN/HC oat	y	n	y	n	10	35% PCW box
RN/HC rice	y	n	y	n	10	35% PCW box
RN/Nips	y	n	y	n	10	35% PCW box
RN/Oat Thins	y	n	y	n	10	35% PCW box
RN/Oysterettes	y	n	y	n	10	35% PCW box
RN/Ritz Bits mini	y	n	y	n	10	35% PCW box
RN/Ritz B cheese	y	n	y	n	10	35% PCW box
RN/Ritz B PB	y	n	y	n	10	35% PCW box
RN/Royal Lunch	y	n	y	n	10	35% PCW box
RN/Sociables	y	n	y	n	10	35% PCW box
RN/Swiss Cheese	y	n	y	n	10	35% PCW box
RN/Triscuit wafers	y	n	y	n	10	35% PCW box
RN/Triscuit Bits	y	n	y	n	10	35% PCW box
RN/Tr. Deli Rye	y	n	y	n	10	35% PCW box

RN/Tr. lowsalt	y	n	y	n	10	35% PCW box
RN/Tr. wheatnbran	y	n	y	n	10	35% PCW box
RN/Twigs	y	n	y	n	10	35% PCW box
RN/Uneeda	y	n	y	n	10	35% PCW box
RN/Vegetable thins	y	n	y	n	10	35% PCW box
RN/Waverly	y	n	y	n	10	35% PCW box
RN/Waverly lowsalt	y	n	y	n	10	35% PCW box
RN/Wheatsworth	y	n	y	n	10	35% PCW box
RN/Wheat Thins	y	n	y	n	10	35% PCW box
RN/WT lowsalt	y	n	y	n	10	35% PCW box
RN/WT multigrain	y	n	y	n	10	35% PCW box
RN/WT nutty	y	n	y	n	10	35% PCW box
RN/Zings chips	y	n	y	n	10	35% PCW box
RN/Zings cheddar	y	n	y	n	10	35% PCW box
RN/Z ranch	y	n	y	n	10	35% PCW box
RN/Zwieback	y	n	y	n	10	35% PCW box
RN/Mister Salty pret.	y	n	y	n	10	35% PCW box
RP/Hostess Brownie	y	n	n	n	10	35% PCW box
RP/H. cupcakes	y	n	n	n	10	35% PCW box
RP/H. crumb coffee ck.	y	n	n	n	10	35% PCW box
RP/H. frosted donuts	y	n	n	n	10	35% PCW box
RP/H. HoHos	y	n	n	n	10	35% PCW box
RP/H. Mini muffins	y	n	n	n	10	35% PCW box
RP/H. Suzy Qs	y	n	n	n	10	35% PCW box
RP/H. Twinkies	y	n	n	n	10	35% PCW box
RP/H. Twinkies light	y	n	n	n	10	35% PCW box

RP/Ralston Oat Krisp	y	n	n	n	10	35% PCW box
RP/RyKrisp natural	y	n	n	n	10	35% PCW box
RP/RyKrisp seasoned	y	n	n	n	10	35% PCW box
RP/RyKrisp sesame	y	n	n	n	10	35% PCW box
RP/Wheat Krisp	y	n	n	n	10	35% PCW box
RP/Chex Mix bbq	y	n	n	n	10	35% PCW box
RP/Chex Mix cheddar	y	n	n	n	10	35% PCW box
RP/Chex sc&onion	y	n	n	n	10	35% PCW box
RP/Chex traditional	y	n	n	n	10	35% PCW box
Sn/Animal crackers	y	n	n	n	10	35% PCW box
Sn/Bonnie short	y	n	n	n	10	35% PCW box
Sn/Cheez-it	y	n	n	n	10	35% PCW box
Sn/Grahams cinnamon	y	n	n	n	10	35% PCW box
Sn/Grahams Dino	y	n	n	n	10	35% PCW box
Sn/Grahams milkhoney	y	n	n	n	10	35% PCW box
Sn/HiHo	y	n	n	n	10	35% PCW box
Sn/Krispy saltines	y	n	n	n	10	35% PCW box
Sn/K. cheddar	y	n	n	n	10	35% PCW box
Sn/K. unsalted	y	n	n	n	10	35% PCW box
Sn/Krispy wheat	y	n	n	n	10	35% PCW box
Sn/Lemon Coolers	y	n	n	n	10	35% PCW box
Sn/Lil chips	y	n	n	n	10	35% PCW box
Sn/Mini butter	y	n	n	n	10	35% PCW box
Sn/Mini chocolate	y	n	n	n	10	35% PCW box
Sn/Super Mario	y	n	n	n	10	35% PCW box
Sn/Vanilla	y	n	n	n	10	35% PCW box

FILM PRODUCTS						
EK/Kodak 35mm boxes	y	n	n	n	12	35% PCW
EK/Kodak Funsavers	n	y	y	n	12	rec. con.
Fuji Film 35mm boxes	y	n	y	n	-	rec. con.
Fuji Quicksnaps	n	y	y	n	-	rec. con.
GUMS, CHEWING						
Tootsie Roll/T rolls	n	n	y	n	-	red. pac.
TR/Tootsie Pops	n	n	y	n	-	red. pac.
WL/Bubblicious	y	n	y	n	12	50% PCW OP.
WL/Certs	y	n	y	n	12	50% PCW OP.
WL/Chiclets	y	n	y	n	12	50% PCW OP.
WL/Dentyne	y	n	y	n	12	50% PCW OP.
WL/Trident	y	n	y	n	12	50% PCW OP.
Wr/Big Red	n	n	y	n	8	red. pac.
Wr/Doublemint	n	n	y	n	8	red. pac.
Wr/Extra	n	n	y	n	8	red. pac.
Wr/Juicy Fruit	n	n	y	n	8	red. pac.
Wr/Spearmint	n	n	y	n	8	red. pac.
DESSERT PRODUCTS Company/Product	**RP**	**Rb**	**SR**	**SC**	**EFR**	**Notes**
CB/ThankYou puddings	y	y	n	n	10	steel cans
DF/Country Charm IC	n	n	y	n	10	red. pac.
DF/Dean Fatfree IC	n	n	y	n	10	red. pac.
DF/Fieldcrest	n	n	y	n	10	red. pac.

DF/Frozen Yogurt	n	n	y	n	10	red. pac.
Gl/BettyCrockercakes	y	n	y	n	14	35% PCW paper.
Gl/BC brownies	y	n	y	n	14	35% PCW paper.
Gl/BC classics	y	n	y	n	14	35% PCW paper.
Gl/BC Light	y	n	y	n	14	35% PCW paper.
Gl/BC Muffins	y	n	y	n	14	35% PCW paper.
Gl/BC Softasik	y	n	y	n	14	35% PCW paper.
Gl/BC Supermoist	y	n	y	n	14	35% PCW paper.
Gl/Bisquick	y	n	y	n	14	35% PCW paper.
Gl/Bisquick red. fat	y	n	y	n	14	35% PCW paper.
Gl/bread mixes	y	n	y	n	14	35% PCW paper.
Gl/chiffon	y	n	y	n	14	35% PCW paper.
Gl/Microrave mixes	y	n	y	n	14	35% PCW paper.
Gl/BC frosting	n	y	y	n	14	HDPE, reusable
GM/Pillsbury breads	y	n	y	n	10	35% PCW paper.
GM/P brownies	y	n	y	n	10	35% PCW paper.
GM/P bundt cakes	y	n	y	n	10	35% PCW paper.
GM/P cupcakes	y	n	y	n	10	35% PCW paper.
GM/P Lovinlites	y	n	y	n	10	35% PCW paper.
GM/P microwave mixes	y	n	y	n	10	35% PCW paper.
GM/P Plus	y	n	y	n	10	35% PCW paper.
GM/P Baketopsfrost	n	y	y	n	10	HDPE, reusable
KG/Cool Whip tub	n	n	y	n	10	reusable
KG/Jell-O gelatins	y	n	y	n	10	35% PCW paper.
KG/Jell-O nobake	y	n	y	n	10	35% PCW paper.

KG/Jell-O puddings	y	n	y	n	10	35% PCW paper.
KG/Jell-O sugarfree	y	n	y	n	10	35% PCW paper.
KG/Minute tapioca	y	n	y	n	10	35% PCW paper.
KG/Breyer's IC	n	n	y	n	10	red. pac.
KG/Breyer's light	n	n	y	n	10	red. pac.
KG/cheesecake mix	y	n	y	n	10	35% PCW paper.
KG/Sealtest IC	n	n	y	n	10	red. pac.
Ne/Stouffersic 1/2g	n	y	y	n	10	HDPE
RN/Royal gelatins	y	n	y	n	10	35% PCW paper.
RN/Royal nobake	y	n	y	n	10	35% PCW paper.
RN/Royal puddings	y	n	y	n	10	35% PCW paper.
RN/Royal real cheese	y	n	y	n	10	35% PCW paper.
RN/Royal sugar fr. gel.	y	n	y	n	10	35% PCW paper.
RN/R sugarfr pudn.	y	n	y	n	10	35% PCW paper.
PG/Duncan Hines cmix	y	n	y	n	12	35% PCW paper.
PG/DH Delights	y	n	y	n	12	35% PCW paper.
PG/DH Moist deluxe	y	n	y	n	12	35% PCW paper.
PG/DH microwavemix	y	n	y	n	12	35% PCW paper.
PG/DH frosting	n	y	y	n	12	HDPE, reusable
SL/Sara Lee poundck	y	y	y	n	10	alum. tin
SL/desserts	n	n	y	n	10	red. pac.
GARBAGE BAGS Company/Product	**RP**	**Rb**	**SR**	**SC**	**EFR**	**Notes**
Argon/series C	y 80%	n	n	y	-	10% PCW

Ca/Ruffies Eco kit.	y	n	y	n	-	33% PCW
Ca/Rf Eco lg. trash	y	n	y	n	-	33% PCW
Ca/Rf trash	y	n	y	n	-	33% PCW
Ca/Rf Sure St. kit.	y	n	y	n	-	15% PCW
Dyna-Pak/Best Buy leaf & grass	y 80%	n	n	y	-	11% PCW
DP/lg. trash	y 80%	n	n	y	-	11% PCW
DP/tall kitchen	y 80%	n	n	y	-	11% PCW
DP/trash	y 80%	n	n	y	-	11% PCW
DP/Full Circle liner	y 80%	n	n	y	-	11% PCW
DP/Full Circle leaf	y 80%	n	n	y	-	11% PCW
DP/FC large trash	y 80%	n	n	y	-	11% PCW
DP/FC tall kitchen	y 80%	n	n	y	-	11% PCW
DP/FC trash	y 80%	n	n	y	-	11% PCW
Earthwise trash	y 60%	n	n	n	18	60% PCW
FB/Glad kitchen	n	n	y	n	10	less material
FB/G kitchen h. tie	n	n	y	n	10	less material
FB/G sandwich	y	n	n	n	10	rec. box
FB/sandwich pleated	y	n	n	n	10	rec. box
FB/trash	n	n	y	n	10	less material
FB/trash hvywt.	n	n	y	n	10	less material
FB/trash large	y	n	y	n	10	less material
NA/Harmony trash	y 80%	n	n	y	10	30% PCW
NA/Recycle 1 trash	y 80%	n	n	y	10	30% PCW
NA/Ironhold trash	y	n	n	n	10	70% rec.
CT/Brawny lg. kit.	y	n	y	n	-	5–15% PCW

CT/Brawny lg. trash	y	n	y	n	-	5–15% PCW
CT/Brawny trash	y	n	y	n	-	5–15% PCW
CT/Brawny scent kit.	n	n	n	n	-	5–15% PCW
Mobil/Hefty, Kordite	y	n	y	n	10	rec. pac.
Petosky/Resour. kit	y 30%	n	n	n	10	10% PCW
PA/Husky Re. kit.	n	n	n	n	-	20% PCW
PA/Husky lg. trash	n	n	n	n	-	20% PCW
PA/Husky trash	n	n	n	n	-	20% PCW
PA/Husky Yard	n	n	n	n	-	20% PCW
Stone/Yardmstr. lawn	y	y	n	n	-	14% PCW
Strout/KLEENSITE	y 95%	n	n	y	-	15% PCW
Strout/Mr Neat rec.	y 95%	n	n	y	-	15% PCW
Strout/Mr Neat trash	y 95%	n	n	y	-	15% PCW
Wb/Renew draw kit.	y 80%	n	n	y	12	24% PCW
Wb/Renew draw lawn	y	n	n	y	12	30% PCW
Wb/Renew. dr. lg. trash	y 80%	n	n	y	12	24% PCW
Wb/Renew trash	y 80%	n	n	y	12	24% PCW
Wb/Renew dr. tall kit.	y	n	n	y	12	30% PCW
Wb/Renew kit.	y	n	n	y	12	30% PCW
Wb/Renew Lawn	y	n	n	y	12	30% PCW
Wb/Renew lg. trash	y	n	n	y	12	30% PCW
Wb/Renew lg. kitchen	y	n	n	y	12	30% PCW
Wb/Renew trash	y	n	n	y	12	30% PCW
Wb/Ultra GS kit.	y	n	n	y	12	30% PCW

Wb/Ultra GS lg. trash	y	n	n	y	12	30% PCW
LIGHT BULBS Company/Product	**RP**	**Rb**	**SR**	**SC**	**EFR**	**Notes**
GE/EnerChoice cir.	y 80%	n	n	n	8	energy sav.
GE/EC Compax 52w	y	n	n	n	8	energy sav.
GE/EC 15w	y	n	n	n	8	energy sav.
GE/EC 20w	y	n	n	n	8	energy sav.
GE/EC 26w	y	n	n	n	8	energy sav.
GE/EC 40w	y	n	n	n	8	energy sav.
GE/Q halogen 300w	y	n	n	n	8	energy sav.
GE/halogen 50w flood	y	n	n	n	8	energy sav.
GE/a-line hgen. 50w	y	n	n	n	8	energy sav.
GE/a-line hgen. 90w	y	n	n	n	8	energy sav.
GE/EC 34w tube	y	n	n	n	8	energy sav.
GTE/Sylvania CF 18w	n	n	n	n	10	energy sav.
GTE/S CF 22w	n	n	n	n	10	energy sav.
GTE/S ES 34w tube	n	n	n	n	10	energy sav.
GTE/S nl. halogen 50w	n	n	n	n	10	energy sav.
GTE/S nl. hgen. 55w	n	n	n	n	10	energy sav.
GTE/S nl. hgen. 60w	n	n	n	n	10	energy sav.
GTE/S nl. hgen. 75w	n	n	n	n	10	energy sav.
GTE/S nl. hgen. 100w	n	n	n	n	10	energy sav.
GTE/S nl. hgen. 45w fl.	n	n	n	n	10	energy sav.

GTE/S nl. hgen. 45w sp.	n	n	n	n	10	energy sav.
Philips/Earth L 15w	n	n	n	n	10	energy sav.
Philips/EL 20 watt	n	n	n	n	10	energy sav.
Philips/EL 23 watt	n	n	n	n	10	energy sav.
MISCELLANEOUS Company/Product	**RP**	**Rb**	**SR**	**SC**	**EFR**	**Notes**
Db/Saran Wrap	y	n	y	n	12	35% PCW paper.
Db/Ziploc bags	y	n	y	n	12	35% PCW paper.
Ek/Victor es mouse tr.	y	n	n	n	10	nontoxic 35% PCW paper.
Ek/V metalbait mouse	y	n	n	n	10	nontoxic 35% PCW paper
Ek/V live catch mt.	y	n	n	n	10	nontoxic 35% PCW paper
Ek/V Rat trap	y	n	n	n	10	nontoxic 35% PCW paper
Ek/V Rodent glue trap	y	n	n	n	10	nontoxic 35% PCW paper
Ek/V Tincat re. mt.	y	n	n	n	10	nontoxic 35% PCW paper
Ek/V roach glue trap	y	n	n	n	10	nontoxic 35% PCW paper
Ek/V flying ins. trap	y	n	n	n	10	nontoxic 35% PCW paper
Ek/V fly catcher	y	n	n	n	10	nontoxic 35% PCW paper

Ek/V roach traps	y	n	n	n	10	nontoxic 35% PCW paper
Ek/Ekco kitchen tools	y	n	y	n	10	rec. card.
Emsco/Rescue broom	y	n	y	n	-	rec. plastic
Em/Rescue angle br.	y	n	y	n	-	rec. plastic
Manco/self-ad. labels	y	n	n	n	10	25% PCW paper.
Ma/tissue wrap	y	y	n	n	10	80% rec. paper.
Ma/mounting putty	y	n	n	n	10	reusable
Ma/kraft paper	y	y	n	n	10	100% rec. paper.
Ma/bubble wrap	y	n	n	n	10	10% PCW plastic
Ma/photo mailers	y	y	n	n	10	100% rec.
Ma/padded envelopes	y	y	n	n	10	60% rec.
Ma/mailing tubes	y	y	n	n	10	90% rec.
Ma/Caremail boxes	y	y	n	n	10	20% rec.
Ma/Tyvek envelopes	y	y	n	n	10	reusable
Re/Reynolds wrap af.	y	y	y	n	12	low-VOC inks
Re/R plastic wrap	y	n	y	n	12	low-VOC inks
Re/R SureSeal bags	y	n	y	n	12	low-VOC inks
Re/R Micro wrap	y	n	y	n	12	low-VOC inks
Re/Oven bags	y	n	y	n	12	35% PCW paper.
Re/R Cut-Rite wax pr.	y	n	y	n	12	35% PCW paper.
Re/R CR sand. bags	y	n	y	n	12	35% PCW paper.
Re/R SureSeal zipper	y	n	y	n	12	35% PCW paper. reusable

Re/R freezer paper	y	n	y	n	12	35% PCW paper.
Re/Redi-Pan	n	y	y	n	12	alum. pans
Ri/Safer violet insect killer	n	n	n	y	-	biodegradable
Ri/S Aphid killer	n	n	n	y	-	biodegradable
Ri/S Flea soap	n	n	n	y	-	biodegradable
Ri/Insect killer	n	n	n	y	-	biodegradable
Ri/Insect trigger	n	n	n	y	-	biodegradable
Ri/Mite killer	n	n	n	y	-	biodegradable
Ri/Moss & Algae killer	n	n	n	y	-	biodegradable
Ri/Moss killer	n	n	n	y	-	biodegradable
Royal/rubber matts	y	n	y	y	-	80% PCW rubber
UltraPac/Prod. cont.	y	y	y	y	-	100% rec. PETE
UltraPac/Shaws tub	y	y	y	y	-	100% rec. PETE
Visy/brown wr. paper	y	y	y	y	-	100% PCW paper.
WoodFuel/Na. bbq briq.	n	n	y	y	-	100% rec. wood
OVER-THE-COUNTER REMEDIES Company/Product	RP	Rb	SR	SC	EFR	Notes
AH/Dimetapp bottle	n	y	n	n	8	glass
Ah/Robitussin bottle	n	y	n	n	8	glass
AH/Anbesol	n	y	n	n	8	glass
BM/Bufferin	y OP	n	y	n	12	50% PCW pac.

BM/Bufferin AFN	y OP	n	y	n	12	50% PCW pac.
BM/Comtrex	y OP	n	y	n	12	50% PCW pac.
BM/Nuprin	y OP	n	y	n	12	50% PCW pac.
BM/Theragran-M	y OP	n	y	n	12	50% PCW pac.
BW/Actifed	n	n	y	n	10	red. pac.
BW/Neosporin	n	n	y	n	10	red. pac.
BW/Sudafed	n	n	y	n	10	red. pac.
JJ/Imodium AD	n	n	y	n	12	red. pac.
JJ/Mylanta	n	y	n	n	12	HDPE
MD/Citrucel	n	y	y	n	10	HDPE
PG/Metamucil	n	y	y	n	12	PETE
PG/Vicks Nyquil	n	y	n	n	12	PETE
PG/Pepto-Bismol	n	y	y	n	12	PETE
RR/Maalox	n	y	y	n	10	HDPE
Sandoz/Dorcol	n	y	y	n	10	PETE
Sandoz/Triaminic	n	y	y	n	10	PETE
SK/Tums tablets	n	y	y	n	10	HDPE
Sterling/Milk of Mag.	n	y	y	n	10	HDPE
Upjohn/Kaopectate	n	y	n	n	12	HDPE
Upjohn/Motrin	n	y	y	n	12	HDPE
WL/Anusol	y part.	n	y	n	12	20% PCW OP
WL/Benylin	y part.	n	y	n	12	20% PCW OP
WL/Effergrip/Efferd.	y part.	n	y	n	12	20% PCW OP
WL/Benydryl Cold	y part.	n	y	n	12	20% PCW OP
WL/Medi-Flu	y part.	n	y	n	12	20% PCW OP
WL/Rolaids	n	y	y	n	12	HDPE

WL/Tucks	y part.	n	y	n	12	HDPE
TOOTHPASTES						
Ch/Aim	y box	n	n	n	14	35% PCW box
Ch/Closeup	y box	n	n	n	14	35% PCW box
Ch/Pepsodent	y box	n	n	n	14	35% PCW box
CD/Arm&Hammer d. care	y box	n	n	n	12	35% PCW box
CP/Baking Soda	y box	n	n	n	12	35% PCW box
CP/Colgate	y box	n	n	n	12	35% PCW box
CP/Col. standup tube	n	n	y	n	12	20% less pac.
CP/Peak	y box	n	y	n	12	35% PCW OP
CP/Ultrabrite	y box	n	y	n	12	35% PCW OP
Lion/Checkup Zact	y box	n	n	n	-	rec. box
PG/Crest	y box	n	n	n	12	rec. box
PG/Crest pump	n	n	y	n	12	red. pac.
UNDERARM DEODORANTS						
BM/Ban Fresh n'Dry	n	n	y	n	12	rem. carton
BM/Ban w/carton	y OP	n	n	n	12	35% PCW box
BM/Ban wide solid	n	n	y	n	12	rem. carton
Ch/Faberge Lady Pow.	n	n	y	n	14	rem. carton
Ch/Faberge power st.	n	n	y	n	14	rem. carton
Gi/Dry Idea	n	n	y	n	12	rem. carton
PG/Old Spice	n	n	y	n	12	rem. carton
PG/Secret	n	n	y	n	12	rem. carton
PG/Sure	n	n	y	n	12	rem. carton

PAPER GOODS Company/Product	RP	Rb	SR	SC	EFR	Notes
AT/private lab. bath	n	y	n	y	-	80% PCW
AT/facial	n	y	n	y	-	80% PCW
AT/napkin	n	y	n	y	-	30% PCW
AT/towel	n	y	n	y	-	30% PCW
CI/Cascades bath	n	y	n	y	-	80% PCW
CI/facial	n	y	n	y	-	80% PCW
CI/kitchen towel	n	y	n	y	-	80% PCW
CI/napkin	n	y	n	y	-	80% PCW
CI/paper towel	n	y	n	y	-	100% PCW
CI/Cycle 2 kitchen	n	y	n	y	-	100% PCW
CI/Doucelle bath	n	y	n	y	-	80% PCW
CI/kitchen towel	n	y	n	y	-	80% PCW
Cf/Today's Choice b.	n	y	n	y	-	11% PCW
Cf/facial	n	y	n	y	-	11% PCW
Cf/napkin	n	y	n	y	-	11% PCW
Cf/towel	n	y	n	y	-	11% PCW
FH/Green Forest bath	n	y	n	y	10	10% PCW
FH/GF napkin	n	y	n	y	10	10% PCW
FH/GH towel	n	y	n	y	10	10% PCW
Georgia Pacific	n	y	n	n	10	PCW not avail.
JR/Brawny towels	n	y	n	n	8	PCW not avail.
JR/Rennaisance bath	n	y	n	n	8	PCW not avail.
JR/Ren. towels	n	y	n	n	8	PCW not avail.
Keyes/Chinet plates	n	y	n	n	-	95% rec.

KC/Hi-Dro Towels	n	y	n	n	10	100% rec.
KC/Kleenex facial	y 60%	y	n	n	10	PCW not avail.
KC/Kleenex bath	n	y	n	n	10	PCW not avail.
Marcal bath	n	y	n	n	-	60% PCW
Marcal facial	n	y	n	n	-	60% PCW
Marcal towels	n	y	n	n	-	60% PCW
Morcon/generic bath	n	y	n	y	-	60% PCW
Mn/lunch napkin	n	y	n	y	-	60% PCW
Mn/Mor-Soft bath	n	y	n	y	-	60% PCW
Mn/Mor-Soft napkin	n	y	n	y	-	60% PCW
Mn/Morning Gl bath	n	y	n	y	-	60% PCW
Mn/Morning Gl napkin	n	y	n	y	-	60% PCW
Mn/private bath	n	y	n	y	-	60% PCW
Mn/Rose Soft bath	n	y	n	y	-	60% PCW
Mn/trad. napkin	n	y	n	y	-	60% PCW
PT/Capri bath	n	y	n	y	-	28% PCW
PT/Capri facial	n	y	n	y	-	28% PCW
PT/Capri napkin	n	y	n	y	-	28% PCW
PT/towel	n	y	n	y	-	28% PCW
PT/Gayety bath	n	y	n	y	-	28% PCW
PT/Gayety napkin	n	y	n	y	-	28% PCW
PT/Gayety towel	n	y	n	y	-	28% PCW
PT/Gentle Touch bath	n	y	n	y	-	28% PCW
PT/GT cube facial	n	y	n	y	-	28% PCW
PT/GT facial	n	y	n	y	-	28% PCW
PT/GT napkin	n	y	n	y	-	28% PCW

PT/GT towel	n	y	n	y	-	28% PCW
PT/Nature's Choice b.	n	y	n	y	-	28% PCW
PT/NC facial	n	y	n	y	-	28% PCW
PT/NC napkin	n	y	n	y	-	28% PCW
PT/towel	n	y	n	y	-	28% PCW
PT/Pert bath	n	y	n	y	-	28% PCW
PT/Pert napkin	n	y	n	y	-	28% PCW
PT/Pert towel	n	y	n	y	-	28% PCW
PT/generic bath	n	y	n	y	-	28% PCW
PT/g. facial	n	y	n	y	-	28% PCW
PT/g. napkin	n	y	n	y	-	28% PCW
PT/g. towel	n	y	n	y	-	28% PCW
St/TreeFreeAware b.	n	y	n	y	12	10% PCW
St/A boudoir facial	n	y	n	y	12	10% PCW
St/A facial	n	y	n	y	12	10% PCW
St/A napkin	n	y	n	y	12	10% PCW
St/A towel	n	y	n	y	12	10% PCW
St/CARE bath	n	y	n	y	12	10% PCW
St/C boudoir facial	n	y	n	y	12	10% PCW
St/C facial	n	y	n	y	12	10% PCW
St/C napkin	n	y	n	y	12	10% PCW
St/C towel	n	y	n	y	12	10% PCW
St/Envirocare b.	n	y	n	y	12	10% PCW
St/E boudoir facial	n	y	n	y	12	10% PCW
St/E facial	n	y	n	y	12	10% PCW
St/E napkin	n	y	n	y	12	10% PCW

St/E towel	n	y	n	y	12	10% PCW
St/Enviroquest b.	n	y	n	y	12	10% PCW
St/En facial	n	y	n	y	12	10% PCW
St/En napkin	n	y	n	y	12	10% PCW
St.En towel	n	y	n	y	12	10% PCW
St/Forever Green b.	n	y	n	y	12	10% PCW
St/FG facial	n	y	n	y	12	10% PCW
St/FG napkin	n	y	n	y	12	10% PCW
St/FG towel	n	y	n	y	12	10% PCW
St/Green Meadow b.	n	y	n	y	12	10% PCW
St/GM facial	n	y	n	y	12	10% PCW
St/GM napkin	n	y	n	y	12	10% PCW
St/GM towel	n	y	n	y	12	10% PCW
St/New Day Choice b.	n	y	n	y	12	10% PCW
St/ND facial	n	y	n	y	12	10% PCW
St/ND napkin	n	y	n	y	12	10% PCW
St/ND towel	n	y	n	y	12	10% PCW
St/Proj. Green towel	n	y	n	y	12	10% PCW
St/Safe bath	n	y	n	y	12	10% PCW
St/S facial	n	y	n	y	12	10% PCW
St/S napkin	n	y	n	y	12	10% PCW
St/S towel	n	y	n	y	12	10% PCW
St/Tree-Free bath	n	y	n	y	12	10% PCW
St/TF boudoir facial	n	y	n	y	12	10% PCW
St/TF facial	n	y	n	y	12	10% PCW
St/TF napkin	n	y	n	y	12	10% PCW

St/TF towel	n	y	n	y	12	10% PCW
Webster Renew bath	n	y	n	y	12	40% PCW
Scott Bath Tissue	n	y	y	n	12	20% PCW
Sc/Scottowels	n	y	y	n	12	20% PCW
Sc/Job Squad towels	n	y	y	n	12	20% PCW
Sc/Viva towels	n	y	y	n	12	20% PCW
Sc/Viva napkins	n	y	n	n	12	20% PCW
Sc/Cottonelle bath	n	y	n	n	12	20% PCW
Sc/Scotties facial	n	y	n	n	12	20% PCW
Sc/Sofkins	n	n	n	n	12	20% PCW
Sc/Baby Fresh	n	n	n	n	12	20% PCW
WRITING PAPER/ OFFICE SUPPLIES						
Astro-Valcour mailer	y	n	n	n	-	15% PCW
Dt/Memo Pad	y	y	n	n	-	rec. paper
Dt/Pencil tablet	y	y	n	n	-	rec. paper
Dt/Scribble tablet	y	y	n	n	-	rec. paper
Dt/Writing tablet	y	y	n	n	-	rec. paper
EP/Earthwise binders	n	y	n	n	-	10% PCW
EP/EW folders	y	y	n	n	-	10% PCW
EP/EW ex. wallets	y	y	n	n	-	10% PCW
EP/EW file pock. lt.	y	y	n	n	-	10% PCW
EP/EW hanging bind.	y	y	n	n	-	10% PCW
EP/EW report covers	y	y	n	n	-	10% PCW
EP/EW portfolios	y	y	n	n	-	10% PCW
EP/EW column pads	y	y	n	n	-	22% PCW

EP/EW comp. books	y	y	n	n	-	10% PCW
EP/EW wire note.	y	y	n	n	-	10% PCW
EP/EW wire memo.	y	y	n	n	-	20% PCW
EP/EW binder 3-ring	y	n	n	n	-	93% PCW
EP/EW binder index	y	n	n	n	-	93% PCW
EP/EW data binder	y	n	n	n	-	55% PCW
EP/EW binder index	y	y	n	n	-	10% PCW
EP/EW border cover	y	y	n	n	-	15% PCW
EP/EW file folders	y	y	n	n	-	15% PCW
EP/EW folders man.	y	y	n	n	-	10% PCW
EP/EW folder part.	y	y	n	n	-	15% PCW
EP/EW folder pressb.	y	y	n	n	-	15% PCW
EP/EW border cov. 3h	y	y	n	n	-	15% PCW
EP/EW twinpoc. port.	y	y	n	n	-	15% PCW
EP/EW record book	y 72%	n	n	n	-	48% PCW
EP/EW ledger book	y	n	n	n	-	48% PCW
EP/EW cash book	y	n	n	n	-	48% PCW
EP/EW journal book	y	n	n	n	-	48% PCW
EP/EW ex. wallet ledger	y	y	n	n	-	10% PCW
EP/EW ew velcro	y	y	n	n	-	10% PCW
EP/EW ew leg. velcro	y	y	n	n	-	10% PCW
EP/EW ew comp. vel	y	y	n	n	-	10% PCW
EP/EW ew ltr. vel.	y	y	n	n	-	10% PCW
EP/EW ex. file ltst.	y	y	n	n	-	10% PCW
EP/EW ex. file ledg.	y	y	n	n	-	10% PCW

EP/EW ex. file lst.	y	y	n	n	-	10% PCW
EP/EW paper rec. vdt.	y	y	n	n	-	100% PCW
EP/EW paper rec. hdt	y	y	n	n	-	100% PCW
EP/EW paper rec. box	y	y	n	n	-	100% PCW
EP/EW stg. file ltr.	y	y	n	n	-	100% PCW
EP/EW stg. file ledg.	y	y	n	n	-	100% PCW
EP/EW stg. file lt./ledg.	y	y	n	n	-	100% PCW
EP/EW bb hfld. ltrg.	y	n	n	n	-	15% PCW
EP/EW bb hfld. ltrn.	y	n	n	n	-	15% PCW
EP/EW bb hfld. legg	y	n	n	n	-	15% PCW
EP/EW bb hfld. legn	y	n	n	n	-	15% PCW
EP/EW indcard blank	y	y	n	n	-	20% PCW
EP/EW incard ruled	y	y	n	n	-	20% PCW
EP/EW ic. 4x6 blank	y	y	n	n	-	20% PCW
EP/EW ic. 4x6 ruled	y	y	n	n	-	20% PCW
EP/EW 1/5 tab clear	y	n	n	n	-	PCW not avail.
EP/EW 1/5tab blue	y	n	n	n	-	PCW not avail.
EP/EW 1/5tab red	y	n	n	n	-	PCW not avail.
EP/EW 1/5tab natur.	y	n	n	n	-	PCW not avail.
EP/EW 1/5 tab violet	y	n	n	n	-	PCW not avail.
EP/EW 1/3 tab clear	y	n	n	n	-	PCW not avail.
EP/EW 1/3tab blue	y	n	n	n	-	PCW not avail.
EP/EW 1/3tab red	y	n	n	n	-	PCW not avail.
EP/EW 1/3tab natur.	y	n	n	n	-	PCW not avail.
EP/EW 1/3 tab violet	y	n	n	n	-	PCW not avail.
EP/EW sticknote 3x3	y	n	n	n	-	15% PCW

EP/EW sticknote 3/5	y	n	n	n	-	15% PCW
EP/EW sticknote 2x3	y	n	n	n	-	15% PCW
EP/EW sn. 1.5x2	y	n	n	n	-	15% PCW
TYPING/WRITING PAPER						
Fox River Circa '83	n	y	n	y	-	15% PCW
FR/Circa Select	n	y	n	y	-	15% PCW
FR/Confetti	n	y	n	y	-	25% PCW
FR/Eaton bond	n	y	n	y	-	15% PCW
FR/Early American	n	y	n	y	-	25% PCW
PAPER, OFFICE Company/Product	**RP**	**Rb**	**SR**	**SC**	**EFR**	**Notes**
GP/Proterra felt	n	y	n	y	10	20% PCW
GP/Proterra laid	n	y	n	y	10	20% PCW
GP/Proterra linen	n	y	n	y	10	20% PCW
GP/Proterra vellum	n	y	n	y	10	20% PCW
Mead/Post 100% theme	y	y	n	n	12	100% PCW
Md/Post 100% filler	n	y	n	n	12	100% PCW
Md/Post 100% memo	y	y	n	n	12	100% PCW
Md/Green Cycle note	y	y	n	n	12	10–20% PCW
Md/GC tablets	y	y	n	n	12	10–20% PCW
Md/GC envelopes	n	y	n	n	12	10–20% PCW
Md/GC memo book	y	y	n	n	12	10–20% PCW
Md/Muppets notebook	y	y	n	n	12	100% PCW
Md/Muppets memo	y	y	n	n	12	100% PCW

Md/Muppets portfolio	n	y	n	n	12	100% PCW
Md/Simply Miss Piggy	n	y	n	n	12	10% PCW
Md/Sequel carbonless	n	y	n	n	12	10% PCW
Md/Harmony Xerograph	n	y	n	n	12	10% PCW
Md/Gilbert bond	n	y	n	n	12	15% PCW
Md/Gilbert ESSE	n	y	n	n	12	50% PCW
Md/Gilbert Oxford	n	y	n	n	12	40% PCW
Md/Gilcrest recycled	n	y	n	n	12	40% PCW
PP/Duralite Rmailer	y	n	n	y	-	25% PCW
PP/Nature mailer	y	n	n	y	-	25% PCW
PP/Polymail dispatch	y	n	n	y	-	25% PCW
PP/PM Rig. oefmail	y	n	n	y	-	25% PCW
PP/PM Rig. osfmail	y	n	n	y	-	25% PCW
AD/Postlite mailer	y part.	n	n	n	-	15% PCW
AD/Jiffylite mail 4x8	y part.	n	n	n	-	15% PCW
AD/Jlite mailer 5x10	y part.	n	n	n	-	15% PCW
AD/Jlite mailer 6x10	y part.	n	n	n	-	15% PCW
Safco/Duofile	n	y	n	y	-	30% PCW
Sf/Pers. Re. file b	n	y	n	y	-	30% PCW
Sf/Pers. Re. file	n	y	n	y	-	30% PCW
Sf/Recycle It	n	y	n	y	-	30% PCW
3M/Post-it Notes	n	n	n	n	12	10% PCW
Stuart Hall/filler p.	n	y	n	n	10	60% PCW
SH/notebook 80	y	y	n	n	10	60% PCW

SH/wire notebook	y	y	n	n	10	60% PCW
SH/notepad	y	y	n	n	10	60% PCW
Paper Greet. Cards						
AG/Just My Style	y	y	n	n	10	rec. cont.
AG/78th St.	y	y	n	n	10	rec. cont.
AG/seasonal lines	y	y	n	n	10	rec. cont.
AG/wrapping paper	y	y	n	n	10	rec. cont.
Hallmark/Ambassador	y	y	n	n	10	10% PCW
Hm/Christmas	y	y	n	n	10	10% PCW
Hm/Christmas Natur.	y	y	n	y	10	90% red. pac.
Hm/My Thoughts Exact	y	y	n	n	10	10% PCW
Hm/Shoebox Greetings	y	y	n	n	10	10% PCW
PERSONAL CARE Feminine Products Company/Product	**RP**	**Rb**	**SR**	**SC**	**EFR**	**Notes**
JJ/Carefree napkins	y	n	y	n	12	35% PCW box
JJ/Modess napkins	y	n	y	n	12	35% PCW box
JJ/Stayfree maxipads	y	n	y	n	12	35% PCW box
JJ/Sure n' Natural	y	n	y	n	12	35% PCW box
KC/Depends under.	y part.	n	y	n	10	red. pac.
KC/Kotex	n	n	y	n	10	red. pac.
KC/Kotex New Freedom	n	n	y	n	10	red. pac.
KC/Light Days Long	n	n	y	n	10	red. pac.
KC/Kotex ultrathin	n	n	y	n	10	red. pac.

PG/Always pantiliner	y	n	y	n	10	red. pac.
SL/L'Eggs panty hose	y	n	y	n	12	38% less pac.
Tambrands/Tampax	y	n	y	n	10	biod. applic.
SHAVERS, Disposable						
BIC/shaver 10 pack	y part.	n	y	n	10	red. pac.
BIC/dispos. shaver	y part.	n	y	n	10	red. pac.
BIC/Lady shaver	y part.	n	y	n	10	red. pac.
BIC/Sensitive shaver	y part.	n	y	n	10	red. pac.
Gi/Atra shaver	n	n	y	n	12	red. pac.
Gi/Braun Clean Spray	n	n	n	n	12	CFC free
Gi/Trac II blades	n	n	y	n	12	red. solvents
LOTIONS						
Jergens Ad. therapy pouch	n	n	y	n	10	78% less pac.
Jergens/Vit. E pump	n	n	y	n	10	refill.
Jergens/Extra Dry	n	n	y	n	10	refill.
PG/Noxzema	n	n	y	n	12	red. pac.
SC/Curel	n	y	n	n	-	HDPE
SC/Softsense	n	y	n	n	-	HDPE
WL/Lubriderm	n	y	y	n	12	HDPE
MOUTHWASHES						
CP/Fluorigard	n	y	y	n	12	PETE
CP/Viadent	n	y	y	n	12	PETE
Dep/Lavoris	n	y	y	n	10	PETE
Dep/Crystal Lavoris	n	y	y	n	10	PETE

MD/Cepacol	n	y	y	n	10	PETE
Pfizer/Plax	n	y	y	n	10	PETE
PG/Scope	n	y	y	n	12	PETE
PG/Scope mint	n	y	y	n	12	PETE
WL/Listerine 64 oz.	n	y	y	n	12	PETE
WL/Lister. Coolmint	n	y	y	n	12	PETE
WL/Listermint	n	y	y	n	12	PETE
SHAMPOO/ CONDITIONER						
Ab/Selsun Blue	n	y	n	n	10	HDPE
Ab/Selsun Extramed	n	y	n	n	10	HDPE
BM/Clairol herbal	n	y	y	n	12	HDPE
BM/Clairol 3 in 1	n	y	y	n	12	HDPE
BM/Clairol cond.	n	y	n	n	12	HDPE
Ch/Rav	n	y	n	n	14	HDPE
Ch/Rav sh. & cond.	n	y	n	n	14	HDPE
Cosmair/L'Oreal	n	y	n	n	10	HDPE
Dl/Breck sh. & cond.	n	y	n	n	12	HDPE
Dl/Breck cond.	n	y	n	n	12	HDPE
Db/Permasoft	n	y	n	n	10	HDPE
Dep/Nature's Family	n	y	n	n	10	biodeg.
Gi/White Rain	n	y	n	n	12	HDPE
Gi/White Rain balsam	n	y	n	n	12	HDPE
HC/Salon Selectives	y part.	y	y	n	12	25% rec. HDPE
HC/Finesse	n	y	y	n	12	HDPE
HC/Suave balsam	n	y	y	n	12	HDPE

HC/Suave sh. & cond.	n	y	y	n	12	HDPE
HC/Vibrance	n	y	y	n	12	HDPE
Jherri Redd. (Conair)	n	y	n	n	12	HDPE
JJ/Pooh shampoos	n	y	n	n	12	HDPE
PG/Head & Shoulders	n	y	n	n	12	HDPE
PG/Ivory	n	y	n	n	12	HDPE
PG/Pantene	n	y	n	n	12	HDPE
PG/Pert Plus	n	y	n	n	12	HDPE
PG/Pert dandruff	n	y	n	n	12	HDPE
PG/Prell	n	y	n	n	12	HDPE
PG/Shamtu	n	y	n	n	12	HDPE
PG/Vidal Sassoon	n	y	n	n	12	HDPE
HAIR SPRAYS						
BM/Clairol mist	n	y	n	n	12	non-airpump
Ch/Aquanet spray	y part	y	n	n	14	25% PCW HDPE
Ch/Rave mist/spritz	n	y	n	n	14	HDPE pump
Conair/Jr. Red. p.s.	n	y	n	n	-	HDPE pump
Cos/L'Or. megspritz	n	y	n	n	10	HDPE pump
Demert Allset Extra	n	y	n	n	-	HDPE pump
Dl/Breck pump	n	y	n	n	12	HDPE pump
Db/Permasoft mois.	n	y	n	n	10	HDPE pump
Gi/White Rain pump	n	y	n	n	12	HDPE pump
HC/Finesse pump	n	y	n	n	12	HDPE pump
HC/Salon Select pump	y part	y	n	n	12	25% rec. HDPE
HC/Suave pump	n	y	n	n	12	HDPE
Pl/Jhirmack spritz	n	y	n	n	-	HDPE

PG/Pantene p.&s.	n	y	n	n	12	refillable
PG/Shamtu p.&s.	n	y	n	n	12	refillable HDPE
PG/Vidal Sassoon p.&s.	n	y	n	n	12	refillable HDPE
HAND SOAPS						
CP/Irish Spring	y	n	y	n	12	58% PCW pac.
CP/Palmolive	y	n	y	n	12	58% PCW pac.
CP/Softsoap	n	n	y	n	12	refillable
Dl/Liquid Dial	n	n	y	n	12	refillable
Jergens/Liquid Soap	y	n	y	n	10	100% rec. cart.
PG/Ivory liquid	n	n	y	n	12	refillable
LOTIONS & CREMES						
Bm/Keri	n	n	y	n	14	refillable
Ch/Vaseline In. Care	n	y	y	n	14	HDPE
Ch/Vaseline I.C. pump	n	y	y	n	14	refill. HDPE
Ch/Brut bottle	n	y	y	n	14	HDPE
Dl/Tone pump	n	n	y	n	12	refillable
Dl/Mos. Riche pump	n	n	y	n	12	refillable
HC/Suave ex. relief	n	y	y	n	12	HDPE
HC/Suave Aloe	n	y	y	n	12	HDPE
HC/Suave Cocoa	n	y	y	n	12	HDPE
PET FOODS **Company/Product**	**RP**	**Rb**	**SR**	**SC**	**EFR**	**Notes**
GM/Alpo dog food	y	y	n	n	10	alum. cans
GM/Alpo	y	y	n	n	10	steel cans

Hz/9 Lives cat	y	y	n	n	12	alum. cans
Hz/Skippy dog	y	y	n	n	12	steel cans
Hz/Vets dog	y	y	n	n	12	steel cans
Mars/Kal Kan Ped.	y	y	n	n	10	steel cans
Ne/Bone-anza dog trt.	y	n	n	n	10	rec. paper.
Ne/Chef's Blend cat	y	n	n	n	10	rec. paper.
Ne/Chew-eez dog trt.	y	n	n	n	10	rec. paper.
Ne/Fancy Feast cat	y	y	n	n	10	54% rec. alum.
Ne/Fresh Catch cat	y	y	n	n	10	54% rec. alum.
Ne/Frisk buffet 6 oz.	y	y	n	n	10	54% rec. alum.
Ne/Fr. buff. 13 & 22 oz.	y	y	n	n	10	25% rec. steel
Ne/Fr. dry cat	y	n	n	n	10	rec. paper.
Ne/Fr. dry kitten	y	n	n	n	10	rec. paper.
Ne/Fr. Masters Ch.	y	n	n	n	10	rec. paper.
Ne/Grand Gourmet dog	y	y	n	n	10	25% rec. steel
Ne/Mighty Dog 6 oz.	y	y	n	n	10	54% rec. alum.
Ne/Mighty Dog 13 oz.	y	y	n	n	10	25% rec. steel
Ne/PrimeChoice dog t.	y	n	n	n	10	rec. paper.
Ne/Wagtime dog bis.	y	n	n	n	10	rec. paper.
QO/Ken-L-Ration dog	y	y	n	n	12	steel cans
RP/Nature's Course	y	n	n	n	10	rec. paper.
RP/Cat Chow	y	n	n	n-	10	35% PCW
RP/Dog Chow	y	n	n	n	10	35% PCW
RP/Horse chow	y	n	n	n	10	35% PCW

PROCESSED FOODS Company/Product	RP	Rb	SR	SC	EFR	Notes
Bo/Orleans clams	y	y	y	n	8	steel cans
Bo/Orleans crab	y	y	y	n	8	steel cans
Bo/Orleans	y	y	y	n	8	steel cans
Bo/Pasta	n	n	y	n	8	22% red. pac.
CA/Armour dinner	n	n	y	n	12	red. pac.
CA/Armour franks	n	n	y	n	12	red. pac.
CA/Banquet dinners	y part.	n	y	n	12	red. pac.
CA/Butterball meats	n	n	y	n	12	red. pac.
CA/Country Pr. chick.	n	n	y	n	12	red. pac.
CA/Ekrich meats	n	n	y	n	12	red. pac.
CA/Healthy Balance	y part.	n	y	n	12	red. pac.
CA/Healthy Choice fat-free dinners	n	n	y	n	12	PETE tray red. pac.
CA/HC dinners	n	n	y	n	12	PETE tray red. pac.
CA/HC lunch meats	n	n	y	n	12	red. pac.
CA/HC sauces	n	n	y	n	12	red. pac.
CA/HC soups	y	y	y	n	12	steel cans
CA/Swiss Miss	y part.	n	y	n	12	rec. paper.
CA/Ul. Slimfast	y	y	y	n	12	steel cans
CC/Knorr sauces	y	n	n	n	12	rec. paper.
CC/Muller's pasta	y	n	n	n	12	rec. paper.
Cm/Franco American	y part.	y	y	n	12	steel cans

Cm/Healthy Budget f.d.	n	y	y	n	12	PETE tray
Cm/Hungry Man f.d.	n	y	y	n	12	PETE tray
Cm/LeMenu dinners	n	y	y	n	12	PETE tray
Cm/Pork & Beans	y part.	y	y	n	12	steel cans
Cm/Soups	y part.	y	y	n	12	steel cans
Cm/Pepp. Farm crumbs	y	n	y	n	12	rec. OP
Cm/Swanson can. meats	y	y	y	n	12	steel cans
Cm/Swanson f. dinners	n	y	y	n	12	PETE tray
Cm/Swanson pies	y	y	y	n	12	alum. tins
Cm/Swanson pizzas	n	n	y	n	12	red. pac.
DF/Freshlike f. vegs.	y	y	y	n	10	steel cans
DF/Vegall. f. vegs.	n	n	y	n	10	steel cans
Dl/Armour beef	y	y	y	n	12	steel cans
Dl/Armour chili	y	y	y	n	12	steel cans
Dl/Armour C.B. hash	y	y	y	n	12	steel cans
Dl/Armour prep. meat	y	y	y	n	12	alum. cans
Dl/Armour Treet	y	y	y	n	12	alum. cans
Dl/Armour Vienna sa.	y	y	y	n	12	alum. cans
GM/Green Giant vegs.	y	y	y	n	10	steel cans
GM/Joan of Arc vegs.	y	y	y	n	10	steel cans
GM/LeSeur vegs.	y	y	y	n	10	steel cans
Hz/Ore-Ida pot.	n	n	y	n	12	red. pac.
Hz/Starkist tuna	y	y	y	n	12	steel cans

Hz/Weight Wtrs. din.	n	n	y	n	12	red. pac.
Hs/San Giorgio pasta	y	n	n	n	12	rec. paper.
Ho/Hormel chili	y	y	y	n	8	35% rec. steel
Ho/chunk meats	y	y	y	n	8	35% rec. steel
Ho/Dinty Moore stews	y	y	y	n	8	35% rec. steel
Ho/Hormel can. hams	y	y	y	n	8	35% rec. steel
Ho/ham patties	y	y	y	n	8	35% rec. steel
Ho/Mary Kitchen hash	y	y	y	n	8	35% rec. steel
Ho/tamales	y	y	y	n	8	35% rec. steel
Ho/bacon pieces	y	y	y	n	8	35% rec. glass
Ho/Chi Chis sauces	y	y	y	n	8	35% rec. glass
HO/sliced dried beef	y	y	y	n	8	35% rec. glass
Ho/Sloppy Joe sauce	y	y	y	n	8	35% rec. glass
Ho/smoked sausage	y	y	y	n	8	35% rec. glass
Ho/Spam cans	y	y	y	n	8	50% rec. alum.
Ho/Spam Lite	y	y	y	n	8	50% rec. alum.
Ho/spread prod.	y	y	y	n	8	50% rec. alum.
Ho/Vienna sausage	y	y	y	n	8	50% rec. alum.
Ho/Top Shelf	y	n	n	n	8	35% PCW paper.
Ho/Dinty Moore class.	y	n	n	n	8	35% PCW paper.
Ho/Quick Meal sand.	y	n	n	n	8	35% PCW paper.
Ho/pepperoni	n	n	y	n	8	35% less pac.
Ho/pork loin	n	n	y	n	8	20% less pac.
Ho/micro. bacon	n	n	y	n	8	40% less pac.
KG/Budget Gourmet	n	n	y	n	10	least pac.
KG/Kraft micro. entree	n	y	y	n	10	PETE tray

KG/Light & Healthy	n	n	y	n	10	red. pac.
KG/Oscar Mayer meats	n	n	y	n	10	red. pac.
KG/OM Lunchables	n	n	y	n	10	red. pac.
KG/Macaroni & Cheese	y	n	y		10	rec. paper.
KG/Velveeta dinners	n	n	y	n	10	red. pac.
KG/Velveeta cheese	n	n	y		10	reusable
LU/Lipton Cup a Soup	y	n	y	n	14	35% PCW paper.
LU/Recipe soup	y	n	y		14	35% PCW paper.
LU/Sunkist Fun Fruit	y		y		14	35% PCW paper.
Ne/Libby's chili	y	y	y	n	10	25% rec. steel
Ne/L chili w/beans	y	y	y	n	10	25% rec. steel
Ne/L corned beef	y	y	y	n	10	25% rec. steel
Ne/L C. B. hash	y	y	y	n	10	25% rec. steel
Ne/L potted meat	y	y	y	n	10	54% rec. alum.
Ne/L red salmon	y	y	y	n	10	25% rec. steel
Ne/L Sloppy Joe	y	y	y	n	10	25% rec. steel
Ne/L Spreadables	y	y	y	n	10	54% rec. alum.
Ne/L tamales	y	y	y	n	10	25% rec. steel
Ne/Vienna sausages	y	y	y	n	10	54% rec. alum.
Ne/Stouffer's L.C. lasg.	y	y	y	n	10	54% rec. alum.
RN/Del Monte dr. fruit	y part.	n	y	n	10	part. rec.
RN/DM canned vegs.	y	y	y	n	10	50% rec. alum.
RN/DM can. vegs.	y	y	y	n	10	25% rec. steel
RN/DM bottles	y	y	y	n	10	45% rec. glass

SL/Ball Park franks	n	n	y	n	10	red. pac.
SL/Hillshire Fm. sa	n	n	y	n	10	red. pac.
SL/Jimmy Dean sa.	n	n	y	n	10	red. pac.
SL/Hillshire Deli	n	n	y	n	10	red. pac.
SL/Sara Lee hams	n	n	y	n	10	red. pac.
SL/Sara Lee turkeys	n	n	y	n	10	red. pac.
SL/Mr. Turkey d. cuts	n	n	y	n	10	red. pac.
Tyson/f. dinners	n	n	y	n	10	red. pac.
SNACKS: CHIPS, NUTS Company/Product	**RP**	**Rb**	**SR**	**SC**	**EFR**	**Notes**
AB/Eagle chips	n	n	y	n	12	red. pac.
AB/Eagle minipretz.	n	n	y	n	12	red. pac.
AB/Eagle ranch	n	n	y	n	12	red. pac.
AB/Eagle ripples	n	n	y	n	12	red. pac.
AB/Eagle tortilla	n	n	y	n	12	red. pac.
AB/Eagle nuts 10 oz.	y	y	y	n	12	steel cans
Bo/Graingers	n	n	y	n	8	red. pac.
Bo/Jay's chips	n	n	y	n	8	red. pac.
Bo/Jay's cornpops	n	n	y	n	8	red. pac.
Bo/Jay's pretzels	n	n	y	n	8	red. pac.
Bo/Jay's tortilla	n	n	y	n	8	red. pac.
Bo/Krunchers	n	n	y	n	8	red. pac.
Bo/La Famous	n	n	y	n	8	red. pac.
Bo/Quinlan's pretz.	n	n	y	n	8	red. pac.
Bo/Seyfert's pretz.	n	n	y	n	8	red. pac.

GM/Bugles	y	n	n	n	12	35% PCW paper.
Ke/O'boises	n	n	y	n	10	red. pac.
Ke/pretzels	n	n	y	n	10	red. pac.
Ke/Quingles	n	n	y	n	10	red. pac.
Ke/Piazzarias	n	n	y	n	10	red. pac.
Ke/Ripplins	n	n	y	n	10	red. pac.
Pe/Frito Lay Cheetos	n	n	n	n	12	red. pac.
Pe/FL Fritos	n	n	n	n	12	5% red. pac.
PE/FL Funyums	n	n	y	n	12	red. pac.
Pe/Lay's chips	n	n	n	n	12	25% red. pac.
Pe/Tostitos	n	n	n	n	12	red. pac.
Pe/FL Rold Gold	n	n	y	n	12	red. pac.
Pe/Ruffles	n	n	y	n	12	25% red. pac.
Pe/FL Sanitas	n	n	y	n	12	25% red. pac.
Pe/FL Sun Chips	n	n	y	n	12	25% red. pac.
PG/Fisher nuts 11 oz.	y	y	y	n	12	steel cans
PG/Fisher flav. 16 oz.	y	y	y	n	12	glass
RN/Planters nuts 12 oz.	y	y	n	n	10	glass
RN/P. sunflower	y	y	n	n	10	glass
RN/P honey roasted	y	y	n	n	10	glass
RN/P light	y	y	n	n	10	glass
RN/P unsalted	y	y	n	n	10	glass
RN/P peanuts can	y	y	n	n	10	glass
POPCORN						
AH/Jiffy Pop	y	y	n	n	8	alum. tray
CA/Golden Valley	y	n	n	n	12	rec. box

CA/Orville Red. 45 oz	n	y	y	n	12	PETE
CA/Orville Red. box	y	n	n	n	12	rec. box
GM/BC Pop Secret	y	n	n	n	12	rec. box
McCormick/TV Micro	y	n	n	n	10	rec. box
Newman's Own	y	n	n	n	-	rec. box
SOFT DRINKS **Company/Product**	RP	Rb	SR	SC	EFR	Notes
Campbell's tomato j.	y	y	y	n	12	alum. cans
Cm/V8	y	y	y	n	12	alum. cans
Cm/V8	y	y	y	n	12	steel cans
Cd/Canada Dry ginger	n	y	y	n	12	PETE
Cd/Mott's juice cans	y	y	y	n	12	alum. cans
Cd/Orange Crush	n	y	y	n	12	alum. cans
Cd/Sunkist	n	y	y	n	12	alum. cans
Cd/Schweppes soda	n	y	y	n	12	alum. cans
Cd/Schweppes ginger	n	y	y	n	12	alum. cans
Cd/Schweppes tonic	n	y	y	n	12	alum. cans
Canfield's/cola	n	y	y	n	10	alum. cans
Ca/club soda	n	y	y	n	10	alum. cans
Ca/club s. cran.	n	y	y	n	10	alum. cans
Ca/club s. lemon	n	y	y	n	10	alum. cans
Ca/club rasp.	n	y	y	n	10	alum. cans
Ca/Swiss Creme	n	y	y	n	10	alum. cans
Coca-Cola 21 PETE	y part.	y	y	n	12	not wide. avail.
Co/Coke Classic	n	y	y	n	12	PETE
Co/Cherry Coke	n	y	y	n	12	PETE

Co/Coke II	n	y	y	n	12	PETE
Co/Diet Coke	n	y	y	n	12	PETE
Co/Minute Maid or.	n	y	y	n	12	PETE
Co/Minute Maid fr.	n	y	y	n	12	PETE
Co/Minute Maid nat.	n	y	y	n	12	PETE
Co/Sprite	n	y	y	n	12	PETE
DS/Dr Pepper	n	y	y	n	10	PETE
DS/Dr Pepper diet	n	y	y	n	10	PETE
DS/7-Up	n	y	y	n	10	PETE
DS/7-Up cherry	n	y	y	n	10	PETE
DS/7-Up diet	n	y	y	n	10	PETE
Dole fruit ju. pine.	y	y	n	n	12	steel cans
Dole grapefruit	y	y	n	n	12	steel cans
Dole orange	y	y	n	n	12	steel cans
GH/LaCroix waters	y	y	n	n	-	glass
Ne/Libby's Juicy 12 oz.	y	y	y	n	10	alum. cans
Ne/Libby's mango	y	y	y	n	10	alum. cans
Ne/Libby's orange	y	y	y	n	10	alum. cans
LU/Nestea	y part.	y	y	n	12	glass
LU/Nestea diet	y part.	y	y	n	12	glass
Ocean Spray/cran.	y part.	y	n	n	12	glass
OS/rasp.	y part.	y	n	n	12	glass
OS/Refreshers	y part.	y	n	n	12	glass
OS/ruby red	y part.	y	n	n	12	glass
OS/Mauna 1	y part.	y	n	n	12	glass

OS/Cranapple	y part.	y	n	n	12	glass
OS/Crangrape	y part.	y	n	n	12	glass
OS/Cranstraw	y part.	y	n	n	12	glass
PE/Pepsi Cola 21 PETE	y part.	y	y	n	12	not wide. avail.
Pe/Pepsi Cola	n	y	y	n	12	PETE
Pe/Diet Pepsi	n	y	y	n	12	PETE
Pe/Pepsi caf.-free	n	y	y	n	12	PETE
Pe/Mountain Dew	n	y	y	n	12	PETE
Pe/Diet Mountain Dew	n	y	y	n	12	PETE
Pe/Orange Slice	n	y	y	n	12	PETE
Pe/Lemon Slice	n	y	y	n	12	PETE
Pe/Diet Slice	n	y	y	n	12	PETE
Perrier min. waters	y part.	y	y	n	10	glass
PG/Hawaiian Punch	n	y	y	n	12	steel cans
QO/Gatorade	n	y	y	n	12	PETE
QO/Gatorade bottles	y part.	y	y	n	12	glass
Snapple juices	y part.	y	y	n	-	glass
Sunsweet prune	y part.	y	y	n	-	glass
Sunsweet juices	y part.	y	y	n	-	alum. cans
Tropicana grapefruit	y part.	y	y	n	-	25% rec. glass
Trop. orange	y part.	y	y	n	-	25% rec. glass
Trop. Twister	y part.	y	y	n	-	25% rec. glass
Veryfine juices	y part.	y	y	n	-	glass
Welch's juices	y part.	y	y	n	-	glass

TRASH, RECYCLE BINS Company/Product	RP	Rb	SR	SC	EFR	Notes
Rb/Roughneck 20 gn.	y	y	n	n	14	100% PCW
Rb/Roughneck 32 gn.	y	y	n	n	14	60% PCW min.
Rb/Roughneck 42 gn.	y	y	n	n	14	100% PCW
Rb/Roughtote RC 18 gn.	y	y	n	n	14	20% PCW
Rb/Roughtote 22 gn.	y	y	n	n	14	20% PCW
Rb/Roughtote 34 gn.	y	y	n	n	14	20% PCW
Rb/Newspaper Rec.	y	y	n	n	14	15% PCW min.
Rb/Stack n' Cycle	y	y	n	n	14	15% PCW
Sf/Mobile 98 rec.	y	y	n	y	-	88% PCW HDPE
Sf/Paper Pal	y	y	n	y	-	10% PCW HDPE
Sf/Public Square rec.	y	y	n	y	-	14% PCW steel
Sf/PS rec. lid	y	y	n	y	-	14% PCW steel
Sf/rec. contain.	y	y	n	y	-	20% PCW HDPE
Sf/mini-waste	y	y	n	y	-	20% PCW HDPE
Sf/rec. baskets	y	y	n	y	-	20% PCW HDPE
Sf/rec. maxi-bins	y	y	n	y	-	50% PCW HDPE
Sf/standard rec.	y	y	n	y	-	20% PCW HDPE
Mobil/Tucker garbage	y	n	n	n	10	100% rec.

REC. GARDEN HOSES						
Aquapore/Complete	y	y	n	y	-	65% PCW rubber
Aq/Deluxe weeping	y	y	n	y	-	65% PCW rubber
Aq/rubber soaker	y	y	n	y	-	65% PCW rubber
Aq/Weeping system	y	y	n	y	-	65% PCW rubber
Aq/Weeping starter	y	y	n	y	-	65% PCW rubber

Part 6

RATING THE SUPERMARKETS

Chapter 17

What Your Supermarket Is Doing to Help the Earth

The green-consumer revolution has spread to local supermarkets. In a survey conducted by the New Consumer institute, it became clear that most major (and some minor) supermarket chains are responding to the green consumer in numerous ways. The variety of available programs truly reflects not only how much green marketing has become part of the commercial culture of the 1990s, but how much consumers can influence large corporations. There are more than 31,000 supermarkets in the United States. They range from the town market to "hypermarts" that sell everything from drugs to diapers. There's no question that supermarkets are the most powerful retail force in the country. When you consider that most households patronize markets at least once a week and that we buy most of our staples through them (milk, food, meat, poultry, etc.), you'll realize that the industry can influence how people consume, what they consume, and show customers ways to help the environment.

Unlike the major consumer goods manufacturers, however, the biggest companies do not necessarily have the best environmental records. In fact, some smaller regional and metropolitan chains seem to be making a proportionally larger effort than their big brothers. What are supermarkets doing to become better environmental citizens? Most recycle their cardboard boxes. In fact, supermarkets are among the largest recyclers of cardboard in the United States, if not the world. They've been doing so for decades, mostly because of the sheer volume and cost of cardboard they use in a single day. Some chains have taken recycling a step further, by offering everything from plastic bag takebacks and recycling to community recycling for other products. To make an even greater effort, some chains feature recycled materials or packaging in their "private label" goods.

For example, a number of chains are participating in a plastic bag recycling program offered by Sonoco Plastics, a major producer/recycler of low-density polyethylene (LAPE) bags. Of the nation's 16,000 collection sites for bags, Sonoco operates about 8,500. Considering that there are some 31,000 supermarkets, that's slightly more than half of the available market. Although we'd like to see recycling programs for all types of packaging, only the largest chains have the ability, space, and staff to implement the programs. Sonoco says that only chains with sales in excess of $2 million are participating. Nevertheless, the program is a modest success, recovering some 50 million bags a month. The program also takes #2 and #4 plastic bags. Mobil Chemical offers a similar bag recycling program to 4,000 supermarket chains, including A&P, Giant, Eagle, Jewel, Publix, and Safeway.

So, when you shop at the stores that offer this service, it's better to choose plastic bags over paper—if you recycle them. Of course, you can recycle the paper bags as well. Chances are, the paper bags are made of recycled fibers already.

STORES THAT RECYCLE SHOPPING BAGS
(A SAMPLING OF THE SONOCO PROGRAM)

A&P
Alpha Beta
Albertson's
Associated Foods
Bartell Drug
Big Bear
Big "V"
Bi-Lo
Brookshire
    Brothers
HE Butt
Chief's & Rays
Ernst
Fairway
First National
    (Finest)
Food Barns
Foodland
Food Lion
Fry's

Giant
Giant Eagle
Golub
Harris-Teeter
Heinen's
Homeland
Houchens
Hughes
Hy-Vee
Ingles
Jewel
King Kullen
Kroger
Lucky
Marsh
Military
    Commissaries
P&C
Piggly-Wiggly
Price Chopper

Publix
QFC
Red
Riser
Thriftway
Safeway
Schnucks
Seaway
    Foodtown
Shopko
Shop 'n Save
Spartan
Superfresh
Super Valu
Von's
Ware
Weis
Wetterau
Winn-Dixie

ENVIRONMENTAL PIONEERS: THE GREENEST
SUPERMARKET CHAINS

Recycling shopping bags is but one aspect of a well-rounded environmental program. For the purposes of our survey, we looked for chains with full environmental programs.

High marks were given to those having "environmental task force" committees that planned and carried out action that would (1) reduce the overall waste the chain created, (2) reduce energy usage, (3) interact with the community to promote recycling and recycled goods, (4) educate customers on environmental matters. Few chains did all of these things well. The highest-rated chains were:

1. Safeway
2. Von's
3. Fred Meyer
4. Meijer
5. Nature's Fresh Northwest
6. Dominick's
7. Big Bear
8. Giant Foods
9. Giant Eagle
10. Raley's
11. Ralph's
12. Roundy's
13. Scrivner
14. Shaw's
15. Spartan
16. Wegman's
17. Associated Grocers
18. Kroger
19. Publix
20. HE Butt

Chapter 18

The Green Supermarket Chain Survey

SURVEY SUMMARY

102 chains surveyed
65 sold reusable shopping bags
54 recycled office paper
53 provided recycling bins, pick-ups, or bag-return programs
40 sponsored plastic bag "rebate" programs
35 started environmental task forces
35 recycled shrink wrap
34 recycled meat renderings
33 recycled motor oil from truck fleet
29 recycled batteries
27 stocked private-label recycled paper products
23 started environmental education programs
22 conducted shelf-labeling programs
21 sponsored community recycling/redemption programs
20 started environmental school programs
17 recycled scrap metal
15 recycled silver from photo departments
11 composted organic waste

11   recycled cooking oil
9   conducted environmental store tours

WHAT MAKES ONE STORE GREENER
THAN ANOTHER

In conducting our supermarket survey, we found that, similar to the 1990 wave of green advertising and product introductions, supermarket chains go to great lengths to show the public how environmentally adept they are. Some plant trees around Earth Day. Others trumpet the fact that they recycle a lot of cardboard (but they all do). What separates the leaders from the laggards is an overall sense of purpose. We found few chains that go the extra mile to act on environmental ideals. However, the best chains are environmentally informed on every level of the operations. They don't do just the things they have to do, they get the community involved and talk to suppliers about reducing packaging. The most aggressive chains have even retrofitted their stores and trucking fleets to save energy.

Most of the ten largest supermarket chains (measured by sales volume) in the Forbes 500 are actively recycling. Some aggressive chains—mostly on the West and East coasts—have launched programs that feature in-store labeling, printed brochures, and tagging of green products. The top three chains—American, Kroger, and Great A&P—are actively pursuing green consumers through marketing, merchandising, and recycling efforts. But their efforts vary widely. American, a $21 billion holding company, is actually a parent company for several large regional chains, including Acme Markets, Jewel Foods, and Osco Drugs (Midwest), Star (East), and Lucky (West). A spokesman for American said that no central corporate program is in place for this reason.

What separates the hangers-on from the real innovators is the degree of their environmental commitment. The smaller chains have excelled in this area. In many instances, the small to medium chains have surpassed their richer cousins. California chains Raley's and Ralph's have joined with Fred Meyer of Portland to have SCS certify and label their products as to recycled content, recyclability, and overall environmental soundness.

Because of the place supermarkets occupy in the community, they *should* be leaders in environmental education. After all, they produce mountains of waste, consume thousands of kilowatts of electricity, release ozone-eating CFCs into the atmosphere (from refrigeration equipment), and have huge trucking fleets that consume millions of gallons of diesel fuel and oil. In short, supermarket chains are mammoth environmental consumers—and polluters. That's why they need to be more responsible than nearly all other community institutions. On the CFC issue alone, major chains have taken action to recycle CFCs and switch to HCFC refrigerants, which are less damaging than CFCs but are not the best solution.

Our idea of an above-average green supermarket chain was Raley's, based in Sacramento, California. In addition to recycling the usual cardboard boxes and wooden pallets, they use more than 63 million feet of recycled cash register tape and have saved 10 million gallons of water since the inception of the program. Winn-Dixie, in Jacksonville, Florida, has installed computer controls to lower energy costs on its refrigeration equipment. Von's, in Los Angeles, uses recycled paper in the printing of its annual report. Dominick's, in

Northlake, Illinois, uses computers to identify the most efficient trucking routes to save on fuel costs.

The chains that are most serious about greening their operations have set up environmental task forces or committees. They then set in motion a range of actions around the company as part of an agenda. At the very least, a green chain recycles everything it can from the office to the meat department. As an incentive to customers, it also provides recycling of shopping bags and other items such as cans and bottles. We found it even more significant when a chain recycles rarely recycled items such as shrink wraps or polystyrene (foam). Most community recyclers won't take these "problem" plastics.

In evaluating the largest chains in the country, we looked at the whole scheme of environmental responsibility. We considered everything from recycling to energy conservation. We even discounted things that most chains already do, such as recycle cardboard and wooden pallets. We rated actions that were already "in the bag," or daily activities that weren't considered additional green efforts. Then we looked at extraordinary measures in our Green Grocer Actions category.

"IN THE BAG":
STANDARD SUPERMARKET PRACTICES

- Cardboard box baling/recycling
- Pallet recycling/reuse
- Bakery leftover donations
- CFC recovery (federal law requires it)
- Stocking recycled paper products (national brands)
- Grocery bag "choice" programs (plastic or paper)

- Produce, milk, or other product crate reuse
- Plastic pail recycling
- Stocking recycled plastic products (national brands)

GREEN GROCER ACTIONS:
ENVIRONMENTAL PROGRAMS THAT WORK

- Environmental advertising, education, brochures, labeling
- Use of third-party certification of green claims
- Full-scale energy conservation programs
- Complete company recycling in office, fleet (oil, batteries), refrigeration (CFCs), warehouse, and all store departments (produce, meat, etc.)
- Water conservation programs
- Silver recycling from photo departments
- Use of recycled paper for printing, advertising, brochures
- Community recycling (cans, bottles, paper, etc.)
- Recycled plastic or paper egg cartons
- Community education, speakers' bureaus, school involvement
- Recycling of grocery bags, scrap metal, cooking oil
- Setting up environmental/waste reduction task force
- Composting organic waste

CHAIN STORE ACTIVITY SUMMARIES

For sampling purposes, we polled not only the Top 10 stores in the Forbes 500 but small and medium regional chains throughout the country.

We'd like to see the major chains maintain an environmental program that expands to meet community and cus-

tomer needs, not something that rears its head only around
Earth Day. This means a steady stream of environmental surveys, brochures, recycling services, and third-party certification of green claims. Eventually, we'd like to see something
akin to the German system in which any package can be returned to the store for recycling. Such a program would include everything from foam meat trays to drink boxes.
Supermarkets would do an even bigger service if they ex-
panded their selection of bulk goods (the largest chains already have) to eliminate packaging. Refillable and reusable
packaging should also be emphasized.

We made an attempt to contact all of the largest chains.
Only three major chains did not respond to our direct inquiries: Bruno's, Albertson's, and Wal-Mart. It's worth noting that Food Lion was featured in an ABC-TV *Prime-Time
Live* feature that presented some evidence of unsanitary operations. The company refuted the report. Wal-Mart is listed
because it sells supermarket products. That company, too,
was cited by a television program (NBC's *Dateline*) as having bought foreign-made goods despite their "Buy America"
advertising. Wal-Mart has denied the allegations.

The Food Marketing Institute provided an extensive list of
(unaudited) chain activities. We summarized the most significant activities of the programs. For a complete list of environmental activities, call the companies or ask the customer
service department where you shop.

ABCO, Phoenix, AZ (602) 222-1780
- Features SCS–certified products
- Recycling programs

Albertson's, Boise, ID (208) 385-6200
- In-store labeling, signs, information booths

- Environmental surveys, brochures, letter-writing campaigns
- Bag, community recycling
- Recycled egg cartons

Fred Albrecht Grocery, Akron, OH (216) 733-2861
- Environmental education program

Alfalfa's, Boulder, CO (303) 321-2877
- Shelf labeling, signs, information booths
- Consumer surveys, brochures

Apple Tree, Houston, TX (713) 460-5000
- Recycled egg cartons

Associated Grocers, Seattle, WA (206) 764-7610
- Recycled egg cartons
- Recycles bags, oil, batteries, scrap metal, shrink wrap
- Environmental education
- Environmental task force

Baker's, Omaha, NE (402) 397-4321
- Earth Day program
- Advertising, brochures
- Telephone book recycling
- Environmental committee

Bassett's IGA Markets, Oak Harbor, OH (419) 898-4891
- Shelf tags
- Recycling programs (in-house and community)
- Local school education programs
- Canvas bags

Bel Air Markets, Sacramento, CA (916) 929-6342
- Shopping bag reuse credit (5 cents)
- Plastic bag recycling

- Community recycling, clean-up
- Shopping bag recycling

Big Bear Stores, Columbus, OH (614) 464-6500
- Community, office recycling
- Employee education
- Plastic and paper bag recycling
- Canvas bags

Big Star (Malone & Hyde/Fleming) (601) 342-4296
- Recycling planning

Bi-Lo, Mauldin, SC (803) 234-1600
- Shopping bag reuse credit (5 cents)
- Shopping bag, community recycling
- Canvas bags
- Environmental education

Bozzuto's, Chesire, CT (203) 272-3511
- Canvas bags
- Office, community recycling
- Oil, battery recycling

Brown & Cole Stores, Ferndale, WA (206) 384-5915
- Environmental task force
- Recycling advertising, information
- Composts organic waste
- Office, community recycling

Circle K, Phoenix, AZ (602) 253-9600
- Stocks "photodegradable" shopping bags
- Supports community recycling

City Market, Grand Junction, CO (303) 241-0750
- Office, community recycling
- Battery, scrap metal recycling

- Environmental education
- Bag rebate program

Christy's Market, Elwood City, PA (412) 758-1010
- Community recycling
- Environmental education

Clemens, Lansdale, PA (215) 855-9960
- Office, community recycling
- Environmental task force
- Composts organic waste
- Environmental education

Copps Corporation, Stevens Point, WI (715) 344-5900
- Shopping bag rebates (5 cents)
- Bag recycling
- Environmental task force, education
- Office, community recycling

Dan's Foods, Salt Lake City, UT (801) 272-8455
- Office, community recycling
- Environmental education, policy
- Shrink wrap recycling
- Recycled egg cartons

Dillon Stores (Kroger), Wichita, KS (316) 663-6801
- Egg cartons made of recycled paper
- Community recycling
- Offers customers 3 cents per grocery sack (returned)
- Recycled egg cartons

Dominick's Finer Foods (& OMNI), Northlake, IL (708) 562-1000
- Community, office recycling, environmental/energy program
- Canvas bags

- Shopping bag recycling program
- Recycled egg cartons

Dorothy Lane Market, Dayton, OH (513) 299-3561

- Shopping bag rebates
- Environmental education

Eagle Foods, Rock Island, IL (309) 794-1416

- Stocks recycled paper products
- Stocks biodegradable soaps

G&R Felpausch, Hasting, MI (616) 945-3485

- Shopping bag rebates (5 cents)
- Environmental education
- Environmental task force
- Office, community recycling

Fiesta Mart, Houston, TX (713) 869-5060

- Environmental education
- Community recycling
- Scrap metal recycling

Fleming Companies, Oklahoma City, OK (405) 840-7200
(also Malone & Hyde, Big Star)

- Environmental education
- Office, community recycling
- Bag rebate program
- Battery, motor oil recycling

Food Barn, Greenwood, SC (803) 227-2631

- Environmental advertising

Food City/Oshwawa Group, Toronto, Canada
(416) 236-1971(Bolands, Codville, Elliott Marr)

- Bag rebate program
- Recycled paper products
- Office recycling

Foodland Supermarket, Honolulu, HI (808) 732-0791
- Environmental education, advertising
- Reusable bags
- Shelf labeling

Food Lion, Salisbury, NC (704) 633-8250
- Office, bag recycling
- Recycled paper shopping bags, produce trays
- Plastic egg carton recycling pilot

Fred Meyer, Portland, OR (503) 232-8844
- Private-label products with recycled content
- Community, office recycling, information
- SCS–labeling program
- Recycled egg cartons

Gateway Foods, LaCrosse, WI (608) 785-1330
- Office, community recycling
- Recycle oil, scrap metal, antifreeze, batteries
- Environmental education, advertising
- Private-label recycled line

Giant Eagle, Pittsburgh, PA (412) 963-2542
- Office, community recycling
- Composts organic waste
- Environmental task force

Giant Foods, Washington, DC (301) 341-4100
- Environmental committee, information
- Community, office, photo, oil, warehouse recycling
- Asked suppliers to cut back on packaging
- Bag recycling program

Goodings Supermarkets, Orlando, FL (407) 869-8300
- Office, warehouse, community recycling
- Recycles shrink wrap

- Environmental education, task force
- Private-label recycled products

Great A&P, Montvale, NJ (201) 930-4236
- Environmental task force, energy conservation
- Office, oil, battery, store recycling
- Private-label recycled products
- Store sign program, education

Hannaford Brothers/Shop 'N Save, Portland, ME (207) 761-5965
- Environmental education, waste reduction programs
- Private-label recycled products
- Office, store, battery, shrink wrap, scrap metal recycling
- Composts organic waste

Harris-Teeter, Charlotte, NC (704) 845-3429
- Offers three bagging alternatives
- Recycling information, advertising
- Paper and plastic recycled egg cartons
- Shrink wrap, batteries, scrap metal recycling

HE Butt Grocery, San Antonio, TX (512) 270-8000
- Adopt-a-Tree program
- Environmental task force, energy conservation
- Community recycling, education, composting
- Bag recycling program, recycled egg cartons

Hughes Markets, Los Angeles, CA (213) 227-8211
- Environmental education

Hy-Vee Food Stores, Chariton, IA (515) 774-2121
- Shopping bag rebates
- Office recycling
- Private-label recycled products
- Asked suppliers to reduce packaging

IGA (distributor), Chicago, IL (312) 693-4520
- Has a program to plant 1 million trees
- Recycled egg cartons
- Office recycling
- Private-label recycled products

Jewel Foods (American Stores), Melrose Park, IL (708) 531-6000
- Community, office recycling
- Private-label recycled paper goods
- Environmental task force, information
- Bag recycling program, recycled egg cartons

Kash n' Karry, Tampa, FL (813) 621-0200
- Environmental education ("Nature Friendly" kit)
- Recycled egg cartons

King Soopers (Kroger), Denver, CO (303) 778-3100
- Community, office recycling
- Environmental education, signs, booths, brochures
- Environmental task force, advertising, workshops
- Community projects, speaker's bureau

King Super Markets, West Caldwell, NJ (201) 808-4204
- Environmental education, advertising
- Private-label recycled products
- Office recycling
- Environmental task force

Kroger, Cincinnati, OH (513) 762-4000
- CFC recycling program
- Recycles tires into bumper guards
- Community, battery, oil, shrink wrap recycling
- Educational booths in stores

Larry's Markets, Seattle, WA (206) 243-2951
- Environmental brochures, education, tags
- Promotion of organic gardening
- Private-label recycled products
- Paper bag reuse credit (4 cents)

Lees Supermarket, Westport, MA (508) 636-3348
- "Bring your own bag" program
- Nonchlorine-bleached paper products
- Bag rebate program

Loblaw Companies, Toronto, Ontario, Canada
(416) 967-2557
- Recycled product line
- Recycling programs

Lucky Stores (American), Dublin, CA (510) 833-6328
- Plastic and paper bag recycling programs
- Environmental task force, education, advertising
- Shrink wrap, battery, oil, tires, community recycling
- Private-label recycled products

Macey's, Salt Lake City, UT (801) 262-5446
- Canvas bags

Marketplace Foods, Virginia Beach, VA (804) 490-0413
- Community, office recycling
- Canvas bags
- Recycled egg cartons
- Bag rebate program

Marsh Supermarkets, Yorktown, IN (317) 594-2100
- Office, community recycling
- Reusable shopping bags
- Environmental education

Martin's Super Markets, South Bend, IN (219) 234-5848
- Environmental education, advertising
- Private-label recycled products
- Office, community recycling
- Bag rebate program

Meijer, Grand Rapids, MI (616) 453-6711
- Environmental task force, waste minimization, education
- Metal, oil, battery, shrink wrap, scrap, office recycling
- Recycled egg cartons
- Water-use reduction, photographic-silver recovery

Minyard Food, Coppell, TX (214) 393-8700
- Office recycling
- Photo silver, battery, shrink wrap recycling
- Environmental education

Mrs. Gooch's Natural Food Markets, Sherman Oaks, CA
(818) 501-8484
- Environmental education

National Grocers, Weston, Ontario, Canada (416) 240-3211
- Office, oil, battery, scrap metal, community recycling
- Private-label recycled products
- Environmental education, task force
- Bag rebate program

Nature's Fresh Northwest, Portland, OR (503) 281-7485
- Community, plastic, aseptic box recycling
- Postcards for manufacturer recycling information
- Environmental education, information
- Bag rebate program

Oshawa Group, Etobicoke, Ontario, Canada (416) 236-1971
- Office, oil, battery, shrink wrap, community recycling
- Environmental education, advertising

- Composts organic waste
- Shelf labeling

P&C Food Markets, Syracuse, NY (315) 453-0325
- Environmental task force, policy statement
- Community, office recycling
- Environmental information, packaging reduction
- Recycled egg cartons

Pratt Foods, Shawnee, OK (405) 275-9831
- Enviromarket program

Prevos Family Markets, Traverse City, MI (616) 943-8011
- Office, shrink wrap recycling
- Bag rebate program
- Private-label recycled products
- Reusable shopping bags

Price Chopper Supermarkets, Schenectady, NY
(518) 356-9435
- Plastic, oil, shrink wrap, office recycling program
- Composting, Styrofoam recycling test programs
- Environmental education, advertising
- Shopping bag reuse credit program

Publix, Lakeland, FL (813) 688-1188
- Environmental task force, information
- Bag, oil, metal, silver, shrink wrap, office recycling
- Reusable bags
- Private-label recycled products

Purity Supreme, N. Billerica, MA (508) 663-0750
- Testing "Green Lane" checkout lane

Raley's, Sacramento, CA (916) 373-3333
- SCS/Green Cross labeling program

- Water saving, office recycling program
- Bag reuse program (5 cents)
- Telephone book recycling

Ralph's Grocery, Compton, CA (310) 605-2994
- Environmental task force, community, office recycling
- SCS/Green Cross labeling program
- Recycled egg cartons
- Bag reuse credit program (5 cents)

Roundy's, Milwaukee, WI (414) 453-8200
- Environmental task force, survey, education
- Office recycling, recycled paper in printing
- Tree for aluminum cans exchange
- Recycled egg cartons

Safeway Stores, Oakland, CA (510) 891-3000
- Community, office, fleet-oil recycling
- Packaging reduction program, energy conservation
- Environmental education, signs, booths, surveys
- "Environmental Options" education program

Save-A-lot, Ellwood City, PA (412) 758-1010
- Environmental education

Save Mart Supermarkets, Modesto, CA (209) 577-1600
- Solid waste task force, education
- Packaging reduction
- Bag rebate program (5 cents), reusable bags
- Office, community recycling

Schnuck Markets, St. Louis, MO (314) 994-9900
- Environmental education

Scotchman Stores, Watseka, IL (815) 432-6161
- Participates on county recycling committee

Seaway Food Town, Maumee, OH (419) 891-4223
- Community, cooking oil, fleet oil, bag recycling
- Environmental advertising
- Recycled advertising pages

Scrivner, Oklahoma City, OK (405) 841-4295
- Office, community recycling
- Recycles shrink wrap, oil, batteries, photographic silver
- Environmental task force, education, advertising
- Private-label recycled products

Shaw's Supermarkets, East Bridgewater, MA
(508) 378-7211
- Office, community recycling
- Recycles shrink wrap, oil, batteries
- Environmental task force, education, advertising
- Private-label recycled products

Shop 'N Save, Greensburg, PA (412) 836-8707
- Donated 100,000 trees
- Bag reuse credit program, recycling
- Uses recycled paper in flyers
- Private-label recycled products

Shoprite Supermarkets, Edison, NJ (908) 417-0850
- Environmental brochure, gasoline-saving program
- Bag reuse credit program (2 cents)
- Environmental advertising, education
- Reusable shopping bags

Spartan Stores, Grand Rapids, MI (616) 878-2000
- Community, office, bag, battery, oil, printing recycling
- Energy conservation, education programs
- Solid waste/recycling task force
- Community speakers, publications

Star Market (American), Cambridge, MA (617) 661-2310
- Office, bag recycling
- Packaging reduction program
- Flyers printed on recycled paper
- Environmental committee, brochures, advertisements

Supermarkets General (Pathmark), Woodbridge, NJ
(908) 499-3500
- Private-label recycled paper products
- Office recycling

Super Valu Stores/Stop N' Shop, Minneapolis, MN
(612) 828-4000
- Office, community recycling
- Private-label recycled products
- Environmental task force, education
- Recycles batteries, oil, scrap metal

Tops Markets, Buffalo, NY (716) 827-3271
- Office, community recycling
- Private-label recycled products
- Reusable shopping bags
- Environmental task force, advertising, tours

Von's Stores (Pavilions, Tianguis, Williams Bros.),
Los Angeles, CA (818) 821-7290
- Office, community, bag, CFC, battery, oil, scrap recycling
- Energy conservation, noise pollution, alternative fuels
- Environmental education, recovery programs, tours
- Hazardous materials clean-up team

Wakefern Food, Elizabeth, NJ (908) 527-7742
- Office, community recycling
- Shrink wrap, oil, battery, scrap, photographic-silver recycling

- Composts organic waste
- Bag rebate program

Wal-Mart, Bentonville, AR (501) 273-4000

- Recycling programs
- Environmental education, information
- Will build a "green" store

Wegmans Food Markets, Rochester, NY (716) 328-2550

- Environmental education, fund-raising, advertising
- Office, community, oil, shrink wrap recycling
- Private-label recycled products
- Environmental task force

Wettereau, Hazelwood, MO (314) 524-5000

- "Earthcare" infomercials, environmental education
- Community, bag recycling
- Green labeling program

Winn-Dixie, Jacksonville, FL (904) 783-5000

- Office recycling
- Alternative fuel fleet, energy conservation
- Tree-planting program
- Recycled egg cartons

Part 7

HOW TO RATE AND SUPPORT COMPANIES THAT PRACTICE SUSTAINABILITY

Chapter 19

The Power Behind Your Purchase

Nothing is more powerful than an individual acting out of conscience, thus helping to bring the collective conscience to life.—Norman Cousins

I keep arguing with my "green" printer Richard Gould over the state of the environment. I insist it's getting better because millions more people worldwide are getting involved in environmental issues. He counters that there's no way it's getting better simply due to explosive population growth. Too many people, too few resources. The earth gets the short end of the stick. While Richard and I are confident we're doing our part (his Sunshine Printing, in Highland Park, Illinois, uses soy-based ink, natural solvents, and recycled paper), neither of us is so sure about the 5 billion others procreating on the planet. At times I almost feel that environmental concerns are "somebody else's problems."

Our ongoing "debate" brings to mind some very good reasons why we can't buy our way out of our environmental problems at the supermarket. The first reason is simple: There are too many people involved. Every twenty-four hours, enough people are added to the earth to fill a city the size of Newark or Akron, according to the group Zero Population Growth. I'm not going to invoke the litany of guilt depicting starvation in the Third World, so think of two words: *resources* and *sustainability*. These words are critical to the survival of the human race. Here's how you fit in.

As with all societies, there are saints and sinners, but most people are in the middle, deciding where they want to go. You can have an impact on their direction in improving the planet. But first you need to understand your motivation for doing so. We all want to do our fair share. We Western consumers, however, are doing our *unfair* share. The bottom line is that we consume more than our share in pursuit of consumption itself. We pay a price for convenience, although most of us don't know what that means—or how we can change the balance in favor of the rest of the planet.

Although you may not catch even a glimmer of the crisis as you shop, you should know that Americans consume eleven times the world's average in energy, six times the steel, and four times the grain. Despite our Dionysian consumption, the United States represents only 5 percent of the world's population. Is that a fair share? What are the resources being used for? Consumer products, the bedrock of two-thirds of our economy. Everything from gasoline to groceries consumes energy and natural resources. It's one of the curses of prosperity. Even our love affair with beef has a steep price. According to the Beyond Beef Campaign, some 1.3 billion cattle are emitting some 60 million tons of global-warming methane gas and causing the burning and desertification of rain forests, where at least one-half of the earth's plant and animal species lives. While it's hard to tell if not eating a hamburger will help the planet, it's important to realize that this type of consumption is linked with a resource gluttony that characterizes our high standard of living. Although most of us don't feel wealthy, our standard of living is vastly higher than that of most developing countries.

Consider Mexico City, with 22 million people (and climbing), the world's most populous city. For all of its considerable resources, nearly 40 percent of the city lives in slums with substandard sewage treatment, pollution control, and utilities. Of course, if you wanted to look at the whole picture, you'd have to consider China's 1.1 billion-plus people, India's more than 900,000 people, and the masses of Africa, Asia, and Eastern Europe, who are starving for their share of natural resources and consumer products. Do these people have two cars, a refrigerator, and a stove per family? What if they did? This snapshot of humanity is not meant to elicit guilt but a sense of awareness. People, no matter where they live, consume resources and pollute. It's a fact of life. With world population expected to hit 6 billion by 1997 (there were only 2 billion folks in 1927), the most powerful industrial nations must set an example for the developing ones. There's plenty of opportunity for you to do your part.

According to author and futurist Robert Theobald, your decisions in the marketplace are more powerful than a vote. As he states in his recent book *Turning the Century: Personal and Organizational Strategies for Your Changed World* (Knowledge Systems, 1992): "Our consumption decisions are 'votes' about the future of ourselves and our society. If we perceived our purchases in this way, we would be far more careful about our choices."

Because you have economic power every time you step into a store, it extends beyond your hometown. The products you choose are made by international corporations run by people just like you. Executives and directors of these companies must spend some time in the supermarket sometime in their lives. They may not care much about the planet or the other people on it as you do, but they face the same reality.

So you may be thinking the same thing as a director of Procter & Gamble or the Queen of England. We all have to live on this planet. We all have to eat.

Consider the positive social change that has come about because consumers decided to become "revivers."

- We demanded foods with lower fat, salt, and cholesterol so that we could give our circulatory systems a break and live longer.
- We demanded (and were willing to pay for) safer cars and got airbags, antilock brakes, computer-controlled traction, and side-impact protection. What were once bitterly fought by the auto industry as unnecessary costs are moving from options to standard equipment.
- We demanded and received comprehensive laws on energy-saving appliances, pollution, and community toxic disclosure. What's next? A complete system that supports energy and resource conservation, sustainability, recycling, and waste reduction. Who's going to do this? We are, through the government and the industries that serve your best interests.

Choosing a company that thinks like you do is like preparing a grocery list. First, you determine your staple needs for the week (milk, sugar, coffee, etc.). Then you move on to any special ingredients for recipes. After you've prepared your list, you ask other household members what they'd like. Then you're off to the store.

As we've discussed, two of the staple needs for the planet are sustainability and resource conservation. These terms are intimately linked. Sustainability means efficient use of resources such as water, forests, air, energy, etc. Instead of chopping down trees that can't be replaced, tree farms are re-planted and as much paper is recycled as possible. Instead of using as much fossil fuel as possible, manufacturers retrofit their plants to save energy and use less raw material. Of course, you're not likely to find any of this on the side of a cereal box or on a bread wrapper. Like a grocery list, you need to be organized and know what you want, or you'll waste a lot of time.

If a manufacturer's product does not promote sustainabil-ity and causes irreparable damage to the planet, it hurts your life and home as well. It pays to tell a company that (1) you endorse what they do by buying their products, and that (2) they can still improve.

A COMPANY IS WHAT IT DOES, NOT WHAT IT SAYS

If we had a nickel for each word of bluster generated by multinational corporations over their environmental commit-ment, we'd have enough money to start our own multina-tional concern. So, we place a lot more stock in what a company does than in what it says. In most cases, companies pump up their public relations to the point that whatever they originally wanted to say about their environmental activities is obscured by how loudly and often they get their message out.

What a company does in its factories and offices is far more important than what it spends on media campaigns, public television sponsorship, and the usual spate of environ-mental-group handouts. In other words, any company can promote itself or write big checks. Few companies, however, put their money where it can do the most good.

For example, for the last two years, SC Johnson & Son—makers of Raid, Glade, Pledge, and dozens of other household products—commissioned high-profile polls with the Roper Organization on environmental attitudes. While the surveys were first-rate, it's more important to look at what SC Johnson as a company is doing to make its products and operations more environmentally sound. Since the company is privately held, there were no annual reports or SEC documents to inspect. For all of its environmental "image making," no one at SC Johnson's consumer hotline could tell us what the company was doing to make its products more environmentally sound. All they could tell us was that some aerosols didn't contain CFCs. That's hardly a bold claim. Some 98 percent of aerosol products don't contain CFCs, as they were largely banned by the government in 1978. We wanted to know what the company was doing to make Raid less toxic or to improve packaging on its expanding line of products. Johnson bought the Drackett company—makers of Windex and other cleaning products—late in 1992 for more than $1 billion. Ironically, we were able to obtain more information from Drackett than from Johnson. We also called and wrote to Johnson's headquarters in Racine, Wisconsin, several times, thinking that their "worldwide environmental center" would give us a response. We had reason to believe that such information was forthcoming since Johnson is a subscriber to our *Conscious Consumer* newsletter. No information was given, however.

Johnson isn't alone in its clouded image making. Several companies that have spent millions on positive green public relations came up short where it counts. Mobil, a $63 billion corporation, produces top-drawer brochures and literature trumpeting that "our commitment to a cleaner and safer environment dates back to 1956, when we adopted our first formal policies and initiatives." After we waded through their glossy "Target: Environmental Excellence" report, we asked two simple questions: Do your Hefty trash bags contain any recycled plastic, and do your polystyrene products contain any postconsumer recycled product (they did contain some preconsumer content or plant waste)? The answer was no, although Mobil is a dominant player in making plastic shopping bags and polystyrene foam containers. Mobil even owns a subsidiary called Tucker Housewares, which makes plastic garbage cans. How many of Tucker's products contain recycled material? One. Is Mobil typical of other producers of garbage bags and plastics? Hardly. We counted no fewer than five other companies that have lines of recycled garbage bags. One tiny company (Webster Industries) even has a line of 100 percent recycled bags. Why doesn't Mobil? We asked a Mobil representative that question. The reply was, "We can't get enough recycled product for our volume." Just think if Mobil *could* make all of its garbage bags from recycled plastic. Recycling centers would be hustling every supermarket customer for every neglected bag and discarded milk bottle and scavenge for every scrap of shrink wrap.

Once a company's management decides that environmental concerns can be part of its business, it can appeal to consumers and shareholders. Rubbermaid, a $1.6 billion company based in Wooster, Ohio, offers dozens of recycled plastic products and allows outside auditors to check its plants for environmental problems. Rubbermaid does not produce a full report on its environmental commitment, but we could see in the supermarket how it was acting on whatever environmental policy it has in a way that can be measured by everyone from plant managers to supermarket shoppers. That's closer to our definition of a true environmental management program. We were pleased to note that Rubbermaid has posted record sales for forty straight years and averages a new product introduction every day of the year. More important, the company is developing its products with a strict environmental focus. To quote from their 1991 annual report: "Environmental trends have also created commercial opportunities . . . Our plastic recycling efforts will grow significantly as the infrastructure expands to collect, sort, and reprocess postconsumer plastics."

To a large degree, environmental management comes from the highest level of management and works its way down. In our survey of companies' environmental policies, we noted that when there wasn't an environmental management committee, or an executive charged with leading an environmental program or companywide effort, the company didn't pay enough attention to environmental issues. Surprisingly, some large corporations that we expected to have extensive environmental operations either didn't report them or weren't doing much at all. Since we didn't have access to company records or facilities, we had no way of telling.

American Home Products, a $7 billion concern that produces famous brands such as Chef Boyardee, Jiffy Pop, Chap Stick, Dristan, Robitussin, and Anacin, sent us a four-page brochure that told us little. It was boilerplate language that essentially meant that they were interested in complying with all environmental laws. When we checked their 1991 "10-K" report (for information not always given in the annual report), we discovered that the company was facing an $8.2 million fine in the state of New York for "alleged unlawful air emissions" and was "involved in various antitrust suits and investigations relating to its marketing and sale of infant formula." Although the company devoted no fewer than five pages to describing its leadership in dozens of consumer products, we couldn't find one paragraph in the report about the company's ongoing environmental management.

Conversely, Dow, 3M, and Scott Paper had detailed explanations of plant-by-plant improvements in operations. It was clear that these companies had brought their environmental policies into their management and operations. That means devising programs, getting people involved, investing money—and making them work. For example, Dow explained in a special annual report how it spent some "$12 million in 47 waste reduction projects over the last two years, with another 53 projects costing $4 million slated for 1990." Although all these companies are major polluters—and are under pressure to clean up their operations—they are making the projects "pay for themselves"—that is, they're saving money and boosting their profits. That's going to be the "invisible hand" that makes corporate environmentalism successful. The more honest companies are about the process of cleaning up and saving money, the better off we'll be in the supermarket. Less waste in the factory can often translate into less waste in transportation, packaging, and disposal. It's a life cycle that we have to understand if we are to judge fairly what companies are doing and what we should buy in voting for the more responsible producers. More important, we need to restore a balance so that what we consume doesn't overwhelm our environment. Then the planet can begin to restore the very harmony that perpetuates life. In Montaigne's words, "Let us permit nature to have her way; she understands her business better than we do."

Chapter 20

Rating the Companies

Over the past twenty years, there's been phenomenal growth in services that rate companies on their social responsibility, environmental records, and community concerns. Most of that growth is due to the maturing of American culture. The seeds were planted by visionaries like Thomas Jefferson, who believed in prudent farming, a near-vegetarian diet, and the importance of preserving the land and individual freedom. In the nineteenth century, the writings of New England authors Herman Melville, Ralph Waldo Emerson, and Henry David Thoreau appealed to our spiritual quest and our troubled relationship to the planet. In this century, we've wedded the civil rights and environmental movements. Witness the work of Rachel Carson, Wendell Berry, Denis Hayes, Gaylord Nelson, and so many others. We're now examining our "environmental rights." As with all the previous struggles, the greatest battle resides in our hearts and minds. We need to change our attitudes.

It's a quirk of human nature that attitude adjustment can begin with a single person. Look at the work of Martin Luther King, Jr., and you'll get some idea of what one person's words and deeds can mean to people all over the planet. The same reasoning applies when we rate company attitudes. It's important that chief executives listen to their customers. It's even more important that they listen to their children and grandchildren, who will be running the companies (and the planet) soon. It was children who first refused to eat tuna harvested with drift nets that killed dolphins. Under this pressure, multibillion-dollar concerns refused to buy tuna caught in that manner—and advertised that fact.

Never before have individuals expressed their support for responsible corporate environmental behavior on such a scale. In addition to buying environmentally sound products and funding environmental programs and groups, they are investing in companies they believe are environmentally sound. Their concern for the environment in the form of socially responsible investing (SRI) has become a mainstream phenomenon as educated baby boomers are maturing and bringing their principles and social awareness to the marketplace. In 1984, some $40 billion was invested according to socially responsible principles. In 1992, an estimated $650 billion was invested in this way, according to the Social Investment Forum.

THE CERES PRINCIPLES

The SRI movement begat the CERES principles, originally named the Valdez principles. These principles raised corporate accountability to a higher plateau. When the Exxon *Valdez* supertanker ran into a reef and spewed 11 million gallons of oil into Alaska's pristine Prince William Sound in 1989, it impelled a wave of investor activism. The CERES principles crystallized what socially conscious investors had wanted to do for decades: make multinational corporations accountable for their actions. An acronym for Coalition of Environmentally Responsible Economies, CERES has some $150 billion in stockholdings. The group has gained great favor with environmental investors in a short period of time. For example, it attracted 9.5 percent, or 74 million shares, of the Exxon ownership. But the CERES principles are more than a pledge of loyalty to sound environmental management. They are the ideal for environmental operations.

CERES doesn't let any company off lightly. Accountability is stressed because all too often corporations can say one thing and do another. Witness the horde of companies advertising their environmental virtues in 1990 that were also major polluters. The main idea behind the principles is to get a written commitment to become a "responsible steward of the environment by operating in a manner that protects the earth." Here's a summary of the principles, which might help you in evaluating your supermarket chain and favorite brand-name manufacturers.

- **Protection of the biosphere.** We will safeguard all habitats affected by our operations and will protect open spaces and wilderness, while preserving biodiversity.
- **Sustainable use of natural resources.** We will conserve nonrenewable resources through efficient use and careful planning.
- **Reduction and disposal of wastes.** We will reduce and where possible eliminate waste through source reduction and recycling.
- **Energy conservation.** We will conserve energy and improve the energy efficiency of our internal operations and of the goods and services we sell.
- **Risk reduction.** We will strive to minimize the environ-

mental, health, and safety risks to our employees and the communities in which we operate . . .

• **Safe products and services.** We will reduce and where possible eliminate the use, manufacture, or sale of products and services that cause environmental damage. . . . We will inform our customers of the environmental impacts of our products or services. . . .

• **Environmental restoration.** We will promptly and responsibly correct conditions we have caused that endanger health, safety, or the environment. . . .

• **Informing the public.** We will inform in a timely manner everyone who may be affected by conditions caused by our company that might endanger health, safety, or the environment. . . .

• **Management commitment.** We will implement these Principles and sustain a process that ensures that the Board of Directors and Chief Executive Officer are fully informed about pertinent environmental issues and are fully responsible for environmental policy. . . .

• **Audits and reports.** We will conduct an annual self-evaluation of our progress in implementing these Principles . . . which will be made available to the public.

As noble as the principles sound, they are a little daunting for most major corporations. Only one Fortune 500 company has signed on to the principles—the Sun Companies (a petrochemical concern). Most have shied away perhaps for the very reason the principles were established: accountability. For most manufacturers with international industrial complexes, the environmental restoration and audit clauses are difficult to attain. In other words, you can't stop a plant from polluting overnight. It happens over several years with an infusion of millions of dollars and the right technology. Despite this problem with the CERES goals, there's no reason why a company shouldn't aspire to them or embark on the ideal of becoming a responsible environmental citizen. Many companies have done so for a number of reasons, but not primarily for the sake of the planet. In our company survey, only Ben & Jerry's Homemade was among the CERES signatories.

As companies become better environmental citizens, they discover something remarkable. Sound environmental policy makes them more profitable. If they pollute less, they're subject to fewer fines and waste less raw materials and by-products. If they use less packaging, they lower the cost of the product and boost its profitability. If they reduce the amount of materials needed to make a product, the same result is achieved.

For example, one the nation's biggest polluters is the 3M Corporation, makers of Scotch Tape and thousands of other products. The company is held up as a model of corporate environmentalism because of its Pollution Prevention Pays program, which has saved the company some $482 million since 1975 and eliminated some 500,000 tons of waste. Dow Chemical, the makers of Spray n' Wash, installed a $250,000 device to reduce water pollution and saved $2.4 million a year—and reused materials. Other companies didn't fare as well and will need decades to clean up their act. American Cyanamid, which produces vitamins, drugs, and agricultural chemicals, is one of the nation's biggest polluters. It not only has to clean up seventy Superfund toxic waste sites, it's spent $64 million on pollution control (in 1992) alone. Cyanamid has been operating several highly polluting businesses that produce chemicals that make drugs and modern agriculture possible, and it will be years before "clean" ways of producing these chemicals are discovered. So, it's a bit unfair to expect this company and others like it to clean up their acts overnight or to believe that we don't indirectly support what they're doing by buying agricultural products grown with the use of pesticides. Nevertheless, there's a lot of work to be done and we expect these companies to lead the way.

Today, meaningful activity on the corporate level is stronger than ever. A group called the Buy Recycled Business Alliance said it had bought $2.7 billion worth of recycled products in 1991. The twenty-five-member group, led by companies such as Sears, McDonald's, and Bank of America, hopes to add five thousand more member businesses in the next two years.

Environmentalism makes sense for capitalism. Not surprisingly, the best environmental companies are also the most profitable. In a survey conducted by Chicago-based Covenant Investment Management, the 200 companies demonstrating the most corporate responsibility (on the environment and other social issues) consistently outperformed the other companies among the 1,000 largest corporations in terms of total returns to shareholders.

Much work needs to be done. The U.S. Office of Technology Assessment estimates that companies can cut manufacturing waste in half with existing technologies and pare another 25 percent through new technology. Dr. Amory Lovins, the energy savings savant behind the Rocky Mountain Institute, foresees creating an "industrial ecosystem" that emphasizes clean production and reuse of by-products. That should be every company's goal for the future. With more and more informed investors, there are more demands placed on companies besides stock performance.

The Boston-based Domini Social Index Trust, for example, screens companies that not only have good financial prospects but run environmentally clean operations, have good relations with employees, and don't invest in South Africa or in nuclear arms production. This mutual fund is but one of more than a dozen that cater to investors who want "clean and green" companies. This growing movement represents what social thinkers call a "paradigm shift." In other words, people in large numbers are beginning to think and act in a different way, entirely on their own. They are putting individual conscience above the traditional rules of investment that suggest that profit is king. The new thinking suggests that profit must be accompanied by sustainability and social responsibility.

When you buy companies' products, you're underwriting their efforts—good or bad. They cannot exist without your purchases. Remember what happened to the Studebaker and Tucker Motor companies when the public turned away from them. We live in complex times where you can't look at one aspect of a company and judge the whole. You have to consider a number of factors on your green grocery list before you make a buying decision.

CORPORATIONS AS HYDRAS

Remember the Hydra, the many-headed beast from Greek mythology? That's what modern corporations are like. They have operations all over the world. Some facilities may operate responsibly in Third World countries; others may have marketing practices that cause more harm than good in developing countries. Witness the seventeen-year worldwide movement against producers of infant formula. While at first that may sound like a massive altruistic gesture, it's not when you look beyond the public relations releases. Man-made formula, when mixed with local water, carries germs that cause diarrhea, a major killer of children in poor nations. Several social activist groups led by the Interfaith Center on Corporate Responsibility lobbied companies such as American Home Products, Nestlé, Gerber, Abbott Laboratories, and Bristol-Myers Squibb to stop the practice by the end of 1992. They organized an international boycott of these companies' products to affect the change. Eventually involving the World Health organization and Unicef, there's little doubt that the chorus of active consumers had some impact on this unethical corporate practice. Only Nestlé and American Home Products are targets of the boycott as this book goes to press, according to the activist group Action for Corporate Accountability.

SAVING MONEY:
COMPANIES THAT SEND OUT COUPONS

We received a pleasant surprise when we called several of the companies. Although we were requesting information on packaging, they sent us coupons for discounts or free samples of their products. We weren't looking to save money, but if you call these companies, chances are good that you'll receive coupons. Actually, we received the coupons through consumer hotlines, which were originally set up to handle product complaints. Keep in mind, though, that these coupon programs vary from time to time, so we can't guarantee that you'll receive them.

Betty Crocker (General Mills)
Burroughs Wellcome (Actifed)
Celestial Seasonings (teas)
Colgate-Palmolive (Ajax, Fab)

Dial soaps (detergents)
Dial Foods
Diet Pepsi
EarthRite (Benckiser)
General Electric (Energy Choice light bulbs)
Hershey's (chocolate products, Reese's)
Jergens Soap Products (soaps and hand lotions)
Kimberly-Clark (Kleenex, Huggies, Kotex)
Kraft (cheeses, salad dressings)
Lipton Products (tea, soup)
M&M Mars (candies)
Miles Laboratories (SOS pads)
Pillsbury (baking products)
Reynolds
Smuckers Natural Peanut Butter
Vlasic (pickles, Open Pit)

Chapter 21

Action-Oriented
Company Communication

PHONE OR WRITE A LETTER

Tell the company what you'd like changed, what you approve of, and why you think it's important. If you represent a community, church, or environmental group, even better. There's power in numbers. You can write the chief executive of a company, but try the consumer affairs department first—they're more likely to respond. We had only one response to the dozens of letters that were sent out for our survey.

RESEARCH THE COMPANY

Unless a company is privately owned, there's a wealth of information available on it. First, call the company's customer service and shareholder relations department. Ask for all the information they have on environmental programs; community and charitable contributions; and internal programs to reduce waste and energy usage. Some documents you should request include: (1) annual and quarterly reports; (2) 10-K and 10-Q reports (these are filed with the Securities and Exchange

Commission and must reveal any environmental fines or lawsuits); (3) any literature from the consumer affairs department. You can also find company information in the library under Standard & Poor's, Value Line, and investment newsletters (see our resources section at the back of the book).

BUY THE COMPANY (OWN SHARES)

You need buy only one share to get the aforementioned information on a regular basis. More important, you can vote on some company policies (through proxy votes) and the board of directors and attend annual meetings. You also have a more direct route to the company. If you own enough shares, you can start a shareholder resolution designed to get the company to change a policy. Some 350 such resolutions were filed for 199 companies in 1991, according to the Interfaith Center on Corporate Responsibility (ICCR). And the number of proxy ballots is growing. There were only 150 filed in 1988. Subjects for the votes included everything from South Africa divestment to adoption of the MacBride Principles, which direct companies to adhere to fair employment practices in Northern Ireland. One of the top issues was the environment.

For the average American, green investing is a concept that has taken root in every store from Wal-Mart to your local supermarket. When you buy a food product, you're increasing the sales and profit of the manufacturer, wholesaler, and retailer. You're also indirectly endorsing what everyone up to the cashier has done to get it into your hands. If this network of companies has done well by the earth, you're supporting their overall efforts. If they've done poorly, your purchase has the same effect.

Ernest Callenbach, the author of *Ecotopia*, puts it simply.

He's observed that there's a "massive ecological campaign going on. It affects everybody. Now it affects corporate managers. They're all saying yes, we have children, too."

SAMPLE LETTER TO SEND TO COMPANIES

Company Name

Chief Executive Officer

Address

To Whom it May Concern:
I have several concerns about one or more of your products. As an environmental consumer, I would appreciate it if you would address this concern in the interest of keeping me as a customer and helping the earth. Please consider changing the following:

☐ Overpackaged product
☐ No recycled material used in packaging
☐ Unclear what environmental benefits product offers
☐ Packaging is *not* recyclable
☐ Your company's environmental record and management
☐ Lack of information on consumer hotlines
☐ Why you haven't signed CERES principles

Also please send me information on the company's efforts to help the environment through your operations and products.

Sincerely,

HOW HOTLINES EMPOWER YOU

Some $6 billion worth of toll-free calls were placed in 1992. No matter which company you talk to, one call can be an effective message. According to research done by Technical Assistance Research Programs (TARP) in Arlington, Virginia, a call from one person can represent 10,000 others who've had the same idea or problem. That's because most *don't* call companies when they have a complaint or question. TARP found that one of the best hotlines—General Electric—realized a 4-to-1 ratio with its hotline. This means that for every dollar GE spent on the hotline, it earned $4 in sales. In other words, the best hotlines are designed not as help lines but to retain customers and make sales.

Customer retention is a big money issue with companies that use hotlines as marketing tools. According to Performance Research Associates in Minneapolis, companies take their hotlines seriously because it "costs five times more to land a new customer than to keep an old one."

When we called more than 200 of the top consumer hotlines (in most cases we got the phone numbers from product labels) we placed a great value on the response we received. That's because if the company noted we weren't satisfied, that translated into lost business for them—multiplied by the 10,000 other dissatisfied consumers who didn't bother to call. That's why consumer hotlines are an indirect form of empowerment and a vital direct link to a company to tell them what *you* want to change or to know about a product.

The hotline response was so critical that we reduced a company's overall EFACT rating if (1) we had to call more than four times because of a busy signal; (2) were transferred or were put on hold for more than twenty seconds; (3) the specialist had no information or was rude.

There's a connection between how carefully a company listens to its customers and its market share. The best companies take note of what their customers want. And they'll listen to new ideas. Following is a summary of what we found.

THE BEST HOTLINES

Colgate-Palmolive

Informative and accessible, they sent out a well-designed brochure that outlined environmental packaging changes.

Procter & Gamble

Generous product information, multiple phone lines, separate hotlines for certain product groups. Information was received within 5 days of a call. They called back on specific questions.

Kellogg

Their long hours were convenient for after-work callers, although their brochures were lacking in environmental information.

General Electric

Fast, courteous, complete, and well-informed. Surely one of the models for other hotline operations, although their environmental information (and record) is lacking.

Eastman Kodak

The response we received was excellent. Not only did we get two calls back, an environmental affairs executive called us back to follow up. Unfortunately, Kodak's L&F Products (Lysol) hotline had little or no information. Almost all of the information we received was from the Kodak hotline.

Scott Paper

We called them several times. They were consistent and detailed.

Dole Foods

One of the best food company hotlines, they provided detailed information.

DuPont

Although you can certainly take issue with the company's environmental record, their specialists are unusually well-trained to answer information on specific chemicals and subjects.

SC Johnson

While they had a generous amount of product information, they provided little in the way of environmental background. Among the friendliest and most helpful hotlines, though. They called back.

Kraft General Foods

Their specialists were well trained and provided extensive environmental information. Coupons also provided.

THE WORST HOTLINES

These hotlines were nearly always busy, even though we called at least five times at different times of the day. When we did get through, we received little or no information.

Too Busy, Little Information

Bristol-Myers Squibb (Clairol)
Campbell Soup
Chesebrough-Pond's/Unilever
Colgate-Palmolive
Bob Evans Farms: lots of transfers, snippiness
Gerber Products
Mobil: many transfers, little product information, rudeness
Ralston-Purina: little information, always busy

Of course, we realize that many companies don't tell the public everything they're doing on the environmental front, especially on a consumer hotline. It's simply not possible. Nearly every company is attempting to reduce waste on every level as a matter of reducing operating expenses. As I mentioned earlier, the less companies waste and pollute, the more profitable they become. Our first concern, however, was what companies told us as consumers (or revivers). We didn't consider it a positive sign if there was little information forthcoming when we made every effort to ask the company.

HOW YOU ARE MAKING A DIFFERENCE

Your voice is being heard. Under the watchful eye of thousands of grass roots groups, corporate environmental behavior is being monitored as never before. Are they having an impact? Consider the movement to limit the killing of African elephants for ivory. Prior to 1990, it was open season on elephants. The African elephant population dwindled from about 3 million twenty years ago to just 625,000 today. With the push from citizens worldwide, not only did former President Bush sign a presidential order banning the importation of elephant ivory, but Steinway & Sons is asking pianists to forgo real ivory keys on its pianos, and top New York designers and retailers such as Liz Claiborne and Macy's have stopped selling it altogether. All this in the space of one year.

Among manufacturers, Ben & Jerry's Homemade is part of a growing cadre of companies that set aside profits for socially responsible investment. The Patagonia Equipment company follows suit. The firm sells outdoor gear, so it's a natural for them to appeal to people who are environmentally sensitive themselves. These companies' owners and customers want to serve humanity—and make some money in the process. Capitalism can be a force for good.

Part 8

THE FUTURE

Chapter 22

How Products Can Become Greener

If you were going to bake a cake, you'd need to know the ingredients, proportions, and preparation and baking times. In effect, you're manufacturing something using raw materials and a proven formula. After it pops out of the oven and you give it a chance to cool off, you consume it. Apply this thinking to any product you buy and imagine what's to be done with the packaging, the air and water pollution created in the manufacturing, and the wasted raw materials. If we could digest every part of the manufacturing process that wastes resources, we'd be a lot better off. But we can't, so we need to consider what it's doing to the earth.

Using life-cycle analysis (LCA), we can get a better picture of the "care baking process" of nearly every product. Eventually, everyone shopping in the supermarket will be able to determine if one product is better than another in terms of pollution created, packaging, disposability/recyclability, and reuse. At present, we can only make some conclusions on packaging waste and the company's overall environmental record, but the future holds so much. For example, we'll be able to tell what kind of trees were used and if they were grown in a sustainable way—that is, grown on farms specifically for low-grade-paper production, as is the case with most paper production now.

To get an example of what this life-cycle label would look like, we asked Scientific Certification Systems (SCS) to prepare a comparison of a "virgin" bath tissue package (12 rolls, 300 sheets per roll) with a similar-sized 100 percent recycled-paper product. For the purpose of this comparison, we used Tree-Free (Statler) bath tissue and a conventional tissue. Tree-Free was chosen because SCS had conducted research in Statler's mills to obtain information on how their process worked. SCS had already certified that the product had recycled content. The comparison shows how much this recycled paper saves in terms of resources, energy, and pollution over a lifetime use (seventy years) over the virgin product. The comparison is one of the best arguments to date for using recycled products. Read the chart carefully to see why.

Recycled Bath Tissue vs. Virgin Tissue: A Green Choice

Environmental Burdens	100% Recycled Tissue	Virgin
Wood used	3,192 gallons	19,320 gallons
Wood consumed	1 lb.	4,745 lbs.
Coal, oil, nat. gas	220 lbs.	925 lbs.
Other minerals	61 lbs.	109 lbs.
Total energy used	31 million BTUs	84 MBTUs
Energy content of materials (energy released when burned)	12 million BTUs	18 MBTUs

Carbon dioxide produced	4,808 lbs.	12,442 lbs.
Carbon monoxide	6 lbs.	14 lbs.
Sulfur oxides	65 lbs.	185 lbs.
Nitrogen oxides	26 lbs.	64 lbs.
Particulates	8 lbs.	25 lbs.
Hazardous air pollutants	6 lbs.	14 lbs.
Unclassified air emissions	6 lbs.	15 lbs.
Total solids (water pollutants)	9.9 lbs.	38 lbs.
Oxygen-depleting chemicals	13.0 lbs.	3 lbs.
Toxic pollutants	0.1 lbs.	0.6 lbs.
Unclassified water emissions	0.9 lbs.	2.9 lbs.
Product/packaging waste	0.61 cubic feet	84 cu. ft
Hazardous solid waste	1 lb.	3 lb.
Unclassified waste	986 lbs.	623 lbs.

Source: Scientific Certification Systems certification program

THE MIXED BAG OF GREEN PRODUCTS

As the bath-tissue chart shows, in most pollution categories, the earth is much better off with a recycled product. Not only does the recycled product use less water, energy, natural resources, and fossil fuels, it produces less pollution from production to disposal (assuming that packaging is made of recycled material and is recyclable). But this picture is not quite perfect. You'll notice that the recycled product has high levels of oxygen-depleting chemicals (which suffocate aquatic wildlife) and "unclassified waste" (clays and heavy metals found in coated paper that's recycled). Tree-Free also uses 100 percent recycled paper packaging and no wooden pallets. Their operation is so clean that it won an award from the EPA. Their plant is atypical, however. Even in recycling plants, no two are alike. Some are dirtier than others.

Dr. Stanley Rhodes, president of SCS, notes that there are some pollutants that are by-products of paper-recycling plants, which are "still deplorable in terms of water pollution." The plants spew cellulose (a component of wood) fibers into water systems, harming aquatic life. When SCS informed the Statler paper company of this problem, the company said it would install filters at their plants to reduce the pollutants. As for the unclassified wastes, that's something that recycling technology needs to address. Even though the recycling process is generally beneficial to the earth, it's not pollution-free. No manufacturing process is. However, technology continues to create new ways to recover manufacturing wastes. And as we become more aware of the processes behind what we buy, we can help to bring about even greater change.

LIFE-CYCLE ANALYSIS

There's a hidden cost involved in nearly everything we buy. Most manufactured items use up water, deplete nonrenewable resources such as petroleum, and pollute the air and water. The more processed the product, the more resources it uses. When you buy these products, you're contributing to the overall scheme of depletion, pollution, and waste.

The precise environmental impact of each product is difficult to measure because the science of doing so—life-cycle analysis (LCA)—is still developing standards and measurements. The Environmental Protection Agency (EPA) has approved the use of life-cycle analysis to measure specific environmental burdens of products, so it may be only a short time before this science can tell you how each purchase impacts the earth. International research is continuing on this important new topic.

Life-cycle analysis from just one item can be very complex. For example, consider what's involved in just making paper packaging. Paper mills spew pollutants into the environment in volumes most of us can't comprehend. Other chemicals, including cancer-causing dioxins, are released into our waterways. Greenpeace has warned that the very process of bleaching paper (paper's natural color is cardboard brown) with chlorine compounds creates the dioxins and a host of other water-pollution problems. That's why you'll see "unbleached" or "chlorine-free" paper products on the shelf. While the chemistry of the process is being hotly debated, you need to be aware of how manufacturing processes harm the earth.

Chapter 23

The Progress Report

Ironically, what will make products more recyclable is the financial success of recycling. As industries demand more cheap recycled supply, the value of collecting it will climb. William Rucklehaus, a former EPA chief and president of Browning Ferris Industries (the second-largest U.S. waste disposal firm), notes: "If recycling is to be a permanent part of our society, then it has to be economically sustainable. It also has to be meaningful and show a measurable benefit before it's mandated by government."

Companies can make a difference in the meantime. They can and are reducing the amount of packaging they use.

GREEN CHOICES:
DRINKS PACKAGED IN ALUMINUM (THE RECYCLING CHAMP)

A&W Brands: A&W root beer, Diet A&W, Squirt, Diet Squirt, cream soda

Barq's Root Beer

Cadbury-Schweppes/Canada Dry: ginger ale, 50/50, lemon-ade

Canfield's: ginger ale, diet chocolate fudge, Swiss Creme soda, seltzers

Coca-Cola: Coke Classic, Coke II, Diet Coke, Cherry Coke, Sprite, Fresca, caffeine-free varieties, Tab

Diet Rite colas

Hires Root Beer

Lipton Iced Tea, Diet Iced Tea

Nestea, Diet Nestea

Orange Crush, Grape Crush

Pepsico: Pepsi-Cola, Diet Pepsi, Slice, Diet Slice, Orange Slice

Procter & Gamble: Hawaiian Punch, Passion Fruit

Seagram's beverages

7-Up, Dr Pepper, Diet 7-Up, Diet Dr Pepper, Cherry 7-Up, Diet Cherry 7-Up, Mountain Dew, Diet Mountain Dew

Sunkist beverages

Tetley Teas

PRODUCTS IN STEEL CANS
(MAY CONTAIN UP TO 35% RECYCLED CONTENT)

Amore	Boston tea
Antolina artichoke hearts	Boyers
Antolina tomato sauces	Brandywine mushrooms
Argo sweet peas	Brim
Armour chili	Brown Gold
Band-Aids	Bumble Bee tunas
Baxter's clam chowder	Bumble Bee pink salmon
Benchley Teas	Bush beans
Bertolli olive oil	Cadillac
Bookbinder's soups	Campbell's chili
Borden's Egg Nog	Campbell's pork and beans

Campbell's soups

Campbell's tomato juice

Canada Dry sodas

Carnation evaporated milk

Carnation Follow-up formula

Castleberry's corned beef hash

Castleberry's hot dog chili
  sauce

Cento

Chase & Sanborn

Chef Boyardee products

Chicken of the Sea tunas

Chicken of the Sea salmon

Chock Full O'Nuts

Coca-Cola

Colman's mustard

College Inn broths

Contadina

Curity adhesive strips

Dad's

Del Monte

Del Monte fruits

Del Grosso pizza sauce

Del Monte sardines

Dinty Moore beef stew

Dockside clam chowder

Dole fruits

Durkee spices

Ensure Plus

El Rio nacho cheese sauce

Featherweight apple-
  sauce/fruits

Folgers

Food Club

Food Club applesauce/fruits

Food Club juices

Food Club pie fillings

Food Club pork and beans

Food Club salmon

Food Club spices

Franco-American products

Gaines

Geisha clams

Geisha oysters

Geisha shrimp

General Foods International
  coffees

Gerber formula

Grand Gourmet

Green Tree holland ham

Good Start

Harris crab meat

Heinz pork and beans

Hi-C

Hills Brothers

Hollywood carrot juice

Hormel chili

Hormel salmon

Hormel chunk white turkey

Hormel beef stew

Hunt's

Hunt's Manwich

Isomil

Juicy Juice

Ken-L-Ration

Kraft green beans

La Choy bamboo shoots
La Choy bean sprouts
La Choy water chestnuts
Libby's fruits
Libby's juices
Libby's vegetables
Luck's beans
Lucky Leaf apple juice
Lucky Leaf pie fillings
Luzianne
Mancini peppers
Martinson
Maxwell House
McCormick spices
Mead Johnson Enfamil
Medaglia D'Oro
Mega
Mega pork and beans
Musselman's apple sauces
Musselman's orange apricot
    juice
New York Express
Nursoy
Ocean Spray cranberry sauce
Old El Paso beans
Old El Paso green chilis
Oregon fruits
Ortega beans
Pennsylvania Dutchman
    mushrooms
Pepsi
Petclub
Prelate salmon

Progresso
Progresso beans/peas
Progresso soups
Progresso white clam sauce
Prosobee
Puss-n-Boots
Real Sportshake
Redpack
Reese bamboo shoots
Reese crab meat
Reese water chestnuts
Ro Tel
Rumford baking powder
Silver Floss sauerkraut
Similac
SMA
Starkist tunas
S&W sauerkraut sauce, V8
    vegetable juice
S&W Chili Makins
Swanson chicken
Thank You pie fillings
Thompson fruits
Three Diamonds tuna
Twinings tea
VanCamp's pork and beans
Vlasic black olives
Welch's grape juice
Wilson ham, Krakus ham
Whiskas
Weight Watchers soups
7-Up

Afterword

A Revivalist's Agenda

Submitted by the New Consumer Institute
To Further World Peace and Environmental Sustainability

> *Most see that our entire planet is becoming a single, global commons, since we all must share its atmosphere, oceans and electromagnetic spectrum*
> —*Hazel Henderson*, Paradigms in Progress
> *(Knowledge Systems, 1992)*

Great ideas must be borne with the seeds of compassion or they breed dissolution. Such a thought should be the theme of policymakers during the disarmament of the world's great industrial powers.

There is a great moral mandate upon us: Turn our swords into plowshares or tumble headlong into the path of global annihilation that was ushered in fifty years ago. As the empires of the former Soviet Union and the North American Treaty Alliance turned inward to heal mostly economic wounds, there is a precedent that history has never witnessed before. The powers of Europe, Asia, Africa, and the Americas have a political, economic, and spiritual need to unite in this quest.

It's as if the industrial nations of the world have wrestled with the Great White Whale of prosperity, depression, war, and rebirth enough times to know that the next great battle is for a common spiritual destiny—one that guarantees the survival of future generations on this planet. Exploding populations in developing countries and the excessive use of resources among developed countries are pushing the question to the fore. Population has grown 50 percent in the past fifty years alone. And with people come waste- and pollution-generating consumer goods such as autos, refrigerators, and convenience foods.

In 1990, there were 560 million autos on the planet, most of them in the richest nations. What will happen when India, China, and Indonesia attain a level of prosperity that allows even one car per household? Many scientists predict that the resulting carbon dioxide may make coastal regions uninhabitable, due to the greenhouse effect. China is already the third-largest CO_2 producer behind the United States and Russia. India is sixth behind Japan and Germany. But a focus on environmental degradation in developing countries is a polemic best avoided in policy discussions. It leads nowhere and misses the main point: There needs to be a worldwide infrastructure for environmental preservation and resource conversation. It can be financed partially through shifting the money that governments spend on defense.

The economist Hazel Henderson, who believes the world is entering a "Light Age" with respect to technology and forward-thinking philosophy, has long noted that shifting the economics of war into the economics of renewal has always made sense for governments. War, in essence, has been a forced transfer of raw materials. As Daniel Yergin, author of

The Prize, has illustrated in his research on the history of petropolitics, Hitler's drive east into the Soviet Union and the Imperial Japanese Army's thrust into Southeast Asia were quests for natural resources (mainly petroleum). And we need not look very far back in history to uncover similar examples, such as the Persian Gulf War.

Of the $1.475 trillion earmarked for the 1993 U.S. federal budget, $274 billion is set aside for the Department of Defense (DOD). Some $3.5 billion alone is being spent on foreign military aid and $4.1 billion on the Star Wars strategic defense initiative. To put these expenditures into perspective, consider that the cost of one Trident nuclear submarine would pay for immunization and basic health care for all of the needy children of the world. The cost of ten bombers would feed the 100 million people believed by the United Nations to be starving.

Defense funds can be rechanneled into an ambitious program of research and development for alleviating global hunger and for peaceful uses such as the following.

• **Redirect standing military forces to environmental projects.** The defense establishment of the United States has some of the world's greatest resources for global surveillance and technology development. The Pentagon's global "spy" satellite network may be employed to monitor regional and continental environmental maladies. Defense facilities have been part and parcel of environmental degradation, so it's reasonable to make them part of the solution.

• **Redirect defense funding to improve infrastructure.** Since the fall of the Berlin Wall, this has become a well-traveled idea. Global urban building and rebuilding are possible, however, if the United States alone invested 4 to 5 percent of

Gross Domestic Product on infrastructure development (up from 2 percent now).

• **Use military resources and budget to develop energy-efficient technologies.** The startling reality about this suggestion is that the infrastructure already exists. Changing military goals to civilian goals would be a matter of Congress rededicating the Department of Energy's (DOE) national laboratories, which were originally set up to perform nuclear defense and energy research. Becoming energy efficient would cut some $200 billion a year from America's energy bills, according to the Rocky Mountain Institute. Specific projects would include:

1. *Scrap and plastic recycling technologies.* There is currently no infrastructure in place to recycle most consumer nondurable items in the United States (and most other developed countries). Germany now has legislation to develop such an infrastructure. The United States should create one as well, using tax incentives and legislation. The system should favor consumer products that can be recycled and reused. We support Vice President Al Gore's proposal for a Strategic Environmental Initiative, which provides tax incentives for research into new environmental technologies. Energy consumption and product packaging and design should be emphasized in this program.

2. *Biomass processing and energy generation.* Landfills worldwide will not be able to keep up with population growth. Although the EPA set a goal of recycling 25 percent of solid municipal waste by 1992, the country managed to recycle only 17 percent. Nearly one-third of landfill waste by volume is simple yard waste. Defense research facilities could examine new technologies to make composting and biomass heat generation more efficient.

3. *Link military computing facilities into a national network for civilian research.* This "fiberoptic data highway" has been proposed by several technopolicy planners. Connecting the enormous computing power of the military establishment would create a colossus of computing resources for researchers in genetic mapping, biotechnology, population modeling, global warming studies, ozone depletion, rainfall projections, meteorological forecasting, cold/hot fusion energy, efficient desalinization, superconducting materials, solar energy, earthquake prediction, CFC alternatives, electric vehicles, aerogels, lasers, parallel computing, artificial intelligence, and sustainable agriculture.

4. *Redirect DOE and DOD funding, resources, and institutions to develop alternatives to petroleum-based products.* Since the end of World War II, the large industrial nations have become hostage to the supply, price, and politics of oil. When guarding and retaking countries that are major oil producers becomes a national security issue, there's a great incentive to use that same security apparatus to diminish the threat. Two-thirds of the United States' oil consumption is in the transportation sector, and cutting that figure through infrastructure improvements would accomplish a number of socially redeeming goals: (1) create jobs; (2) raise the standard of living; (3) improve the tax base (from the jobs created); (4) spur consumer-goods production and retailing; (5) reduce the U.S. trade deficit; (6) reduce the geopolitical conflicts fomented when oil reserves' security is threatened; (7) diminish the arms race for countries rearming themselves over petro-security issues; and (8) lower world interest rates. Of all the factors, the last point is most critical. The price of petroleum influences world interest rates because it's a key commodity figured in the cost of doing business across the globe. Reducing reliance on this commodity would reduce demand for it, thus lowering its price. That, in turn, would lower interest rates and create a pool for capital for public and private investment. It would also stem and diminish inflation, which ravages incomes and vastly increases government debts.

These are modest proposals that we submit to the world community, the United Nations, the U.S. Congress, and the president of the United States. If you think any of our ideas has merit, as we believe, please feel free to submit them to your congressional representative.

—John F. Wasik, Managing Director,
New Consumer Institute

Largest Manufacturers and Supermarket Chains

A&W Brands (A&W root beer, Squirt, Vernors)
709 Westchester Ave.
White Plains, NY 10604-3100
(914) 397-1700

Abbott Laboratories (Selsun Blue, Ross infant formulas)
1 Abbott Park Rd.
Abbott Park, IL 60064-3500
(800) 227-5767; (708) 937-6100

Alberto-Culver Co. (Alberto VO5, hair care products)
2525 Armitage Ave.
Melrose Park, IL 60160
(708) 450-3000

Albertson's (supermarket chain in western states)
250 Parkcenter Blvd.
Boise, ID 83726
(208) 385-6200

American Brands (tobacco products)
1700 E. Putnam Ave.
Old Greenwich, CT 06870
(203) 698-5000

American Cyanamid (Centrum vitamins)
1 Cynamid Plaza
Wayne, NJ 07470
(201) 831-2000

American Greetings (cards, stationery)
10500 American Rd.
Cleveland, OH 44144
(216) 252-7300

American Home Products (Chef Boyardee, Dimetapp,
    Dristan, Anacin, Advil, Promil, Robitussin, Chap Stick,
    Jiffy Pop, Pam, Denorex)
685 Third Ave.
New York, NY 10017
(212) 986-1000

American Stores (Lucky, Jewel, Osco supermarket chains)
PO Box 27447
Salt Lake City, UT 84127
(801) 539-0112; (800) 541-2863

American Tissue (paper products)
50 Cabot Court
Hauppauge, NY 11688
(516) 435-9000

Anheuser-Busch (Budweiser, Michelob, Bud Light, Eagle
    Snacks)
1 Busch Place
St. Louis, MO 63118
(314) 577-2000

Aquapore Moisture Systems (recycled rubber soaker hoses, systems)
610 S. 80th Ave.
Phoenix, AZ 85043
(602) 936-8083

Argon Industries (garbage bags)
1828 Oak St.
Torrance, CA 90501
(800) 678-2746; (310) 320-1454

Astro-Valcour (bubble packaging)
18 Peck Ave.
PO Box 148
Glens Falls, NY 12801
(518) 793-2524

Avery-Dennison (office products, Post-Lite, Jiffylite mailers)
1 Clark's Hill
Framingham, MA 01701
(800) 336-6476; (508) 879-0511

Bausch & Lomb (Clear Choice mouthwash, contact lens solutions)
1400 N. Goodman St.
Rochester, NY 14692
(800) 553-5340

Benckiser Consumer Products (EarthRite, Electrosol, Scrub-Free)
55 Federal Rd.
PO Box 1991
Danbury, CT 06813-1991
(800) 284-2023; (203) 731-5035

Ben & Jerry's Homemade (ice cream products)
PO Box 240
Waterbury, VT 05676
(802) 244-6957

Bic (disposable pens, shavers, and lighters)
Wiley St.
Milford, CT 06401
(203) 783-2000

Block Drug (Polident)
257 Cornelison Ave.
Jersey City, NJ 07302
(800) 365-6500; (201) 434-3000

Blue Coral (Clear Magic cleaning products)
5300 Harvard Ave.
Cleveland, OH 44105
(216) 641-5490

Borden (Elmer's Glue, Realemon, Cremora, Eagle Brand
  dairy products)
277 Park Ave.
New York, NY 10172
(212) 573-4000

Bristol-Myers Squibb/Mead Johnson (Clairol, Ban, Fresh n'
  Dry, Nuprin, Comtrex)
345 Park Ave.
New York, NY 10154
(800) 422-2902; (800) 468-7746; (800) 223-5800 (Clairol);
  (212) 546-4000

Brown-Forman (Jack Daniel's, Hartman luggage)
PO Box 1060
Louisville, KY 40210
(502) 585-1100; (800) 753-1177

Bumpkin's International (disposable diapers)
1945 E. Watkins St.
Phoenix, AZ 85034
(602) 254-2626

Burroughs Wellcome (Actifed, Neosporin, Sudafed)
3030 Cornwallis Rd.
Research Triangle Pk., NC 27709
(919) 248-3000

CPC International/Best Foods (Skippy peanut butter, Knorr,
   Hellman's, Mazola, Karo syrup, Niagra spray starch,
   Mueller's pasta)
International Plaza
Englewood Cliffs, NJ 07632
(201) 894-4000; (800) 894-2324

Cadbury-Schweppes (Mott's Schweppes/Canada Dry
   beverages)
High Ridge Park
PO Box 3800
Stamford, CT 06905
(800) 426-4891; (203) 968-5895

Campbell Soup Company (Pepperidge Farm, soups, Prego,
   V8, Marie's salad dressing, Franco-American, Open Pit,
   Le Menu, Vlasic pickles)
Campbell Place
Camden, NJ 08103
(800) 257-8443; (609) 342-4800

Canfield's Beverages (Swiss Creme, club soda, cola)
50 E. 89th Place
Chicago, IL 60619
(312) 483-7000

Carlisle Plastics (Ruffies Eco-choice, Re-cycle garbage bags)
1401 W. 94th St.
Minneapolis, MN 55431
(800) 873-3941; (612) 884-7281

Carter-Wallace (Arrid, Trojans)
767 Fifth Ave.
New York, NY 10153
(212) 339-5000

Cascades Industries (tissue products)
467 Marie Victoria, Box 210
Kingsley Falls, Quebec, Canada J0A 1B0
(819) 363-5600

Castle & Cooke/Dole Foods (fruit products)
10900 Wilshire Blvd.
Los Angeles, CA 90024
(213) 842-1500; (800) 232-8888

Celestial Seasonings (teas, Earthwise bags, cleaners)
4600 Sleepytime Dr.
Boulder, CO 80301-3292
(303) 530-5300

Chesebrough-Pond's/Unilever (Pond's creams, Vaseline,
  Rave, Pepsodent)
33 Benedict Place
PO Box 6000
Greenwich, CT 06838-6000
(800) 852-8558 (CT); (800) 243-5804; (203) 625-1849

Chicago Transparent Plastics (Brawny garbage bags)
2700 N. Paulina St.
Chicago, IL 60614
(312) 281-3040

Church & Dwight (Arm & Hammer cleaning products,
    Dental Care)
469 N. Harrison St.
Princeton, NJ 08540-7648
(800) 624-2889 (NJ); (800) 524-1328; (609) 683-5900

Ciba Consumer Pharmaceutical (Doan's pills,
    Eucalyptamint)
581 Main St.
Woodbridge, NJ 07095
(908) 602-6600

Circle K (supermarket chain)
1601 N. 7th St.
Phoenix, AR 85006
(602) 253-9600

Clearly Canadian (bottled waters)
999 W. Hastings St. Suite 1900
Vancouver, BC V6C 2W2
(800) 663-5658; (213) 259-6514

Clorox (bleach, Pine-Sol, Kingsford BBQ, Hidden Valley
    Ranch, KC Masterpiece BBQ sauce)
1221 Broadway
Oakland, CA 94612-1888
(800) 292-2200; (510) 271-7000

Coca-Cola (Minute Maid, Sprite, Diet Coke, Cherry Coke)
1 Coca-Cola Plaza NW
Atlanta, GA 30313
(800) 438-2653; (404) 676-2121

Colgate-Palmolive
(Murphy-Phoenix, Softsoap, Mennen, Ajax, Fab,
Dermassage, Irish Spring, Ultra Britc, Fluorigard, Crystal
White, Fresh Start)
300 Park Ave.
New York, NY 10022
(800) 338-8388; (212) 310-2000

ConAgra/Beatrice Cheese/Armour Swift-Ekrich/Monfort
(Healthy Choice, Armour, Swift's Premium, Hunt's
ketchup, Wesson oils)
1 ConAgra Dr.
Omaha, NE 68102-5001
(800) 325-7424 (Armour-Swift); (714) 680-1430
(Hunt-Wesson); (402) 451-6679 (corporate headquarters)

Conair (Jherri Redding hair care, hair dryers)
150 Milford Rd.
East Windsor, NJ 08520
(609) 426-1300

Confab Company (tissue and paper products)
2301 DuPont Dr., #150
Irvine, CA 92715
(714) 955-0274

Continental Baking/Ralston Purina (Wonder Bread, Hostess)
Checkerboard Square
St. Louis, MO 63164
(314) 982-4953

Adolph Coors (beers and ales)
Golden, CO 80401
(800) 642-6116; (303) 279-6565

Curtice Burns Foods (Brooks chili sauce, Rich & Tangy
    ketchup, Denver Dan, Old Vienna, Light Fantastic,
    Mexican Classics)
90 Linden Place, PO Box 681
Rochester, NY 14603-0681
(716) 383-1850

Dannon (yogurt products)
PO Box 44235
Jacksonville, FL 32256
(800) 321-2174

Dean Foods (dairy products, Veg-All, Freshlike, Peter Piper)
3600 N. River Rd.
Franklin Park, IL 60131
(708) 678-1680

Del Monte/RJR Nabisco Brands (canned goods, ketchup)
PO Box 193575
San Francisco, CA 94119
(800) 543-3090

DeMert & Dougherty (DeMert AllSet, beauty supplies)
5 Westbrook Corp. Center
Westchester, IL 60154
(800) 323-3219

Dep (hair care products)
2102 E. Via Arado
Rancho Dominguez, CA 90220-6189
(800) 367-2855; (213) 604-0777

Descale-It (cleaners)
PO Box 2425
Tucson, AZ 85702
(602) 622-2826

Dial/Purex (Dial soap, Purex, Lunchbucket/Doubletree
   foods)
Dial Tower
Phoenix, AZ 85077-1606
(800) 528-0849 (foods); (800) 457-8739 (laundry);
   (800) 258-3425 (personal care); (602) 207-5518

Dolco Packaging (recycled polystyrene egg cartons)
13400 Riverside Dr., Suite 200
Sherman Oaks, CA 91413
(818) 995-1409

Dow Chemical/DowBrands (Scrubbing Bubbles, Ziploc,
   Freezeloc, Handiwrap, Permasoft, Yes, Saran Wrap, Spray
   n' Wash)
2030 Dow Center
Midland, MI 48674
(800) 258-2436; (800) 428-4795 (DowBrands);
   (517) 636-1000

Dr Pepper/7-Up/Premier Beverages (soft drinks)
PO Box 655086
Dallas, TX 75265-5086
(214) 369-7000

El DuPont De Nemours (DuPont Nylon, Teflon, Kevlar)
1007 Market St.
Wilmington, DE 19880-0010
(800) 551-2355

Duracell (alkaline batteries)
Berkshire Industrial Park
Bethel, CT 06801
(800) 551-2355; (203) 796-4000

Dutton LeBus (recycled paper products)
9871 8th St.
Rancho Cucamonga, CA 91730
(909) 989-5822

Dyna-Pak (garbage bags)
PO Box 682
Lawrenceburg, TN 38464
(615) 762-4016

Eastman Kodak (film products, Lysol, Mop n' Glo)
343 State St.
Rochester, NY 14650
(800) 242-2424; (716) 724-4000

Eberhard-Faber/Faber-Castell (Eco-writer, art supplies)
PO Box 2630
Lewisburg, TN 37091
(615) 359-1583

Ekco Housewares (utensils)
9234 W. Belmont Ave.
Franklin Park, IL 60131
(708) 678-8600

Emsco Group (Rescue recycled plastic brooms)
PO Box 151
Girard, PA 16417
(800) 458-0839; (814) 774-3137

Enforcer Products (cleaners)
PO Box 1068
Cartersville, GA 30120
(404) 386-0801

Esselte Pendaflex (Earthwise file folders, office supplies)
71 Clinton Rd.
Garden City, NJ 11530
(800) 645-6051; (516) 873-3239

Bob Evans Farms (sausages)
3776 S. High St.
PO Box 07863
Columbus, OH 43207
(800) 272-7675

Faultless Starch/Bon Ami (starch, Bon Ami cleaner)
1025 W. Eighth St.
Kansas City, MO 64101-1200
(816) 842-1230

First Brands/Prestone (Glad garbage and sandwich bags)
88 Long Hill St.
East Hartford, CT 06108
(203) 731-2300

Food Lion (supermarket chain)
Salisbury, NC
(704) 633-8250

Fox River Paper (Eaton papers)
PO Box 2215
Appleton, WI 54913
(414) 733-7341

AJ Funk (Sparkle glass cleaner)
1471 Timber Dr.
Elgin, IL 60123
(708) 741-6760

Fuji Photo Film USA (film products, disposable cameras)
800 Central Blvd.
Carlstadt, NJ 07072-3009
(800) 526-9030; (914) 789-8100

General Electric Consumer Lighting (light bulbs, batteries)
Nela Park
Cleveland, OH 44112
(800) 626-2000; (216) 736-4404

Gerber Products (baby food and products)
445 State St.
Fremont, MI 49412
(800) 421-4221; (800) 421-4221; (616) 928-2718

General Mills (Betty Crocker, cereals, Gorton's, Bisquick)
PO Box 1113
Minneapolis, MN 55440-1113
(800) 231-0308 (cereals); (800) 222-6846 (snacks);
    (612) 540-2311

Georgia Pacific (tissue, paper products)
PO Box 105605
Atlanta, GA 30348-5605
(404) 527-0038

Giant Food (East Coast supermarket chain)
PO Box 1804
Washington, DC 20013
(301) 341-4100

Gillette (shaving products, Soft & Dri, Dry Idea)
Prudential Tower, PO Box 61
Boston, MA 02199
(617) 463-3337

Great Atlantic & Pacific Tea (A&P supermarkets, brands)
2 Paragon Dr.
Montvale, NJ 07645
(201) 573-9700

GTE/Sylvania (light bulbs)
100 Endicott St.
Danvers, MA 01923
(203) 965-2000

Guinness Import (beers and ales)
Six Landmark Square
Stamford, CT 06901-2704
(800) 521-1591; (203) 323-3311

Hallmark Cards (greeting cards, stationery)
PO Box 419034
Kansas City, MO 64141-6034
(816) 274-5697

Hannaford Brothers (supermarkets)
145 Pleasant Hill Rd.
Scarborough, ME 04074
(207) 883-2911

Hartz Mountain (pet supplies)
700 Frank E. Rodgers Blvd. S.
Harrison, NJ 07029-9987
(201) 481-4800

G Heilman Brewing (Old Style beer, LaCroix waters)
100 Harborview Plaza
LaCrosse, WI 54602-0459
(608) 785-1000

HJ Heinz USA (Heinz ketchup, Weight Watchers, Starkist)
PO Box 57
Pittsburgh, PA 15230
(412) 456-5700

Helene Curtis (Finesse, Suave, Salon Selectives)
325 N. Wells St.
Chicago, IL 60610-4713
(312) 661-0222

Hershey Foods (Reese's, Lifesavers, San Georgio pasta)
100 Mansion Rd.
Hershey, PA 17033
(717) 534-4000

George Hormel & Company (Spam, Dinty Moore, Light &
    Lean)
501 16th Ave. NE
Austin, MN 55912
(507) 437-5611

Hunt-Wesson/ConAgra (Hunt's ketchup, sauces, Wesson
    oils)
1645 W. Balencia Dr.
Fullerton, CA 92634
(714) 680-1430

International paper (paper and packaging)
2 Manhattanville Rd.
Purchase, NY 10577
(914) 397-1500

James River (Northern tissue, Dixie cups)
PO Box 6000
Norwalk, CT 06856-6000
(800) 243-5384; (203) 854-2469

Jergens/Kao (Jergens lotion, skin care products)
PO Box 14544
Cincinnati, OH 45250
(800) 222-3553

Johnson & Johnson (Tylenol, Band-Aids, baby products,
  feminine hygiene)
199 Grandview Rd.
Skillman, NJ 08558
(800) 526-2433; (800) 526-3967

SC Johnson Wax (Brite, Raid, Glade, Off, Skintastic,
  Windex)
1525 Howe St.
Racine, WI 53403
(800) 558-5252; (414) 631-2000

Kayser-Roth (No-Nonsense pantyhose)
612 S. Main St.
Burlington, NC 27215
(919) 229-2224

Keebler Biscuits (crackers, cookies)
One Hollow Tree Lane
Elmhurst, IL 60126
(708) 833-2900

Kellogg (cereals, Eggo, Mrs. Smith's pies)
One Kellogg Square
Battle Creek, MI 49016
(616) 961-2277; (800) 962-1413

Keyes Fiber (Chinet plates)
301 Merritt 7
Norwalk, CT 06851
(203) 846-1499

Kimberly-Clark (Huggies, Kleenex, Kotex)
PO Box 2020
Neenah, WI 54957-2020
(800) 544-1847; (414) 721-5604

Kraft General Foods/Philip Morris (Oscar Mayer, Post, Breyer's,
   Cool Whip, Louis Rich, Tang, Miracle Whip, Velveeta)
Kraftcourt
Glenview, IL 60025
(800) 323-0768

Kroger (supermarkets, SupeRx drugstores)
1014 Vine St.
Cincinnati, OH 45201
(800) 632-6900; (513) 762-4000

Land O'Lakes (dairy products)
PO Box 116
Minneapolis, MN 55440-0116
(800) 328-4155

L'Eggs Hosiery/Sara Lee (pantyhose)
5660 University Parkway
Winston-Salem, NC 27105
(919) 768-9540

L&F Products/Eastman Kodak (Lysol, Perk, Mop n' Glo,
   Love My Carpet)
225 Summit Ave.
Montvale, NJ 07645
(800) 888-0192; (201) 573-5700

Eli Lilly (pharmaceuticals)
Lilly Corp. Center
Indianapolis, IN 46285
(317) 276-6070

Thomas Lipton/Unilever (teas, soups, Wishbone salad dressing)
800 Sylvan Ave.
Englewood Cliffs, NJ 07632
(201) 567-8000; (800) 697-7897

L'Oreal/Cosmair (cosmetics)
PO Box 98
Westfield, NJ 07091-9987
(800) 631-7358

Lorillard Tobacco (cigarettes)
2525 E. Market St.
PO Box 21688
Greensboro, NC 27420-1688
(919) 373-6669

Lucky Stores/American (supermarket chain)
PO Box BB
Dublin, CA 94568
(415) 833-6000

Manco Products (paper, adhesive products, duct tape)
830 Canterbury Rd.
Westlake, OH 44145
(216) 892-4505; (800) 321-1733

Marion Merrell Dow (Citrucel)
Marion Park Dr.
PO Box 8480
Kansas City, MO 641114
(816) 966-4000

McCain Citrus (Boku drink boxes)
1821 S. Kilbourn Ave.
Chicago, IL 60623
(312) 762-9000

McCormick & Company (spices and seasonings)
11350 McCormick Rd.
Hunt Valley, MD 21031
(301) 771-7301

Mead (paper, stationery, school supplies)
Courthouse Plaza NE
Dayton, OH 45463
(513) 495-6323

Melitta USA (coffee filters)
1401 Berlin Rd.
Cherry Hill, NJ 08003
(800) 451-1694; (609) 428-7202

Merck & Company (pharmaceuticals)
PO Box 2000
Rahway, NJ 07065
(201) 594-4000

M&M Mars (candies, Uncle Ben's Rice, Kal-Kan pet foods)
High St.
Hackettstown, NJ 07840
(800) 852-1000; (201) 222-0293

Mobil (Hefty bags, Tucker housewares)
1159 Pittsford-Victor Rd.
Pittsford, NY 14534
(800) 333-0124 (Hefty bags); (800) 225-7734;
    (716) 248-1368; (212) 883-4242

Monsanto/Nutrasweet/Round-up
800 N. Lindbergh Blvd.
St. Louis, MO 63167
(314) 694-1000; (708) 940-9800 (Nutrasweet)

Morcon (tissue, paper products)
PO Box 302, Rt. 22
Cambridge, NY 12816
(518) 677-8511

Morton Salt (salt products)
100 N. Riverside Plaza
Chicago, IL 60606
(312) 807-2694

Murphy-Phoenix/Colgate-Palmolive (Murphy's oil soap)
101 N. Summit St.
Tenafly, NJ 07670
(800) 432-8226

Nabisco Brands/RJR Nabisco (Saltines, Chips Ahoy cookies,
    Shredded Wheat cereals, Planter's Peanuts, Lifesaver candies)
100 DeForest Ave.
East Hanover, NJ 07936
(800) 932-7800; (201) 503-2659

Nestlé USA (Contadina, Carnation, Hills Brothers, Friskies,
    Libby's, Crosse & Blackwell, Buitoni, Maggi seasoning)
800 N. Brand Blvd.
Glendale, CA 91203
(800) 637-8537; (818) 549-6000

Neutrogena (skin care products)
5760 W. 96th St.
Los Angeles, CA 90045
(800) 421-6857; (213) 642-1150

Newman's Own (salad dressings, sauces, popcorn)
246 Post Rd. Expwy.
Westport, CT 06880
(203) 222-0136

North American Plastics (Ironhold garbage bags)
921 Industrial Dr.
Aurora, IL 60506
(708) 896-6200

Nutrasweet/Monsanto (Nutrasweet and Equal artificial
    sweeteners)
1751 Lake Cook Rd.
Deerfield, IL 60015
(800) 321-7254; (800) 323-5316 (Equal only)

Ocean Spray Cranberries (cranberry products)
1 Ocean Spray Dr.
Lakeville/Middleboro, MA 02349
(508) 946-1000

Outright Industries (Outright stain remover)
4041 W. Ogden Ave.
Chicago, IL 60623
(800) 338-5034; (312) 277-7100

Pepperidge Farm/Campbell (cookies, breads, bakery goods)
595 Westport Ave.
Norwalk, CT 06856
(203) 846-7276

Pepsico (Frito Lay, Pepsi, Slice, Mountain Dew)
1 Pepsi Way
Somers, NY 01589-2201
(914) 767-6000; (800) 433-2652 (Pepsi); (800) 352-4477
    (Frito-Lay)

Perdue Farms (poultry products)
PO Box 1537
Salisbury, MD 21802
(800) 442-2034; (301) 543-3000

Perrier Group (Perrier waters)
777 W. Putnam Ave.
Greenwich, CT 06830
(203) 531-4100

Pet (Progresso, Old El Paso, Underwood)
PO Box 66179
St. Louis, MO 63166-6179
(314) 622-6146

Petosky Plastics (Resource garbage bags)
US 31 South
Petosky, MI 49770
(616) 347-2602

Pfizer (Bengay, pharmaceuticals)
235 E. 42d St.
New York, NY 10017
(212) 573-2323

Philip Morris Companies (Marlboro, Kraft, General Foods,
    Miller beers, Oscar Mayer, Entenmann, Jell-O, Kool Aid,
    Maxwell House, Tang, Velveeta)
120 Park Ave.
New York, NY 10017
(212) 880-3366

Philips Lighting/North American Philips (Earthlight)
200 Franklin Square Dr.
PO Box 6800
Somerset, NJ 08875-6800
(908) 563-3000

Pillsbury/Grand Met (Green Giant, baking products)
PO Box 550
Minneapolis, MN 55440
(800) 767-4466

Planet Products (cleaning products)
Suite 204, 10114 McDonald Park Rd., RR 3
Sidney, British Columbia, Canada V8L 3X9
(604) 656-9436

Playtex Family Products (feminine products, rubber gloves,
   baby products)
215 College Rd.
PO Box 728
Paramus, NJ 07652
(800) 222-0453; (800) 524-0825 (NJ only)

Plochman's (mustard products)
2743 W. 36th Place
Chicago, IL 60632
(800) 843-4566; (312) 254-8989

Polaroid (cameras and film)
784 Memorial Dr.
Cambridge, MA 02139
(800) 343-5000; (617) 577-2000

Poly America (Husky garbage bags)
2000 W. Marshall Dr.
Grand Prairie, TX 75051
(800) 527-3322; (214) 647-4374

Poly Pak America (Duralite mailers)
2939 E. Washington Blvd.
Los Angeles, CA 90023-4277
(800) 826-4000

Pope & Talbot (tissue, paper products)
1500 SW First Ave.
Portland, OR 97201
(503) 228-9161

Procter & Gamble (Ivory, Tide, Crest, Crisco, Prell,
   Pampers, Pepto-Bismol, Max Factor, Cover Girl, Folgers,
   Vicks, Charmin)
PO Box 599
Cincinnati, OH 45201-0599
(800) 543-7310; (800) 638-6204; (800) 843-9657;
   (513) 983-2200

Quaker Oats (cereals, breakfast bars, Van Camp's, Gatorade,
   Aunt Jemima, Celeste, Ken-L-Ration, Gaines)
PO Box 9003
Chicago, IL 60604-9003
(312) 222-7843

Ralston Purina (pet foods, Beech-Nut, Wonder Bread,
   Eveready)
Checkerboard Square
St. Louis, MO 63164
(800) 345-5678; (314) 982-4566

Rayovac (batteries, flashlights)
601 Rayovac Dr.
Madison, WI 53711
(608) 275-3340

Reckitt & Colman (French's mustards, Sani-Flush,
   Easy-Off)
PO Box 945
Wayne, NJ 07474-0945
(201) 633-6700

Revlon (cosmetics, Mitchum speed sticks)
625 Madison Ave.
New York, NY 10022
(212) 527-5644

Reynolds Metals (aluminum, plastic wraps)
6603 W. Broad St.
Richmond, VA 23230
(804) 281-4073 (collect calls accepted)

Ringer (Safer natural pesticides)
9959 Valley View Rd.
Eden Prairie, MN 55344
(612) 9410-4180

AH Robins/AHP (Robitussin, Dimetapp)
1405 Cummings Dr.
Richmond, VA 23261-6609
(804) 257-2000

Roebic Labs (septic, bacterial cleaners)
25 Connair Rd.
PO Box 927
Orange, CT 06477
(203) 795-1283

Rorer Group/RPR (Maalox, pharmaceuticals)
500 Virginia Dr.
Fort Washington, PA 19034
(800) 548-3708; (215) 628-6000

Royal Rubber (recycled rubber mats)
5951 E. Firestone Blvd.
South Gate, CA 90280
(310) 928-7080

Rubbermaid (recycling products, containers, garbage cans)
1147 Akron Rd.
Wooster, OH 44691
(216) 264-6464

Safco Products (file folders, office supplies)
9300 West Research Center Rd.
New Hope, MN 55440
(612) 536-6700

Safeway Stores (supermarket chain)
Oakland, CA 94660
(510) 891-3267

Sandoz Pharmaceuticals (Triaminic, Ex-Lax)
59 Route 10
East Hanover, NJ 07936
(201) 503-7500

Sara Lee (L'Eggs, Hanes, bakery products, Shasta, Kiwi)
70 W. Madison St.
Chicago, IL 60602-4260
(312) 726-2600

Schering-Plough (Coppertone, Solarcaine, Di-Gel, Correctol)
3030 Jackson Ave.
Memphis, TN 38151-0001
(901) 320-2998

Schmid Labs (Feminique)
PO Box 4703
Sarasota, FL 34230
(813) 365-1600

Scott Paper (Scotties, tissues, towels, Washabye Baby)
Scott Plaza Two
Philadelphia, PA 19113
(800) 835-7268; (215) 522-6170

Scott's Liquid Gold (Liquid Gold wood cleaner)
4880 Havana St.
Denver, CO 80239
(800) 227-8111; (303) 373-4860

Joseph E. Seagram (beverages, wine coolers, liquor)
375 Park Ave.
New York, NY 10152
(212) 572-7147

Slim-Fast (diet foods)
919 Third Ave.
New York, NY 10022-3898
(800) 862-4500

SmithKline Beecham (Contact, Aqua Velva, Tums)
PO Box 1467
Pittsburgh, PA 15230-1467
(800) 245-1040; (412) 928-1000

JM Smucker (preserves, jams, jellies)
Strawberry Lane
Orville, OH 44667-0280
(216) 682-0015

Snapple Juices (fruit juices)
175 N. Central Ave.
Valley Stream, NY 11580
(516) 872-4800

Statler Tissue (Tree-Free tissues, papers)
300 Middlesex Ave.
Medford, MA 02155
(617) 395-7770

Sterling Health (Bayer, Philip's Milk, Camphophenique)
90 Park Ave.
New York, NY 10016
(800) 331-4536; (212) 907-2000

Stokley USA (canned foods)
626 E. Wisconsin Ave.
PO Box 248
Oconomowoc, WI 53066-0248
(800) 872-1110; (414) 567-1731

Stone Container (shopping bags, cartons, lawn bags)
150 N. Michigan Ave., Suite 3400
Chicago, IL 60601
(312) 649-7900

Stop & Shop (supermarket chain)
PO Box 1942
Boston, MA 02103
(617) 770-8895

Stouffer Foods/Nestlé (frozen foods)
5750 Harper Rd.
Solon, OH 44139-1880
(216) 248-3600

Stroh Brewery (beers)
100 River Place
Detroit, MI 48207-4291
(313) 446-2000

Strout Plastics (containers)
9611 James Ave. S.
Bloomington, MN 55431
(612) 881-8673

Stuart Hall Paper/Newell (recycled stationery)
PO Box 419381
Kansas City, MO 64141
(816) 221-8480

Sun-Diamond (fruits, Sunsweet fruit juices)
5568 Gibraltar Blvd.
Pleasanton, CA 94566
(510) 463-8200

Sunshine Biscuits (Sunshine and Salerno cookies and
  biscuits)
100 Woodbridge Center Dr.
Woodbridge, NJ 07095-1196
(908) 855-4000

Sunshine Makers (Simple Green cleaners)
15922 Pacific Coast Highway
Huntington Harbor, CA 92649
(714) 840-1319

Supermarkets General (supermarket chain)
301 Blair Rd.
Woodbridge, NJ 07095
(908) 499-3500

Swift-Ekrich/ConAgra (processed meats)
2001 Butterfield Rd.
Downers Grove, IL 60515
(800) 325-7424; (708) 512-1000

Tambrands (Tampax)
One Marcus Ave.
Lake Success, NY 11042
(800) 523-0014; (516) 358-8300

Tetley (teas)
100 Commerce Dr.
PO Box 856
Shelton, CT 06484-0856
(203) 929-9342

Thorn Apple Valley (sausages, meat products)
18800 W. 10 Mile Rd.
Southfield, MI 48075
(800) 227-5828; (800) 823-5616

3M (Post-it Notes, Scotch Tape, Scotchguard, Scotchbrite)
3M Center
St. Paul, MN 55144
(612) 733-1110

Tootsie Roll Industries (candies)
7401 Cicero Ave.
Chicago, IL 60629
(312) 838-3400

Totes (gloves, boots, hats)
10078 E. Kemper Rd.
Loveland, OH 45140
(513) 583-2300

Tropicana (fruit juices)
PO Box 338
Bradenton, FL 34206
(813) 747-4461

Turtle Wax (auto polishes, waxes)
5655 W. 73d St.
Chicago, IL 60638-6211
(800) 323-9883

Tyson Foods (poultry products)
PO Box 2020
Springdale, AR 72765-2020
(800) 233-6332; (501) 756-4714

Ultra Pac (recycled containers)
22051 Industrial Blvd.
Rogers, MN 55374
(612) 428-8340

Universal Foods (yeasts, seasonings, food colors)
433 E. Michigan St.
Milwaukee, WI 53202
(414) 271-6755

Upjohn (Kaopectate, Nuprin, Motrin, pharmaceuticals)
7000 Portage Rd.
Kalamazoo, MI 49001
(800) 253-8600; (616) 323-4000

Van Den Bergh Foods/Unilever (Imperial, Shedd's Spread,
   Ms. Butterworth's, I Can't Believe It's Not Butter,
   Promise)
390 Park Ave.
New York, NY 10022
(800) 735-3554

Van Munching & Company (Heineken beer importer)
1270 Ave. of the Americas, 10th floor
New York, NY 10020
(212) 265-2685

VeryFine (fruit juices)
210 Littleton Rd.
Westford, MA 01886
(508) 692-0030

Visy Recycle (bags)
501 S. Spring St.
Hartford City, IN 47348
(317) 348-5440

Von's Companies (supermarket chain)
PO Box 3338
Los Angeles, CA 90054
(818) 821-7000

Wal-Mart Stores (Sam's, Wal-Marts)
702 SW Eighth St.
Bentonville, AR 72716-0117
(501) 273-4000

Warner-Lambert (Benadryl, Efferdent, Hall's, Schick,
   Clorets, Rolaids, Listerine, Lubriderm, Anusol, Tucks
201 Tabor Rd.
Morris Plains, NJ 07950
(800) 223-0182; (800) 524-2624 (Parke-Davis);
   (800) 742-8377 (Schick razors); (800) 562-0266 (EPT);
   (800) 524-2854 (Trident)

Webster Industries (Renew recycled garbage bags)
58 Pulaski St.
Peabody, MA 01960
(508) 532-2000

Welch's Foods (grape juices, jellies, jams)
100 Main St.
Concord, MA 01742
(508) 371-1001

Winn-Dixie Stores (supermarket chain)
5050 Edgewood Court
Jacksonville, FL 32203
(904) 783-5000

William Wrigley (Doublemint, Juicy Fruit, Freedent gums)
410 N. Michigan Ave.
Chicago, IL 60611
(312) 645-4076

WOC Products (Simply Stain nail polish)
17145 Margay Ave.
Carson, CA 90746
(800) 962-2875

Wood Fuel Processing (recycled fire logs)
2361 Durham Dayton Highway
Durham, CA 95938
(916) 895-1806

Woodstream/Ekco Housewares (Victor traps)
PO Box 327
Lititz, PA 17543-0327
(717) 626-2125

Green Organizations

Alliance to Save Energy
1725 K St. NW, Suite 914
Washington, DC 20006-1401
(202) 857-0666
A rich source of publications and research on energy-saving appliances, building, and policies.

American Paper Institute
260 Madison Ave.
New York, NY 10016
(212) 340-0626
Representing paper companies and packagers, the trade group has some information on paper recycling and waste issues.

American Plastics Council
1275 K St. NW, Suite 400
Washington, DC 20005
(202) 371-5319
Operated in connection with the Society of Plastics Industry, the group provides information on plastics recycling, packaging, and source reduction.

American Solar Energy Society
2400 Central Ave.
Boulder, CO 80301
(303) 443-3130
Membership organization dedicated to the development and promotion of solar energy. Offers a free catalog of publications on the subject and publishes the bimonthly magazine *Solar Today*.

American Wind Energy Assocation
1730 N. Lynn St., Suite 610
Arlington, VA 22209
(703) 276-8334
A trade association for the wind-energy industry. Offers information on research, manufacturers, and installers of wind-power systems.

Aseptic Packaging Council
1000 Potomac St. NW, Suite 401
Washington, DC 20007
(202) 333-5900
A trade group representing a handful of drink-box manufacturers.

Californians Against Waste Foundation
926 J St., Suite 606
Sacramento, CA 95814
(916) 443-5422
One of the largest and most influential state environmental groups, they are sponsoring a Buy Recycled Campaign.

The Calvert Group
4550 Montgomery Ave.
Bethesda, MD 20814
(800) 368-2748

A money management firm, the company offers the largest group of socially responsible/environmentally screened mutual funds.

Citizen/Labor Energy Coalition
1300 Connecticut Ave. NW, Suite 401
Washington, DC 20036
(202) 857-5153
A group that lobbies for fair national energy policies.

Citizens Clearinghouse for Hazardous Wastes
PO Box 6806
Falls Church, VA 22040
(703) 276-7070
A grassroots watchdog group with hundreds of local chapters, it also publishes an excellent newsletter, *Everybody's Backyard.*

Citizens Fund/Citizen Action
1120 19th St.
Washington, DC 20036
(202) 775-1580
The group does investigative reports on pollution regulation and enforcement.

Council for Solid Waste Solutions
1275 K St. NW, Suite 400
Washington, DC 20005
(800) 243-5790; (202) 371-5200
A spin-off of the Society of Plastics Industry, this group promotes plastics recycling programs.

Council on Economic Priorities
30 Irving Place
New York, NY 10003
(212) 420-1133

The group researches, rates, and monitors corporate environmental and social actions.

Council on Plastics and Packaging in the Environment
1001 Connecticut Ave. NW, Suite 401
Washington, DC 20036
An industry-sponsored group that publishes information on plastics packaging and environmental issues.

Econet
3228 Sacramento St.
San Francisco, CA 94115
(415) 923-0900
A nonprofit membership organization that acts as a clearinghouse and electronic information network on energy/environment issues.

Environmental Action Foundation
6930 Carroll Ave., Suite 600
Takoma Park, MD 20912
(301) 891-1100
The group generates research on environmental issues, especially solid waste management. Ask for their *Wastelines* newsletter.

Environmental Defense Fund
1616 P St. NW
Washington, DC 20036
(202) 387-3500
The group has recently formed alliances with major corporations such as McDonald's to help clean up their operations.

Environmental Health Coalition
1717 Kittner Blvd., Suite 100
San Diego, CA 92101-2532
(619) 235-0281
The group offers good information on toxins in the home.

Food Marketing Institute
800 Connecticut Ave. NW
Washington, DC 20006-2701
(202) 429-8263
The trade group behind the nation's largest supermarket
chains, they're a good source of information on recycling
and packaging issues. Ask for their *Reduce, Reuse, Recycle*
brochure.

Friends of the Earth
218 D St.
Washington, DC 20003
(202) 544-2600
An international environmental group.

Glass Packaging Institute
1122 20th St. NW, Suite 321
Washington, DC 20036
(202) 887-4850
The trade group representing glass packagers provides good
background on glass recycling issues and programs.

Government Purchasing Project
PO Box 19367
Washington, DC 20036
(202) 387-8030
A spin-off of Ralph Nader's many organizations, the group
promotes government use of energy-efficient green products
such as recycled paper and safe cleaning supplies.

Greenpeace
1436 U St. NW
Washington, DC 20009
(202) 462-8817

An international environmental group known for its radical activism on nuclear and environmental issues.

Grocery Manufacturers of America
1010 Wisconsin Ave. NW, Suite 800
Washington, DC 20007
(202) 337-9400
A trade association representing manufacturers of most national-brand food and nonfood products.

INFORM, Inc.
381 Park Ave. South
New York, NY 10016-8806
(212) 689-4040
A group dedicated to environmental research and education.

Investor Responsibility Research Center
1755 Massachusetts Ave. NW, Suite 600
Washington, DC 20036
(202) 234-7500
The group publishes in-depth studies on company environmental records and a newsletter.

National Audubon Society
700 Broadway
New York, NY 10003
(212) 979-3000
Once dedicated to preserving bird habitats, the group has a general conservation focus.

National Coalition Against the Misuse of Pesticides
701 E. St. SE
Washington, DC 20003
(202) 543-5450
The group monitors pesticide abuse and applications.

National Consumers League
815 15th St. NW
Washington, DC 20005
(202) 639-8140
This well-established activist group examines consumer and environmental issues. Ask for their pamphlet *The Earth's Future Is in Your Shopping Cart*.

National Recycling Coalition/Recycling Advisory Council
1101 30th St. NW, Suite 305
Washington, DC 20007
(202) 625-6410
Representing industry, government, environmentalists, and consumers, the group is most active in recycling policy.

National Toxics Campaign
1168 Commonwealth Ave.
Boston, MA 02134
(617) 232-0327
Publisher of the newsletter *Toxic Times*, the group monitors toxic issues nationwide.

National Wildlife Federation
1400 16th St.
Washington, DC 20036
(800) 432-6564
A leading international conservation group that protects animal habitats.

Natural Resources Defense Council
1350 New York Ave. NW
Washington, DC 20005
(202) 783-7800
This vocal environmental group files lawsuits on environmental issues and provides background on related topics.

Nature Conservancy International
1800 N. Kent St., Suite 800
Arlington, VA 22209
(703) 841-5300
A large and wealthy group that buys and manages land for conservation and restoration.

Pennsylvania Resources Council
PO Box 88
Media, PA 19063
(215) 565-9131; (800) 468-6772
A group that's extremely well informed on "environmental shopping" issues. Ask for their brochure *Become an Environmental Shopper: Vote for the Environment*.

People for the Ethical Treatment of Animals (PETA)
PO Box 42516
Washington, DC 20015
(301) 770-7444
A leading animal rights group that publishes a list of manufacturers that don't test on animals.

Polystyrene Packaging Council
1025 Connecticut Ave. NW, Suite 515
Washington, DC 20036
(202) 822-6424
The trade group provides information on polystyrene recycling programs, packaging, and reuse.

Public Citizen
215 Pennsylvania Ave. SE
Washington, DC 20003
(202) 546-4996
Ralph Nader's umbrella organization is active on a number of environmental fronts.

Rainforest Action Network
301 Broadway, Suite A
San Francisco, CA 94133
(415) 398-4404
A leading group fighting to save the world's rain forests.

Rocky Mountain Institute
1739 Snowmass Creek Rd.
Snowmass, CO 81654-9199
(303) 927-3851
One of the leading research organizations on energy conservation and renewable resources, the institute also offers energy-conservation consulting services.

Scientific Certification Systems
1611 Telegraph Ave., Suite 1111
Oakland, CA 94612-2113
(800) ECO-FACTS; (510) 832-1415
The company certifies manufacturers' environmental claims and organic produce/pesticide residues and is a major lobbying force behind environmental education and life-cycle analysis.

Sierra Club
730 Polk St.
San Francisco, CA 94109
(415) 776-2211
One of the oldest, largest, and most active environmental groups that's involved on a number of fronts. Also publishes an excellent magazine.

Soap & Detergent Association
475 Park Ave. S.
New York, NY 10016
(212) 725-1262
A trade association that represents the cleaning industry.

Social Investment Forum
430 First Ave. N., #290
Minneapolis, MN 55401
(612) 333-8338
A trade group that represents green and socially responsible investors, planners, and mutual fund managers.

Solar Energy Industries Association
777 N. Capitol St. NE
Washington, DC 20002
(202) 408-0660
A trade group representing solar power companies that publishes a newsletter on the industry.

Sun Day 1993
315 Circle Ave., #2
Takoma Park, MD 20912
(301) 270-2258
Actually a network of organizations, this Public Citizen–sponsored group is pushing for a national energy policy.

Union of Concerned Scientists
26 Church St.
Cambridge, MA 02238
(617) 547-5552
An excellent source of information on energy, nuclear power, and arms issues.

U.S. Federal Trade Commission/Public Reference
Sixth and Pennsylvania Ave. NW
Washington, DC 20580
In addition to regulating misleading green advertising, the agency has guidelines on green marketing. They're free upon request.

World Federalist Association
PO Box 15250
Washington, DC 20003
(202) 546-3950

A group that supports a world system of government that will enforce international environmental and social standards.

World Resources Institute
1709 New York Ave. NW
Washington, DC 20006
(202) 638-6300

A think-tank that does research and issues reports on climate, energy, pollution, forests, biodiversity, and resource management.

World Watch Institute
1776 Massachusetts Ave. NW
Washington, DC 20036
(202) 452-1999

A "big picture" environmentally oriented think-tank that produces an excellent magazine, annual "State of the World" report, and "Environmental Alert" books.

Zero Population Growth
1400 16th St. NW
Washington, DC 20036
(202) 332-2200

The group researches and analyzes world population and resource depletion trends.

Hotlines

Cancer Information
(800) 422-6237; (800) 638-6694 in Maryland
A resource for general information, treatment, and support groups.

Chemical Referral Center
(800) 262-8200
A nonemergency source of information on chemicals. Will locate manufacturer and point of contact.

Energy Technology
(800) 428-2525; (800) 428-1718 in Montana
Provides technical assistance on energy-saving technologies.

Environmental Protection Agency (EPA)
(800) 424-4000
Office of Consumer Affairs
This department handles inquiries and complaints from the public.

EPA Planning & Community "Right-To-Know" hotline
(800) 363-5888; (800) 557-1938

Provides assistance on the law that requires community notification about chemical storage and spills.

Renewable Energy Information & Publications
(800) 523-2929
Sponsored by the Department of Energy, this service offers several publications on alternative energy and conservation.

Resource Conservation & Recovery
(800) 424-9346

Safe Drinking Water (EPA)
(800) 426-4791
Provides information on the Safe Drinking Water Act.

Solid Waste Assistance Program
PO Box 7219
Silver Spring, MD 20907
(800) 677-9424
A useful source of information on recycling, source reduction, composting, legislation, and solid waste disposal.

Publications

BOOKS

Clean & Green, by Annie Berthold-Bond (Ceres Press).
An indispensible guide to natural/nontoxic cleaning.

Consumer's Resource Handbook, Consumer Information
Center, Pueblo, CO 81009.
A free guide that's loaded with company contacts, phone
numbers, and government-agency addresses.

*Costing the Earth: The Challenge for Governments, The
Opportunities for Business,* by Frances Cairncross. (Harvard
Business School Press)
Global environmental issues as seen from a capitalist's per-
spective.

*Energy, Environment and Animal Rights Investment Strategy
Guide,* Good Money Publications, PO Box 363, Worcester,
VT 05682, (800) 535-3551.
A brief primer on how to screen out companies' environmen-
tal, social, and animal rights records. Although geared to in-
vestors, it's a good research tool for everyone.

Environmental Success Index, Renew America, (202) 232-2252.
Published by "a clearinghouse for environmental solutions," the book cites hundreds of examples of programs designed to cut pollution and energy consumption, recycle, the restore natural resources, and reduce the use of toxins.

How Much Is Enough? The Consumer Society and the Future of the Earth, by Alan Durning (WW Norton).
A penetrating look at how our consumer society and over-consumption are ruining the planet.

The 1993 Information Please Environmental Almanac, compiled by the World Resources Institute (Houghton Mifflin).
Everything you ever wanted to know about environmental issues.

Green Marketing Challenges and Opportunities in the New Marketing Age, by Jacquelyn Ottman (NTC Business).
A solid reference on environmental marketing.

Paradigms in Progress: Life Beyond Economics, by Hazel Henderson (Knowledge Systems).
Some eye-opening and visionary ideas on economics, the environment, and our future on the planet.

Rubbish! The Archaeology of Garbage, by William Rathje and Cullen Murphy (HarperCollins).
A remarkable and interesting study of landfills and what they reveal about our society and our relationship to waste.

Save Our Planet: 750 Everyday Things You Can Do to Help Clean Up the Planet, by Diane McEachern (Dell).
Packed with good, actionable ideas.

Save the Animals! 101 Easy Things You Can Do, by Ingrid Newkirk (Warner).
A good source of information on "cruelty-free" products that have not been tested on animals.

The Social Investment Almanac, A Comprehensive Guide to Socially Responsible Investing, edited by Peter Kinder, Steven Lydenberg, and Amy Domini (Henry Holt).
A complete volume on socially responsible investment, corporate environmentalism, and related resources.

The Solution to Pollution: 101 Things You Can Do to Clean Up the Environment, by Lawrence Sombke (Mastermedia, Ltd.).
Practical green advice that's concise and easy to read.

State of the World, by Lester Brown and the World Watch Institute (WW Norton).
An indispensable guide to the state of the planet's resources and population. Updated yearly by the staff of the World Watch Institute, a forward-thinking research organization.

Tackling Toxins in Everyday Products: A Directory of Organizations, Inform, Inc., 381 Park Ave. S., NY, NY 10016.
A comprehensive guide on toxins in the home and what you can do about them.

Turning the Century: Personal and Organizational Strategies for Your Changed World, by Robert Theobald, (Knowledge Systems).
Robust thinking on our place on the planet and the future.

MAGAZINES

Business Ethics
1107 S. Hazeltine Blvd., Suite 530
Chaska, MN 55318
(612) 448-8864
Whether you work for or manage a company, this magazine is the best in profiling socially responsible corporate actions.

E magazine
PO Box 5098
Norwalk, CT 06851
(203) 854-5559
A clearinghouse of information on ecological topics.

Earth Island Journal
300 Broadway, Suite 28
San Francisco, CA 94133
(415) 788-3666
A magazine for global conservation, published by one of the most outspoken environmental groups.

Garbage
2 Main St.
Gloucester, MA 01930
(508) 283-3200
An objective journal that looks at the practical side of recycling, solid waste, toxins, and green products.

Recycling Times
PO Box 10540
Portland, OR 97210
(503) 227-1319

A leading publisher of periodicals on recycling, the company also publishes *Resource Recycling* and *Bottle/Can Recycling Update*.

World Watch
World Watch Institute
1776 Massachusetts Ave. NW
Washington, DC 20036
(202) 452-1999

A highly influential and informative magazine that reviews world resources, energy conservation, and population issues.

Also see previous listings for the National Audubon Society, Environmental Defense Fund, Environmental Action, National Wildlife Federation, Natural Resources Defense Council, Nature Conservancy, Sierra Club, and Zero Population Growth. All have publications.

NEWSLETTERS

The Conscious Consumer
PO Box 51
Wauconda, IL 60084
(708) 526-0522
The quarterly newsletter evaluates and criticizes green/socially responsible products and marketing.

Earth Day 2000
116 New Montgomery St., Suite 530
San Francisco, CA 94105-3607
(800) 727-8619
A good general resource guide that's easy to read.

The Earthwise Consumer
PO Box 1506
Mill Valley, CA 94942
Features information on "clean and green" lifestyles.

The Green Consumer Letter; The Green Business Letter
1526 Connecticut Ave. NW
Washington, DC 20036
(800) 955-4733
Two useful monthlies that review green products and practices.

Green MarketAlert
345 Wood Creek Rd.
Bethlehem, CT 06751
(203) 266-7209
Oriented toward marketing concerns, this is the best available newsletter on green marketing and product regulation.

Good Money
PO Box 363
Calais Rd.
Worcester, VT 05682
(800) 535-3551
One of the most complete publications on socially and envi-
ronmentally responsible investing research.

Pollution Prevention News
EPA Office of Pollution Prevention
401 M St. SW (PM-219)
Washington, DC 20460
The EPA-published newsletter does excellent profiles of
companies attempting to cut pollution and reduce energy
consumption.

Reusable News (EPA)
(800) 424-9346
A free periodical that covers solid-waste management, source reduction, and recycling.

EPA PUBLICATIONS

EPA
401 M St. SW
Washington, DC 20460
(800) 424-9346
The following free guides can be ordered from the agency's RCRA hotline (above). The publications listed below are but a sampling. Ask for their publications list and *Green Advertising Claims* brochure.

PUBLICATION	EPA #
Adventures of the Garbage Gremlin	530/SW-90-024
Characterization of Mun.	
Solid Waste 1992	530/SW-92-042
Consumers Handbook for	
Reducing Solid Waste	530-K-92-003
Facts on Degradable Plastics	530-SW-90-017C
Household Hazardous Waste	530/SW-88-014
Let's Reduce & Recycle	530/SW-90-005
Methods to Manage & Control	
Plastic Wastes	530/SW-89-051A
Plastics: The Facts about Production	530-SW-90-017A
Plastics: The Facts on	
Source Reduction	530-SW-90-017C
Recycle	530/SW-88-050

Glossary

Aerosol—A product that uses a propellant to force the product out of the package. While most aerosols don't contain ozone-eating CFCs, many contain hydrocarbons, which contribute to smog. A good alternative to an aerosol is a pump spray or a solid.

Aseptic packaging—The kind of technology used in fruit-drink boxes. Consisting of paper, foil, and plastic, this "shelf stable" package requires no refrigeration and can stay fresh on the supermarket shelf for weeks. Unbreakable, lightweight, and designed to prevent spoilage, the boxes are said to use less material to make than glass. Retailers and manufacturers prefer them because they reduce transportation, refrigeration, and distribution costs. Environmentalists dislike them because they are difficult and uneconomical to recycle, although a few industry-sponsored pilot programs exist in trial operations across the country.

Biodegradable—What a product does if it breaks down to simple minerals, water, and carbon dioxide. The underlying meaning is that what a product breaks down to is not harmful to the environment. Since there are no universally accepted and policed technical or government definitions for "biodegradable," manufacturers have been using the term loosely.

Blister packs—A type of packaging that combines a plastic covering with a cardboard card that may be hung or shelved. Generally not recyclable, it's designed largely for the convenience of the retailer, although it's often a wasteful form of packaging.

Carcinogen—A substance known by researchers to cause cancer. There are two classes of carcinogens: "known" and "suspected." The former is verified to cause cancer in humans; the latter in animals (through testing). There are about 3,500 carcinogens. Although many of them are man-made and found in compounds such as gasoline, others are naturally occurring.

CFCs (chlorofluorocarbons)—Chemicals that are used in the refrigeration/cooling process. Although inert and nontoxic, these chemicals devour the earth's protective ozone layer. This layer of gas partially shields ultraviolet (UV) light from entering the atmosphere. The less ozone there is, the more UV light reaches us, causing sunburn, skin cancer, cataracts, and crop failure. While no CFCs can be found in most consumer aerosols, they are still used in refrigeration and vehicle air conditioning. The government banned the use of CFCs as propellants in most consumer aerosols in 1978. They are still used in medical aerosols. When a company claims it uses "no CFCs," it's a pretty empty claim. An agreement called the Montreal Protocol is mandating the international phase-out of production of CFCs by 1995, but until a workable substitute is found, CFCs and their cousin chemicals—HCFCs (hydrochlorofluorocarbons)—will continue to pose a problem to the ozone layer, scientists believe.

Composting—The biochemical process that ultimately produces humus, a nitrogen-rich material that's a concentrated plant fertilizer. Since home yard waste comprises nearly one-third of U.S. landfill space, communities have opened up composting facilities. Several manufacturers such as Procter & Gamble have invested millions in garbage composting technology, which takes difficult-to-dispose-of wastes such as disposable diapers and attempts to compost them in an industrial process. The process is still largely in the trial phase. It will be years before large-scale composting will be a viable economic alternative to landfilling solid waste. You can, however, start your own composting pile for grass, clippings, and kitchen waste. Most hardware and home-center stores sell composting appliances and chemicals.

Concentrated, superconcentrated—Types of detergents that use chemicals that allow you to use less detergent per load. The products are packaged in smaller containers, which produce less disposable waste.

Closed-loop recycling—A process that continuously recycles a product. For example, aluminum cans are melted down to make more aluminum cans in a closed-loop process. This process is deemed more environmentally sound than "open-loop" recycling.

Degradable (also biodegradable, photodegradable)—What a product does if exposed to sunlight, water, and air. In theory, it should break down into harmless chemicals such as water and carbon dioxide. The U.S. Federal Trade Commission and several state attorneys general, however, have sued companies such as Mobil over the use of the term on garbage-bag boxes. Research has found that in most landfills, these degradable products (typically plastic or paper) do nothing because there's no water, light, or air to make the process work.

Global warming/greenhouse effect—The heating of th earth's atmosphere that is believed to be caused by overaccu mulation of carbon dioxide and other gases. The burning o fossil fuels and build-up of other man-made gases is acceler ating the effect, scientists believe. Although the subject o much debate, global warming may lead to a rise in th earth's temperature by 9 degrees F. by the year 2050, sea level rise, droughts, and crop failures.

Green Lights—A voluntary program sponsored by the EPA designed to reduce energy usage through the installation of en ergy-efficient technologies and lighting in commercial/indus trial facilities. Ask your local supermarket chain and call you favorite consumer goods companies to find out if they're par ticipating. Reduced energy consumption translates into lowe consumption of fossil fuels and nuclear power, which lessen the burden on the environment (less air and land pollution).

Groundwater—Water that's naturally stored in under ground pools or aquifers. In some cases, landfills and indus trial waste sites have seriously polluted groundwater sources This is a difficult resource to replace because of growing population demands. The U.S. Water Council estimates tha by the year 2,000, water supplies will be severely inadequate in 17 of the nation's 106 water supply regions.

Heavy metals—Elements such as cadmium, chromium mercury, and lead that are found in batteries and printing inks. These metals are poisonous to humans and wildlife and can leach from landfills that contain paperboard, batteries and industrial wastes.

HDPE (high-density polyethylene)—A plastic resin used in milk jugs, detergent bottles, and supermarket bags. It can be re cycled into pipes, playground equipment, and shopping bags.

Integrated pest management—A "biorational" process that uses the least-toxic method to control insects in agriculture. An old and accepted way of farming, IPM employs use of natural predators, plant varieties, and natural pesticides such as garlic, marigolds, and rosemary. It's considered an alternative to extensive use of synthetic pesticides, which are leached into groundwater supplies and form residues on produce.

Life-cycle analysis (LCA)—A scientific process that looks at the total impact of a product from natural resources to disposal. This cradle-to-grave study examines energy use, transportation, pollution, and disposability.

Ozone "friendly" or "safe"—Product claims that imply that a product's aerosol propellants do not harm the earth's protective ozone layer. Government agencies and environmental groups have found, however, that such claims may be misleading. Companies may substitute hydrocarbon-based propellants that cause smog. See *VOCs*.

Paperboard—Cardboard that's either made flat for boxes or corrugated for cartons. The majority of paperboard made in the United States is made from recycled paper and can be found in most outer packaging of products. Although highly recyclable, it may not be taken by most recyclers if it's printed with colored inks, which contaminate the recycling process.

PETE or PET (polyethylene terephthalate)—The most commonly recycled plastic resin that's usually found in soft-drink bottles. It can be recycled into carpeting, egg cartons, insulation, or garbage cans. It's identified on bottles as #1 resin.

Phosphates—Chemical compounds that enhance the cleaning ability of detergents and promote algae growth in waterways, thus choking off animal life. While most detergents do not contain phosphates (because of laws banning them), they may contain other chemicals that are not environmentally friendly.

Postconsumer, preconsumer waste—The former term refers to waste that is thrown away by consumers in household garbage. The latter refers to waste that's found in factories and mills. Environmentalists maintain that postconsumer waste content is the more significant factor in recycled products since it diverts waste from landfills and slightly eases the burden on the environment. Preconsumer waste may also include mill scraps, which are not destined for landfills but may be included in manufacturers' claims of recycled content.

Rain forest—A type of forest that grows only in regions with high annual rainfall. In developing countries, rain forests are being cleared for crop and grazing land at the rate of 27 million acres per year. Rain forests support unique ecosystems that may account for half of all the plant and animal species on earth. Some of the plant species contain important medicines. This is a particularly pressing concern since rain forest acreage is destroyed every minute. As a result, some 17,500 species of plants and animals become extinct every year.

Recyclable—Generally, a product that can be recycled by a commonly available industrial process. Usually denoted by the "chasing arrows" on packaging, by practical definition, products can be recycled only where facilities exist to handle them. Some paper and plastic products—such as milk cartons and vinyl shampoo bottles—are not widely recycled, so it's misleading to suggest that they are easily recycled. See Part 3, The Packaging Problem.

Recycled—Generally, something that contains recycled content. While the percentage of recycled content varies, there is no single law that dictates how much recycled content a product—or its packaging—should contain. Also see *Post-*, *reconsumer waste*. To date, the EPA has issued standards on percentage of postconsumer recycled content only in making printing paper. Private groups such as SCS and Green Seal monitor claims on recycled content in other products.

"Reduce, Reuse, Recycle"—The slogan used to encourage better use of resources. If you can cut back your use of wasteful products and packaging, reuse whatever you can, and recycle the rest, it will represent a meaningful personal contribution to environmental progress.

Refillable—A container that may be returned to the retailer for reuse as a container or refilled with the original product. Examples include returnable soft-drink bottles and glass milk bottles (still available in some parts of the United States).

Solid waste management—This term refers to efficient disposal or diversion of waste from landfills. As the cost of maintaining (and closing) landfills rises, solid waste management becomes more critical.

Source reduction—The process by which the amount of material used in packaging is reduced by some degree. Also known as "lightweighting," the process results in less material ending up in landfills. The process is a priority among manufacturers and the EPA in cutting down the weight and volume of product packaging.

Sustainable agriculture—A set of practices that ensure the continual, environmentally balanced use of land. For example, sustainable agriculture practices maintain topsoil, groundwater, and soil fertility through prudent use of fertilizers and pesticides. Another example is avoiding the harvesting of old-growth or rain forest tress that can't easily be regrown. This problem is especially acute because each year

farmers must feed 93 million more people with 24 billio
fewer tons of topsoil.

10-K—A document required by the Securities and Exchang
Commission for most U.S.–based public (widely availabl
stock-issuing) corporations. Among other pertinent fact
about the company, the document will list the company's en
vironmental and civil liability, or suits and actions pendin;
against the company. The document is available to the publi
(by request only) through the company's shareholder or in
vestor relations department.

33/50 Program—The voluntary waste-reduction progran
sponsored by the EPA that was designed to reduce the re
lease of seventeen highly toxic chemicals by 33 percent b;
the end of 1992 and 50 percent by 1995. More than 500 in
dustrial companies have signed up for the program.

Toxic Release Inventory (TRI)—A set of statistics com
piled by the EPA that tracks a group of chemicals releasec
by industrial companies. The inventory focuses on a smal
group of toxic chemicals, although there are some 70,000
man-made chemicals being produced.

VOCs (volatile organic compounds)—A group of chemi
cals that, when evaporated into the atmosphere, react witl
other compounds to create smog. Common VOCs includ
isobutane, butane, propane, and alcohols. Products that con
tain VOCs include nail polish removers, paints, windshiel
washer fluid, floor polish, hair-styling gel/mousse, charcoa
lighting fluid, painting inks, and paint strippers.

Water-based (soluble) ink—A type of ink that uses wate
as a base instead of petroleum solvents. The environmenta'
benefit is that water-based inks do not emit or reduce smog
producing VOCs. Inks that use soybean oil are other petro
leum-ink substitutes.

How You Can
Participate in Our Work

GREEN PRODUCTS SURVEY

We would like to know how you feel about green marketing and in which areas you feel uninformed. We will use the
information in future publications.

(Send to New Consumer Institute,
PO Box 51, Wauconda, IL 60084)

. Would you be willing to contact a company concerning a
product's environmental soundness?   [ ] Yes   [ ] No
[ ] Maybe
. If so, how would you contact them? By Phone____ By
Letter____ By Fax____
. Do you think your contact with a company concerning
environmental product quality will effect a change in the
product design, manufacture, or packaging?   [ ] Yes
[ ] No   [ ] Maybe
. What concerns you most about products?
Price [ ]
Quality [ ]

    Nutritional value (where pertinent) [ ]
    Labeling [ ]
    Manufacture [ ]
    Packaging [ ]
    Utility [ ]

5. Would you pay more for a product deemed environmentally sound? [ ] Yes [ ] No [ ] Maybe
6. Would you like more information on:
    (A) Environmentally sound home improvement products (paints, materials, strippers, etc.) [ ]
    (B) Environmentally sound investments [ ]
    (C) Environmentally sound gardening products [ ]
    (D) Environmentally sound personal care products (cosmetics, deodorants, over-the-counter remedies) [ ]

The New Consumer Institute
Wants You to Join its Green Network
Members will receive a two-year subscription to the *Conscious Consumer* newsletter and discounts on special publications and other green guides.

[ ] $19.95 two-year sub. includes quarterly newsletter
[ ] $1.95 for newsletter sample only
[ ] Please send me information about your dynamic speakers and research!
[ ] Please send information to friend or loved one.

Name _____ Address _____
City, State & Zip _____
Age ____ Occupation _____ Education _____

YET ANOTHER EASY WAY TO HELP:
YOUR ENVIRONMENTAL TRANSPORT CARD

We're conducting an important survey that we hope will revolutionize the way you live and impact the earth. In cooperation with Scientific Certification Systems, we'd like you to complete this survey on personal vehicle use. By doing so, you'll be able to measure how much your driving habits contribute to smog, the greenhouse effect, and other air pollution/resource problems.

The survey is simple. Fill in the type of vehicles you own. Include estimated miles per gallon and how much each vehicle is driven. Include your recreational and public transportation use.

The object of the survey is to show how your driving habits create environmental burdens. You'll also be able to determine how much the earth can benefit through more efficient vehicles and the use of public transportation. The idea behind the survey isn't to make you feel guilty. We all need to drive to get to work, drop off children, and run errands. SCS is compiling this research to reveal the differences among vehicles, type of transportation, and amount of driving.

What you need to do: Fill out the survey and return it to SCS (see p. 404). SCS will send you back a "report card" showing how much your driving impacts the earth.

Personal Environmental Transportation Card

Free Evaluation and National Survey

A. Personal Vehicle

For each vehicle you drive, please complete the following. In estimating fuel purchased and miles traveled, include commute to and from work, but exclude any other work-related travel.

Vehicle #1
Year/Make/Model _____
Fuel Bought/Week (gallons) _____
Est. Total Miles/Year _____
Avg. Miles/Gallon _____
Est. Number of Times Vehicle Started/Week _____
Avg. Miles/Hour CITY _____ HIGHWAY _____
Avg. Number of Passengers (use formula below) _____

Vehicle #2
Year/Make/Model _____
Fuel Bought/Week (gallons) _____
Est. Total Miles/Year _____
Avg. Miles/Gallon _____
Est. Number of Times Vehicle Started/Week _____
Avg. Miles/Hour CITY _____ HIGHWAY _____
Avg. Number of Passengers (use formula below) _____

Passenger formula: Estimate the percentage of time you are driving alone or with other passengers. Add up and insert in tables above. Figure for both (or other) vehicles.

	Example			Subtotal
1 Person	×	80	(.80) =	.80
2 Persons	×	10	(.10) =	.20
3 Persons	×	10	(.10) =	.30

Total Avg. Number of Passengers = 1.3

Note: % time must add up to 100%. Convert percents into decimal equivalents and multiply times number of people.

			Subtotal
1 Person ×	___ % =	___	
2 Persons ×	___ % =	___	
3 Persons ×	___ % =	___	
4 Persons ×	___ % =	___	
5 Persons ×	___ % =	___	
6 Persons ×	___ % =	___	
		Total	_____

B. Other Personal/Public Transportation

Please estimate the number of miles traveled by:

Method	Miles		Month or Year
Carpool (avg. 3 passengers)	_____	per	_____
Bus	_____		_____
Taxi	_____		_____
Rental car	_____		_____
Train	_____		_____
Jet	_____		_____
Electric (subway, commuter)	_____		_____

C. Recreational

Please estimate the number of gallons of gas you purchase for:

	Gallons	Month or Year
Boats	_____	_____
All-terrain veh.	_____	_____
Snowmobiles	_____	_____
Motorcycles	_____	_____
RVs	_____	_____
Other	_____	_____
(specify with MPG)	_____	_____

NAME _____

ADDRESS_____

CITY, STATE, ZIP_____

[Optional]

TELEPHONE_____ AGE___ OCCUPATION_____

Please send this survey to Scientific Certification Systems, 1611 Telegraph Ave., Suite 1111, Oakland, CA 94612-2113. For more information, call 1-800-ECO-FACTS or (510) 832-1415. You can fax the survey to (510) 832-0359.

Feel free to copy the survey and pass it along to family, friends, associates, co-workers, and others. The more people that participate, the more we can discover about the environmental impact of driving. SCS will send you back the results, showing how you compare to other survey participants. The organization hopes to be able to paint a picture of how efficiently we use our vehicles and what it means to the environment.

About the Author
and the New Consumer Institute

The author is the publisher and editor of the *Conscious Consumer*, a consumer protection–oriented newsletter that focuses on environmentally sound products and services.

He is a nationally recognized writer/editor well versed in social issues. As senior editor for *Consumers Digest* magazine, he covers the environment, social issues, and personal finance/investing subjects for more than 4 million readers.

The author has contributed to *Reader's Digest*, *HOME*, the *New York Times*, *Popular Science*, *Barron's*, the *Saturday Evening Post*, *Mother Jones*, and *The Progressive*.

He is also the author of *The Green Company Resource Guide*, a reference on environmental marketing.

The author received his B.A. and M.A. from the University of Illinois at Chicago. He's a member of the Chicago Headline Club, the Society of Professional Journalists, and the Sierra Club. He lives with his wife, horses, dog, and groundhogs north of Chicago.

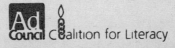